Diving for Pearls

A Thinking Journey with Hannah Arendt

Kathleen B. Jones

Thinking Women Books
San Diego, California

Thinking Women Books
www.ThinkingWomenBooks.com

Publisher's Note: This is a work of non-fiction. This memoir is based on information gleaned from personal journals, research, taped interviews, and conversations with people who appear in the book, and memories of real events and interactions. Some names and identifying characteristics of certain individuals have been changed to preserve their anonymity.

Ordering Information:
Quantity sales. Special discounts are available on quantity purchases by corporations, associations, and others. For details, contact the website above.

Diving for Pearls/ Kathleen B. Jones. -- 1st ed.
ISBN 978-0-9860586-0-8

Dedicated to the memory of Jean Bethke Elshtain, another controversial public intellectual and a dear friend who said she always knew my Arendt would be different.

There are no dangerous thoughts; thinking itself is dangerous.

–HANNAH ARENDT

Acknowledgements

For helping me in various ways through the decade of writing a book, I have many people to thank.

First and foremost, I am grateful for my family's love and patience in listening to me talk about Hannah Arendt all the time.

Thanks to friends and colleagues Bat-Ami Bar On, Paula Bernett, Danielle Celermajer, Oliva Éspin, Susan Burgess, Laurel Corona, Judith Grant, Dan Katkin, Catherine Kineavy, Mona Livholts, Sandra Luft, Lori Marso, Lilly Rivlin, Dieter Rossi, Françoise Vergès, and Gillian Youngs, who discussed or read all or parts of the manuscript in development. And to Kara Saul Rinaldi for housing me more than once in the D.C. area while I was researching Arendt's papers.

Several groups gave me an opportunity to present earlier drafts of chapters—Anna G. Jónasdóttir and GEXcel in Sweden; the feminist theory group of the Western Political Science Association; and Ohio University's Women's and Gender Studies program.

For supporting my seminars for schoolteachers on Hannah Arendt's political theory, special thanks to the National Endowment of the Humanities and to the 100 or so teachers who have been summer scholars in my program.

For providing me, twice, with grants and a creative and supportive environment for writing, thanks also to the Vermont Studio Center.

My research was helped immensely by the professionalism of the special collections librarians and archivists at Olin Memorial Library, Wesleyan, at the Schlesinger Library and the Library of Congress. Special thanks to Maia Ettinger for permission to access her mother's papers.

I am grateful for the incredible design work of Jeanette Vieira (cover) and Joel Friedlander and his team (interior book design).

To my wonderful editor and cheerleader, Louise Bernikow, a huge thanks for your careful reading and encouragement.

Finally, to all the independent authors who have inspired me to keep going, thanks for the supportive community.

Parts of chapter 2 appeared in different form as "Masquerades of Love," in *Emergent Writing Methodolgies in Feminist Studies*, ed. Mona Livholts, New York: Routledge, 2012. Parts of chapter 6 appeared originally in 2003 as "She Lost It at the Movies: Moving Pictures," in *Mr. Bellar's Neighborhood*, http://mrbellersneighborhood.com, and an excerpt from chapter 10 appeared in the *Los Angeles Review of Books.*

Author Photo: Rippee Photography

Contents

{1}

Pearl-Diving

It is with such fragments from the past, after their sea-change, that I have dealt here. That they could be used at all we owe to the time-less track that thinking beats into the world of space and time. If some of my listeners and readers should be tempted to try their luck at the technique of dismantling, let them be careful not to destroy the 'rich and strange,' the 'coral' and the 'pearls,' which can proba-bly be saved only as fragments.

Hannah Arendt, *The Life of the Mind*

EVERYONE WANTS TO MAKE SENSE OF HER LIFE. Some of us do that by telling a story, just like I've tried to do, one sentence at a time. In the dusk of middle age, I chose a peculiar path. Surprising myself by reversing directions, I took a road

I'd abandoned, and found myself exploring again the thinking and life of Hannah Arendt.

One of the most profound and controversial thinkers of the twentieth century, Hannah Arendt defied easy categorization. A brilliant political philosopher, who refused to call herself a philosopher, a woman who never considered her sex an obstacle in her life, a Jew who was called anti-Semitic, and a rigorous thinker who wrote passionately about hatred and love, Arendt tackled some of the thorniest moral and political questions of modern times. And she was as well known in literary and political circles for her brave, powerful prose, as she was among academicians for her philosophical arguments.

I'd first written about her more than three decades ago. Scribbled on my essay in red ink were notes to myself, scarlet traces of a heated dialogue with Hannah Arendt. What had so bothered me then?

In her remarkable essay on authority, Arendt made the bold claim that "authority has vanished from the modern world," and with those words she parted company with the Western tradition of political theory, the very tradition in which I'd been trained. In it, everyone had always agreed "on one essential point: authority is what makes people obey."[1] And on that point, she'd said everyone had been fundamentally mistaken.

The first time I read that essay in my now well-worn copy of *Between Past and Future* (1969) Arendt's bold thinking dazzled me. She traced the fundamental misunderstanding of authority all the way back to the Greeks. In her view, it was Plato and Aristotle who were the villains; those early philosophers of the *polis* hadn't developed an appropriately political notion of authority. Instead, they simply slid the idea of authority as "domination and subjection, command and obedience, ruling and being ruled" from the private into the public realm.

Since I was then looking for a fresh way to view authority, I followed Arendt's argument but then stopped suddenly in my tracks when I realized she had no real objection to a fundamental distinction between public and private life. In fact, she affirmed it.

Reading *The Human Condition*, which she'd published in 1958, further incensed me. Arendt dismissed relationships and activities in the private sphere of everyday life as politically irrelevant and, it seemed to me at the time, even thought them less important to our humanity than what we do and say in public. That claim rankled my feminist core. I shook my fist at the book. Wasn't the personal also political? Didn't creating equality for women in the public arena depend on ending patriarchal relations in the private sphere? I certainly thought so; in fact, I had devoted my entire career to the project of gender equality, which to me meant changing what happened in the "home" was as essential to women's freedom and equality as whether or not women got to be seen and heard in public.

Thus provoked, I took up the challenge Arendt's writing represented and confronted her arguments directly. As refreshingly original as her conceptualization of authority was I considered it of limited use—if not downright threatening!—to my project in feminist theory.

Yet, no matter how much I argued against her, I had to admit I admired her writing. In other essays written in those years, I find myself circling around and then diving deeper into Arendt's writing, each time retrieving some pearl of insight, which shifted my understanding and made me reassess my position. And for the next decade or so I turned to her again and again for inspiration, or just to have a tenacious thinking partner to joust with. But what really threw me was when Arendt thrust herself into my consciousness to become an especially disconcerting interlocutor during the process of writing a memoir.

She wouldn't leave me alone. Every time I penned a line bordering on an all too confident assertion, I'd hear her voice in my head. "Dive deeper, you're not really thinking," it said.

At the time, her intrusion made no sense. After all, I thought, hadn't Arendt once claimed that thinking and emotional introspection were radically opposed? That should make it pretty much impossible for any insights she had to offer to be useful for the emotionally resonant work of confronting the meaning of anyone's personal past.

Yet the more I considered Arendt's life and contemplated the peculiar structure and context of her writing, the more I discovered things that startled and intrigued me. In between the lines of her essays, I began to hear a kind of musical score of life stories. And so, following its rhythms and chords, I embarked on a thinking journey with the traveling companion I've now come to call "Hannah."

Nearly two decades after my first encounter I discovered another Hannah in between the lines of her writing; a Hannah who, intentionally or not, confessed truths about herself, revealed blind spots and displayed emotions she might rather have kept hidden. And when I found that Hannah, she drew me into an intimate and not always welcomed partnership, a disquieting dialogue between two women, one long ago dead, about what and how the heart knows yet prefers to keep to itself. I let my imagination go visiting, entering her life and her work, and began to see the world and my own place in it from an altogether different perspective, asking more and more questions while wondering what Hannah would say.

Through imagined conversations with this Hannah, I began to retrieve anecdotes from her life and mine, finding meanings in them I believe are more universal than applied only to my particular case. Like Hannah, who got caught up in thinking about her own life while writing her biography of Rahel Varnhagen, a nineteenth century Jewish woman who became the host of an important Berlin intellectual salon, reading and writing about Hannah's life and work caught me up in my own, revealing things I had tried to keep even from myself.

So this is the story of my thinking journey with Hannah, a tale at once political and personal, singular and common. Diving below the surface of her writing, the narrative arches and bends, assembling vignettes about Hannah and me into a collage of life stories, a kind of intellectual and emotional scrapbook of travels I took with Hannah through tangled memories of love and action and thought. A collage of life stories; or, in musical terms, a fugue.

Most likely Hannah would judge this a departure from the proper score of life writing. In the preface to her biography of Rahel Varnhagen, she claimed she'd avoided "that modern form of indiscretion in which the writer attempts to penetrate his subject's tricks and aspires to know more than the subject knew about himself or was willing to reveal."[2] I make no such claim. I have been deliberately indiscreet, tried to "know more" about what I have not, so far, been willing to think, whether about Hannah's story or mine. The irony is, while telling Rahel's story even Hannah violated her own principle.

Hannah claimed we come to know who somebody is through a story told by someone who creates a dramatic arc out of the sheer stuff of a life, becoming the author "who...always knows more what it was all about than the participants."[3] Such a story is much more than a simple description of a series of events or occurrences; the whole point is to uncover layers of meaning in the life lived. Then, those always fragmentary reflections, those pearls we narrate in life stories become woven into the wide web of human relationships, binding us together in what Hannah once called the human condition of plurality, where "we are all the same, that is human, in such a way that nobody is ever the same as anyone else...."[4]

We tell stories not to master the past but "to know precisely what [the past] was...endure this knowledge, and then to wait and see what comes of knowing and enduring."[5] Memory, when reified in a story, evokes a kind of transformation of individual acts in anyone's life into a significant whole through a process of re-experiencing or re-suffering those acts by narrating them. The story then becomes a kind of lament, a somewhat melancholic repetition, to quote Goethe, of "Life's labyrinthine, erring course." But to allow memory to speak in an uncensored way—at least as uncensored as humanly possible—one has to get past the point where wellsprings of hurt and anger, or even of joy, "which impel us to action, have been silenced—and that needs time."[6]

Remembering provides no solution to problems nor end to suffering but simply fulfills the all too human need we each have to "recall the significant events in our own lives by relating them to ourselves and others," adding one more item to the world's stock, "where it can live on—one story among many."[7]

So, in the end, my reflections will remain alive and meaningful only if you, dear reader, take up their themes, as I have taken up Hannah's, and, beginning again in a new voice, continue chasing this fugue in different, perhaps unexpected directions.

{2}

Becoming A Conscious Pariah

It was never my intention to write a book about Rahel...What interested me solely was to narrate the story of Rahel's life as she herself might have told it.

Hannah Arendt *Rahel Varnhagen: The Life of a Jewess*

A LONG TIME AGO A WOMAN NAMED HANNAH WROTE A LETTER TO HER LOVER TELLING HIM ABOUT HER BEST FRIEND. Rahel, the close woman friend—who was "unfortunately dead a hundred years now," the letter noted—had once explained something very important to Hannah. Since Hannah had never met Rahel it turns out the explanation Hannah had garnered was one she'd crafted herself from the diaries and letters Rahel left behind. What had Hannah understood from this life lived a century earlier? From Rahel, she said, she'd come to know how important it is that other people, who live in the same time and space as you do, recognize who you are, see you as the person you understand yourself to be, and accept you.

"What a crazy thing," I thought when I first read that letter many years ago. A woman born in another century, dead for a hundred years, whom you'd never met. How could anyone ever call a ghost a close friend? And I continued to think it was crazy until I began to feel the same way. Until, that is, the Hannah in question—Hannah Arendt—became my own closest woman friend.

Hannah's "closest woman friend," Rahel Varnhagen, turns out to have been a Jewish woman born into a late eighteenth century Berlin suffused with Enlightenment ideals about human equality. As an influential figure in German Romanticism Rahel hosted one of the most illustrious salons in her famous garret on *Jägerstrasse.* The major intellectuals of Berlin society, along with many others from all walks of life and classes, came to her rooms to discuss leading cultural and political ideas of the times. They came, and, when the world changed again and Jews were no longer welcome in "polite society," they left.

Though a century separated Hannah and Rahel, these two European women shared a similar fate: they were both born into a world where being a Jew demanded explanation, and, by Arendt's time, could lead to death. Though a shared fate created a bond between them, what drew Hannah to Rahel and intrigued her enough to write Rahel's biography extended well beyond parallels of lineage.

At the time she first discovered Rahel Varnhagen, Hannah had been wrestling with conflicts in her own life, including difficult intimate relationships with men. She was also deepening the exploration of her own identity, asking questions about what it meant to be a Jew in the immediate years before Hitler's ascendancy. I think Hannah came to feel close to Rahel, perhaps closer than to any living woman friend, because the story she told out of fragments from Rahel's life became a narrative arc along which Hannah traveled to discover her own life's truths and make sense of them in the context of the times in which she was living.

While she was his student at Marburg in the 1924, Hannah Arendt had an affair with Martin Heidegger, a man seventeen years her senior who later embraced National Socialism in an ill-fated attempt to secure his academic career. The relationship between Hannah and Martin persisted for several years after she left Marburg to study in Heidelberg. But by 1929 physical intimacy between them had ended. Yet, before his Nazi sympathies emerged, Hannah turned to Martin more than once for comfort and support, explaining how she had taken a journey along a path he had shown her, attempting to find her own way into the world.

> *Heidelberg, 22.IV.28*
>
> *...The path you showed me is longer and more difficult than I thought. It requires a long life in its entirety. The solitude of this path is self-chosen and is the only way of living given me. But the desolation that fate has kept in store not only would have taken from me the strength to live in the world, that is, not in isolation; it also would have blocked my path, which, as it is wide and not a leap, runs through the world...and the path itself is nothing but the commitment our love makes me responsible for. I would lose my right to live if I lost my love for you, but I would lose this love and its reality if I shirked the responsibility it forces on me.*[8]

Reading that letter to Heidegger alongside Hannah's biography of Rahel Varnhagen it became clearer to me how biographical writing helped shape Hannah's commitment "to live in the world" with all the parts of who she was. I began to understand this commitment to be the kind of responsibility Hannah had taken on through her writing: to be responsible to her identity as a Jew. Later, she named this the position of the "conscious pariah."

Such a responsibility meant that a Jew—or anyone, for that matter, who had been excluded from society—had to become aware of her position as an outsider, a pariah, and "conscious of it, become a rebel against it—the champion of an oppressed people...As soon as the pariah enters the arena of politics and translates [her] status into political terms, [she] becomes perforce a rebel. "[9] And a rebel Hannah certainly was.

In 1930s Germany, embracing one's Jewish identity was no simple matter; nor did it become any simpler when Hannah became a stateless person exiled in France and later was sent to an internment camp at Gurs. Nor even in 1940s America, where she escaped from Europe, identifying as a German Jew while resisting any "party line" for what being a German Jew might mean, whether represented by mainstream American Jewish organizations or their more radical Zionist counterparts or, much later, by Jewish survivors of the *Shoah*. I began to think Hannah's life's work was an extended, constantly evolving, sometimes contradictory and not always explicit effort to integrate competing and even conflicting parts of her identity into some kind of whole.

As early as 1926, when she first made the acquaintance of Kurt Blumenfeld, a well-known supporter of the Zionist Movement, Hannah began to cut more deeply into what it meant to be a Jew in a world increasingly inhospitable to Jews. And when the political situation in Germany worsened, she must have felt fragmented, divided into parts it seemed she was expected to choose among. Should she grab onto the German part and abandon the Jewish? And what about being a woman? Where did that part fit in?

In 1929 twenty-three year old Hannah Arendt was living in Berlin with her lover, Günther Stern, a young philosopher she'd met in Heidegger's Marburg seminar a few years earlier. For a while Hannah and Günther survived in the outskirts of Berlin on the pittance of a scholarship she received for a study on German Romanticism, which Hannah had won partly because of strong letters of support, including from Heidegger. Later that year, they moved from Berlin to Heidelberg and after a short while settled in Frankfurt. Before arriving in Frankfurt, they married, in acknowledgement of that city's more provincial culture as much as anything else. Hannah thought Günther companionable enough. He shared many of her intellectual interests. And, she confessed, the match suited her mother. Marriage also gave Hannah some semblance of conformity; at least as a married woman, she might belong to what the world considered "normal."

The couple moved back to Berlin in 1930 and Hannah set to work on several projects. With Blumenfeld's encouragement, she undertook further research on Zionist politics and also began working on *Rahel Varnhagen*.

By early winter 1933, Hannah had nearly finished the biography. She'd already published in *Deutscher Almanach* one chapter from the book as a separate essay on the Berlin salons, along with another piece about Rahel's friendship with Pauline Wiesel, the mistress of Prince Louis Ferdinand, who had been a visitor to Rahel's Berlin salon in the 1790s. Then, Hannah began to grapple with more vexing questions about identity and belonging.

That February had been especially cold in Berlin. The frozen linden trees outside Hannah's window on *Opitzstrasse* swayed and bent in the wind like waltzing skeletons, graceful yet somber, as if gliding toward death. They must have reminded Hannah of Rahel and everything reminding her of Rahel must have also reminded her of being Jewish because, in that winter of 1933, soon after Hitler became Chancellor of Germany, everything had turned into the Jewish Question.

On February 27, 1933, the *Reichstag* was set on fire and Hermann Göring—an early member of the Nazi party who founded the German secret police, or *Gestapo*, later rising to high ranks in the Nazi state—

blamed the fire on Communists, fomenting hostility against them. Years later, Hannah recounted the impact this event had on her life.

> *[I]llegal arrests...followed that same night...People were taken to* Gestapo *cellars or to concentration camps...and from that moment on I felt responsible...I was no longer of the opinion that one can simply be a bystander. I tried to help in many ways.*[10]

A few days after the fire, fearing for his own safety, Günther Stern left for Paris. Hannah stayed behind, working for certain Zionist organizations and allowing her apartment to be used as a sort of underground railway station for fleeing refugees. Those activities soon caught up with her. One day she was taken to the police station at *Alexanderplatz* and held there for eight days. "I was arrested, and had to leave the country illegally...and that was instant gratification for me. I thought at least I had done something! At least I am not 'innocent.' No one could say that of me!"[11]

Yet, later in her life and even long after her death, her harshest critics would accuse her of betraying her principles. Some contended she held to a double standard, applying one to assess her own decisions positively and another to judge negatively those of her own people—other Jews—some of whom, to different degrees, had cooperated with the Nazis, if only to save their own or friends' or families' lives. Who does she think she is to judge the choices Jews were forced to make? After all, she didn't have to make those decisions; when the opportunity came to leave Germany, these critics said, Hannah took the easier way out. She fled.

Yes, she fled, I thought. And she was also lucky and well-known enough to be given a place on Varian Fry's list of famous Jews to be saved and, along with her husband Heinrich Blücher, boarded a ship that sailed from Lisbon to America, becoming one among the last Jews to get out of occupied France alive in 1941.[12] And yet, during her years of exile in Paris, she had also "done something"—been politically active—working for Youth Aliyah, bringing to Palestine in 1935 shiploads of stateless Jewish children and young people.

Figures 1 and 2. Hannah Arendt Accompanying Youth to Palestine. 1935. Source: *Elżbieta Ettinger Papers, 1922-2001 (EEP)*; MC 579, folder 23.8. Schlesinger Library, Radcliffe Institute, Harvard University, Cambridge, Mass.

Had that activity been enough, I wondered, to unburden her conscience of guilt at having escaped the worst? Later, I found a partial answer in her writing.

"There exists in our society a widespread fear of judging...[But] who has ever maintained that by judging a wrong I presuppose myself incapable of committing it?"[13] It seemed to me she'd been aware of the burden of having survived. She had chosen to go on living. I wondered what I might have done under similar circumstances and began to feel certainty in my own righteousness diminish.

After leaving Germany in the fall of 1933, Hannah set aside her biography of Rahel, no closer, I thought, to comprehending the story's full meaning than she had been at the beginning. Five years later, now a stateless person exiled in France and separated from her first husband, she picked up the work again and approached it from a very different angle of vision.

"The thing which all my life seemed to me the greatest shame, which was the misery and misfortune of my life—having been born a Jewess—this I should on no account now wish to have missed."[14] Hannah quoted these words Rahel uttered at the time of her death and placed them at the beginning of the biography. Then, looping backwards, she recounted Rahel's earlier efforts to escape the infamy of her Jewish birth, first by eradicating the fact of being born a Jew from her thinking and then by trying to assimilate through marriage.

Escape. Infamy. Assimilate. Writing these words in Germany in 1933 must have helped Hannah see more clearly how, as she recalled in 1964, "belonging to Judaism had become my own problem, and my own problem was political."[15] Finishing the biography while in exile, her own political consciousness awakened, Hannah judged the price "demanded of the pariah if [s]he wishes to become a parvenu [as] always too high [because it] always strikes at those most human elements which alone made up [a] life."[16] Neither trying to escape being a Jew nor attempting to assimilate, Hannah chose the path of the conscious pariah.

Hannah tried to explain the particular dilemma she faced as a German Jew in a remarkable series of letters exchanged between Hannah and Karl Jaspers, the psychologist and philosopher who was her dissertation advisor and later became a close friend. In January 1933, less than a month before Hitler became Chancellor of Germany, and almost two months before the burning of the Reichstag, she articulated to Jaspers the reasons for her resistance to his book on Max Weber—*Max Weber: Deutsches Wesen im politischen Denken, im Forschen und Philosophieren* (Max Weber: German Character in Political Thinking, Research, and Philosophy):

> *There is a good reason...why I am writing only now to thank you for [the book]: The title and introduction made it difficult for me from the start to comment on the book. It does not bother me that you portray Max Weber as the great German but, rather, that you find the 'German essence' in him and identify that essence with 'rationality and humanity originating in passion'...You will understand that I as a Jew can neither say yes nor no and that my agreement would be as inappropriate as an argument against it...For me, Germany means my mother tongue, philosophy, and literature. I can and must stand by all that. But I am obliged to keep my distance...*[17]

Two days later, came Jaspers' reply:

> *I find it odd that you as a Jew want to set yourself apart from what is German... When I say that German character is rationality, etc., I am not saying that rationality is exclusively German...I made the attempt, hopeless perhaps, to give it ethical content through the figure of Max Weber. That attempt, however, would have proved successful only if you, too, could say: that's the way it is. I want to be a German. When you speak of mother tongue, philosophy, and literature, all you need to add is historical-political destiny, and there is no difference left at all.*[18]

But Hannah continued trying to clarify to Jaspers why she found the term "German character" so disturbing. In the course of her explanation, she began to map out a point of view she defended and embodied throughout the course of her life—the position of a "conscious pariah."

> *I do not have in myself, so to speak, an attestation of 'German character'...I am, of course a German in the sense that I wrote of before. But I can't simply add a German historical and political destiny to that. I know only too well how late and fragmentary the Jews' participation in that destiny has been, how much by chance they entered into what was then a foreign history...Germany in its*

old glory is your past. What my Germany is can hardly be expressed in one phrase, for any oversimplification—whether it is that of the Zionists, the assimilationists, or the anti-Semites—only serves to obscure the true problem of the situation.[19]

How much "by chance" Jews had entered into "what was then a foreign history", and how much more self-consciously and politically Jews needed to engage the course of world events became the centerpiece of Hannah's later work, *The Origins of Totalitarianism.* The seeds of her awareness of the imperative to embrace one's outsider status and develop a political, as opposed to a social, response to it had been sown, in part, by her acquaintance with Blumenfeld's version of Zionism. But I thought it also had roots in her now abandoned relationship with Heidegger.

Jaspers remained uncomprehending of what Hannah claimed.

[Y]ou have drawn conclusions for your interpretation that I cannot go along with. But that is material for another conversation, which I would open with the question of what it is you are really after. We cannot live solely from negations, problems, and ambiguities. All these things need to be informed by something positive.[20]

That other conversation began to take place between them in 1933 Berlin until Hitler's rise to power interrupted it abruptly. It wasn't to continue until after the war, when Hannah discovered to her great relief that Jaspers and his wife, Gertrude, who was also Jewish, had survived. It was a sense of relief Jaspers shared.

"Often over the past years we worried about your fate and for a long time now did not have much hope that you were still alive," Jaspers wrote to Hannah in October 1945.

> *And now not only do we have your reappearance but also a lively, intellectual presence from the wide world! You have, it seems to me, unerringly retained your inner core, whether you had been in Königsberg, Heidelberg or America or Paris. Anyone who is a real human being has to be able to do that.*[21]

As if responding to Jaspers allusion to her "inner core," in her reply Hannah took up again the thread of their earlier exchanges, situating herself in a very particular way:

> *Since I've been in America—that is, since 1941—I've become a kind of freelance writer, something between a historian and a political journalist. In that latter capacity I've focused primarily on questions of Jewish politics. I've written about the German question only when growing hatred toward Ger-*

many and increasing idiocy about it made it impossible to remain silent, especially if one is a Jew.[22]

Jaspers wanted more details: "Tell me about your husband [Heinrich Blücher]. I don't even know what your last name is. In what kind of circumstances are you living?"[23]

"I continue to use my old name," Hannah replied, explaining:

That's quite common here in America when a woman works, and I have gladly adopted this custom out of conservatism (and also because I wanted my name to identify me as a Jew)...I'm still a stateless person...If I had wanted to become respectable, I would either have had to give up my interest in Jewish affairs or not marry a non-Jewish man, either option equally inhuman and in a sense crazy.[24]

And although pleased that Jaspers had invited her in this same letter to contribute an essay to a new journal, *Die Wandlung*, on which he served on the editorial board, Hannah explained why contributing to a German journal would not be an easy thing for her to do:

If Jews are to be able to stay in Europe, then they cannot stay as Germans or Frenchmen, etc., as if nothing had happened. It seems to me that none of us can return (and writing is

> *surely a form of return) merely because people again seem to recognize Jews as Germans or something else. We can return only if we are welcome as Jews. That would mean I would gladly write something if I can write as a Jew on some aspect of the Jewish question.*[25]

She then offered him the German version of her essay, "Organized Guilt and Universal Responsibility," which had been published in English in January 1945 in *Jewish Frontier*.

After Jaspers informed Hannah that the German version of her essay would be included in an upcoming edition of *Die Wandlung*, she wrote back saying that Jaspers' approval was "the most gratifying, indeed the only possible, confirmation of continuity with the past."[26] "*Organisierte Schuld*" (Organized Guilt) became the first piece of writing Hannah published in Germany after the war. And it appeared in *Die Wandlung* in 1945 with a special note Hannah had requested establishing her writing identity unquestionably as that of a Jew.

Less than half a century separates me from Hannah Arendt. Yet, except for the profession of political theory, coming from radically different worlds and eras, we seem to have little in common. Although from the late 1940s to the middle of the 1970s we walked the same New York City streets, we never met. To this day, I regret not having taken her courses at the New School where she was then teaching. Yet as I read through her correspondence with Jaspers, I realized I shared with Hannah a complicated relationship to Judaism, though "complicated" for entirely different reasons from hers.

In 1975, I converted to Judaism, becoming, in the vernacular of our times, a "Jew by choice." Why?

I suppose it was partly because the tradition I'd been born into—my family's Catholic religion—had ceased to have meaning for me. Even in my early adolescence, being a Catholic had become a source of confusion. My earliest memories of the thinly veiled misogyny at the heart of Church orthodoxy, coupled with Church condemnation of my parents' divorce, my mother's remarriage, and my own sexual awakening combined to create a constellation of forces that collided with the highly charged cultural atmosphere of the New York City circles I traveled in at the time—early 1970s women's liberation and socialist radicalism, mixed with a heavy dose of Jewish intellectualism. I was ripe for rebellion.

Except mine was an agnostic's rebellion, a reversal of belief tempered by a transcendentalist longing for community and ritual, the exemplar for which I found, oddly enough, reading Max Weber's *Ancient Judaism* and engaging in lively discussions about Weber's ideas with the rabbi of the conservative synagogue I had started to frequent in Louisville, Kentucky.

I moved to Kentucky in 1975 with my second husband, Mike, who was Jewish, and my son from a previous marriage. It's certainly true that spending time with Mike's parents, who kept Kosher and, at least in the home, celebrated all the major Jewish holidays, gave me a taste of belonging to something at once more worldly and more mundane, more sacred and more profane than my long abandoned ritual Sunday mass. I wanted them to accept me.

But over time what became even more important than their acceptance, which disappeared after our divorce, was finding in Judaism the kind of belonging I needed by attaching myself to a wandering people who, against the odds, had attempted, with differing degrees of success, to sustain themselves as a distinctive community. I felt like a wanderer myself yet held onto the belief, as Hannah once described, that "only within the framework of a people can a man live as a man among men, without exhausting [her]self."[27] Years later, my thinking journey with Hannah renewed my faith in the political ideal that "only when a people lives and functions in concert with other peoples can it contribute to the establishment upon earth of a commonly conditioned and commonly controlled humanity."[28]

Of course, because of her personal experience of the Holocaust, Hannah's own complicated sense of belonging to the Jewish people was rooted in entirely more historically influenced and visceral ways than mine. Redefining her relationship to the religion of her ancestors ruptured forever her perception of the historical era and political and cultural spaces in which she lived and, perhaps more tellingly, led her to abandon anything like a linear view of Jewish history as eternal victimhood or an eschatological justification of the state of Israel, both of which positions make her *persona non grata* in many Jewish circles even today. Yet she insisted she belonged to the Jewish people.

Still, for someone like me—an ardent feminist with leftist predilections, a woman in love with a woman, a grandmother, a person who can spend hours lost in daydreams and introspection—to be obsessed with Hannah Arendt has been disconcerting. She was a woman who ridiculed the women's movement and rejected every form of ideology. She would have considered discussions of the politics of sexuality and love ridiculous. She had no children. And she dismissed interior reflection about one's emotional life as vastly inferior to real thinking. Why then has she captivated me so?

To dispense with the obvious first, her experience as a singular star in the male universe of philosophy is, in itself, an achievement, and one I admired. Her refusal to confine herself to some narrow identity category—Is she a woman, a German, a Jew, a scholar? Is she arrogant or deeply vulnerable at heart?—makes her a distinctively modern role model. And her steadfastness in the face of brutal criticism is a quality I have, more than once, tried to emulate. But none of this really explains why she matters to me or makes me think, again and again, that what she wrote, however dense and difficult to read, and how she lived, however privately and with evident scorn for self-disclosure, might make her matter to anyone trying to make sense of her own life.

We read books at certain times in our lives and they have an impact on us depending on how open we are to what they are saying. In 1977, I was still in graduate school and desperately trying to finish a dissertation on Marx while teaching political science at a public university in North Carolina and raising an eight-year old son. Recently remarried, I also was trying, unsuccessfully, to get pregnant again. Not having much luck with the available fertility consultants in Jacksonville, I traveled that summer to New York to consult another specialist. He scheduled me for a laparoscopy for later in the year and I returned to North Carolina to finish the semester's teaching and, I hoped, my dissertation.

Kathleen B. Jones

In December, I entered a Manhattan hospital for a procedure meant to get things going again in my Fallopian tubes. It so happened I'd taken along a copy of *The New Yorker*. Still under the influence of general anesthesia and dazed by the doctor's news that the operation had been a success, I thumbed through the magazine and came upon an essay entitled "Thinking."

"The faculty of thought...does not ask what something is or whether it exists at all...but what it means to be." I read that line and kept on reading. "By posing the unanswerable questions of meaning, men establish themselves as question-asking beings." (Yes. I admit it. I bridled at the use of the word "men" in that sentence. But, I thought, having forgiven Marx the same language, why shouldn't I also forgive this German woman, who would have been thinking *Menschen*, meaning humans, and not just males).

Later I learned the essay was a posthumously published excerpt from Hannah's last book, *The Life of the Mind*, a book I have now re-read many times, each time uncovering new riches in it. But when I first confronted those words, I misread them as an invitation to avoid the quandary of what it meant to be a woman in those confusing times by escaping into the life of the mind.

In those still relatively early years of women's liberation figuring out how to be both a woman and an intellectual was a task few of us had models to go by. Feeling betrayed by my own body, angry at its needing "redemption" by science, and generally disturbed by my gender, reading Hannah's words in that hospital room seemed to give me a way out. They provided a way for me to think of myself as an intellectual, a disembodied, question-asking being, a person only incidentally female.

Thinking thus, I missed the larger point Hannah had made. I hadn't yet become a question to myself. I hadn't yet asked: what can it mean to be me in this body, at this time, in this place? And I wouldn't really begin to contemplate this question until many years later when I again immersed myself in *Rahel Varnhagen.*

{ 3 }

Slipping into Her Skin

Writing is a matter of seeking understanding.

Hannah Arendt, "*What Remains? Language Remains*"

WHEN I FIRST CAME ACROSS *RAHEL VARNHAGEN: THE LIFE OF A JEWISH WOMAN*, I WAS PUT OFF BY ITS STRANGE FORMAT.[29] The book didn't fit anything I recognized as biography. It seemed a bizarre compilation of facts Hannah had culled from Rahel's correspondence and dreams and then cobbled together into what sounded like a very one-sided story. Only years later, reading the book like a writer, did I begin to understand how its unusual shape made the narrative so compelling: the storyteller had slipped into the story.

"It still comes as a shock to realize," the memoirist Patricia Hampl once wrote, "that I don't write about what I know, but in order to find out what I know." The reader might succumb to the "lovely illusion" that the words fall onto the page as if "inevitably...faultlessly." But the writer knows what the reader forgets: "The heart, the guardian of intuition with its secrets, is the boss. Its commands are what a writer obeys—often without knowing it."[30]

Hampl's lines made me turn back to Hannah's *Rahel* and wonder where Hannah's heart had commanded her to go while she was writing that story. What secrets had her own heart made her confront? Had Hannah's harsh judgment of Rahel's attempts to escape her identity (her fate?) by disappearing into a series of misadventures and unhappy romances been as much an indictment of Hannah herself as of her subject? I decided there was more to be gained from reading the biography again, but this time below the surface of the story of its protagonist's life.

"The thing which all my life seemed to me the greatest shame, which was the misery and misfortune of my life—having been born a Jewess—this I should on no account now wish to have missed." Hardly concealing her hostility Hannah recounted Rahel's earlier efforts to negate her Jewish identity by surrounding herself with the trappings of a cultured life, including her famous *Jägerstrasse* garret, and pursuing romantic liaisons with an aristocratic class of men. To masquerade as a non-Jew, Rahel used the disguise of her sex, yearning to be married to a man of the right culture and bearing "as though," Hannah wrote, "she longed only to be taken away from what and where she was."[31] She belittled Rahel for trying to be exceptional, that is, for seeing herself as an exception among Jews and took her to task for being indifferent to politics, berating Rahel's efforts to find liberation in love. Yet, the one thing Hannah didn't question was the politics of love.

In some ways, it surprised me that Hannah never investigated the politics of love. After all, love—or, more precisely, Augustine's concept of love, *caritas*, as "neighborly love" or the divine command to "love thy neighbor as thyself"—had been the subject of her doctoral dissertation. She defined Augustine's concept of "caritas," or divine love, as rooted in a fundamental equality—an equality "neither of traits nor of talents, but of situation" resulting "in a kinship beyond any mere likeness." Such love was grounded in a radical conception of equality because, she wrote, it "wipes out all distinctions" and "receives a new meaning—love of neighbor." And this love "denotes a change in the coexistence of people…from being inevitable to being freely chosen and replete with obligations," obligations that make "each belong to everyone" and mark the beginning of a "new social life...defined by mutual love."[32]

But if all distinctions are erased in love I wondered why Hannah hadn't considered the possibility that sexual politics might limit love's radical equality? I guess I expected her to be ahead of her times. Throughout her life, or so it seemed, Hannah remained unapologetically adamant that sexuality wasn't a political subject. Love, she insisted, was the most apolitical of attachments.

Even late in life, she wrote to the editors of *The American Review*, who had requested an essay from her responding to Susan Sontag's writing on feminism, that she had "sworn a holy oath not to touch women's liberation." As to 'the woman question,' "it never interested me very much," she admitted in a letter to Claudia Koonz and Renate Bridenthal, thanking them for sending her copies of their pioneering research on European women's history, adding that their book taught her "more than she ever knew." The evidence seemed clear: in Hannah's view, interrogating the status of women wasn't a political question. In this, as in so many other things, Hannah Arendt appeared to part company with feminists both of her own and even earlier generations.

In the latter half of the nineteenth century, feminist progressive reformers were concerned deeply with the politics of love. They criticized romantic love as a dangerous passion that led to conflict and disappointment in a society with gender-based inequalities. And they rejected what was then called "sentimental love" for exalting sexual difference and representing women as passive, idealized objects of men's affection. Instead, these activists advocated an ideal of love based in rational, symmetrical, and egalitarian relations, and not subject to the whims of passion or fantasy.

Contemporary feminists offered new, transformative definitions of love. In bell hooks' words, this means seeing love "as an active force that should lead us into greater communion with the world" and the practice of love as an action that can lead not only to greater life satisfaction for individuals but a way to end domination.[33]

In many ways, hooks's treatise updates earlier feminists' efforts to establish "rational love", egalitarian at its core, as the hallmark of "true love." Yet, hooks pushes past those reformers' intentions to advocate a model of love as

> *the will to nurture one's own or another's spiritual growth, revealed through acts of care, respect, knowing, and assuming responsibility...There is no special love exclusively reserved for romantic partners. Genuine love is the foundation of our engagement with ourselves, with family, with*

friends, with partners, with everyone we choose to love.[34]

This begs the question, not fully answered by hooks: Whom should we choose to love and how? Surprisingly, this question animates Hannah's *Rahel Varnhagen.*

Hannah's life writing displays a fundamental concern with the practice of love expressed as authentic self-awareness and connection to others. One can even trace its ramifications across the trains of her thought from *Rahel Varnhagen* into *The Origins of Totalitarianism*, her monumental work on totalitarianism, and follow it into her reflections in *The Human Condition.* And the reason this question took on such prominence seems to me to have a lot to do with Hannah's life history itself.

As I reread *Rahel Varnhagen* later in my own life I began to think Hannah's insistent lack of interest in the woman question might be covering a deeper truth about her understanding of love and the politics of love.

Underneath the surface lines of Rahel's story I discovered a subterranean narrative, a sort of doppelganger tale where Hannah's life shadowed Rahel's. To write her book, Hannah had slipped into Rahel's skin, becoming the woman in the center of Rahel's story. And by taking on this other woman's life she'd raised questions about the politics of love, even if not directly to herself. The peculiar path Hannah took into biographical writing belied her erasure of sex as a political fact in any woman's life story, no matter how insistently she tried to ignore it.

"She had nothing of the militant feminist," claimed Helen Wolff, the Pantheon publisher and fellow *émigré* and friend of Hannah's for several decades. "Asked once how she felt about being a woman" Hannah's reply was "I am used to it."[35] The prominent American writer and literary critic Alfred Kazin, who became another close friend of Hannah's, concurred. "[D]espite her scorn for such feminist tracts as Simone de Beauvoir's *The Second Sex*, I doubt that she had any more interest in feminism, pro or contra, than Immanuel Kant."[36] But the philosopher Virginia Held countered Kazin's portrait:

> *The record should show that in the last years of her life her views on feminism were beginning to change. I only got to know her a few years before her death, but in several leisurely conversations over dinner she admitted that the woman's movement was making a noticeable and helpful difference in the behavior of her female students: for the first time they were beginning to speak in class. And she did listen with interest to the argu-*

> *ments that I and other women offered on the validity of feminism and the need for a woman's movement.*[37]

Kazin persisted: "Whatever her growing sympathy with feminism—I have to take Professor Held's word for this—I never found Hannah a staunch egalitarian when it came to women whose thinking she could not fully respect."[38] Eight years later, he underscored his point of view: "Every teacher knows how to be nice to students...But when it came to feminism per se... women's righters...you could forget it, you know, nothing of the sort."[39] Of course, Kazin had about as much interest in feminism as Kant. Still, there's no denying Hannah rejected feminism on ideological grounds. Labels aside, her life can be seen as an illustration of how the politics of love affected women in this transitional time.

During the course of my research, I came across a notebook among the papers of Elżbieta Ettinger, a Polish émigré and literature professor who taught in MIT's Humanities Department and was in the process of writing about Hannah Arendt. In that notebook I discovered things shedding further light on Hannah's complicated relationship to "the woman question."

In 1987, soon after the publication of Ettinger's, *Rosa Luxemburg: A Life*, her British publisher suggested she write a biography of Hannah Arendt. Ettinger never completed the task, publishing in 1995 only a much shorter and immensely controversial monograph about the affair between Hannah Arendt and Martin Heidegger. Why Ettinger abandoned the longer biography is complicated to explain. In part, health problems she faced later in life hampered her. But her energy had also been sapped by pursuing an extensive legal case against the German publisher, Verlag, for a book about Heidegger written by Ruediger Safranski, whom Ettinger charged had plagiarized her then unpublished work on the Heidegger affair.

Despite being sidetracked from her original project, Ettinger's archives proved a gold mine of information about Hannah, including notes and transcripts of the many interviews she conducted with Hannah's close friends and acquaintances, along with some of her enemies.

In 1990 Ettinger traveled to Israel to interview the few remaining members of Hannah's family, including Hannah's cousins, Kaethe and Ernst Fuerst. Although nothing in the typescript of the taped interview confirms her notation, Ettinger recorded one small, yet significant piece of information in her notebook that I have never seen mentioned in any biographies of Arendt's life: Hannah had an abortion when she was married to Gunther Stern. And, the Fuersts contended,

Hannah had wanted children; her second husband, Heinrich Blücher, did not.[40]

I kept coming back to this entry, wondering about what this insistent marker of female embodiment might have meant in the life of Hannah Arendt. And the more deeply I dove into the complexity surrounding this fact, the more it occurred to me that by publicly distancing herself from defining gender in political terms Hannah might have been trying to create her own very unique escape into exceptionality.

Like Rahel, Hannah adopted a persona, wore a mask. As a woman, she seemed to stand apart. To many who knew her, she was caricatured as a woman-who-was-not-Woman. Critics, and even some friends, often portrayed her as cold and uncaring, a woman out of touch with her feelings.

One particularly acerbic voice was Diana Trilling's. Through her marriage to Lionel Trilling, Diana became part of the New York intellectual circle of literary critics, writers, and artists who, from the 1930s to the late 1960s, frequented both the pages of New York's most prominent literary magazines (*The New Yorker, Saturday Review, The Atlantic, Harper's,* and *The Nation)* as well as its literary parties. Describing this circle in her memoir of the times, Trilling wrote:

> *With marriage I had entered Lionel's world. It was with his friends that I now chiefly as-*

> *sociated. They were not easy companions, these intellectuals...[O]verbearing and arrogant, excessively competitive; they lacked magnanimity and often...lacked common courtesy. Ours was a cruelly judgmental society, often malicious and riddled with envy.*[41]

That circle included Hannah Arendt, whom Diana Trilling considered especially cruel, having been rebuffed by Hannah on more than one occasion.

"We met over the years a spectacular number of times, maybe a couple of dozen times. She would walk past me, she never said hello...She snubbed me for years," Trilling told Ettinger. As to what explained her being treated so dismissively by Hannah, she offered what she called a "very old-fashioned" explanation: "I think she was very much interested in Lionel...she was sort of a man-eating woman...She addressed her entire conversation to him and never said a word to me." Recalling the earliest occasion when she'd met Hannah Arendt—at a 1946 party for the former Berlin rabbi, Leo Baeck—Trilling continued:

> *I watched her that evening...I was just watching her with Rabbi Baeck...He was a most charming and impressive man...And Hannah kept pressing in on us and pretty soon absolutely took over as if she were the hostess...She was very predatory...a very, very*

> *fierce woman...I thought she was lacking in feminine charm.*[42]

Whatever Hannah may have lacked in ordinary "feminine charm" her fiery intellect gave her an aura of complicated eroticism, attracting both women and men admirers, gay and straight, while at the same time generating jealousy, intense competition, and rivalry. You either loved her or hated her; there was no middle ground.

Irving Howe, who later became a prominent editor and leftist social critic, recollected meeting Hannah when he was a young man. Not yet famous, she was working as an editor at Schocken Books. Howe needed work and Hannah employed him, paying him generously for routine editorial tasks. He recalled them discussing assignments and interesting books in weekly meetings. Howe thought Hannah was a self-confident woman, very generous. Although they differed radically on political viewpoints, Howe then toeing a more orthodox Marxist line, Hannah still sent work his way, even recommending him for a job at *The Nation.* They grew to like each other and became friendly. "I was young, I learned from her; I was then moving from orthodox Marxism."[43]

Hannah was generous, Howe observed, but also "imperious...she liked to be surrounded by admirers and 'disciples' " and to be in the middle of "passionate disputes." After the publication of *Eichmann in Jerusalem* split the intellectual world into supporters and condemners, *Partisan Review* held a panel, inviting Hannah to attend. She declined. Instead, Howe agreed to chair the tense meeting at the Diplomat Hotel in New York. An angry crowd shouted down anyone who spoke in support of Hannah's position. Following that meeting, Hannah refused to have anything more to do with Howe.

But a year or so later, they found themselves at the same party. Howe reached out to shake her hand and Hannah "rather elegantly" indicated with her eyes "No." Nearly a decade passed before they found common ground for a different kind of relationship—what Howe called one based on the political critique of the "anti-intellectualism of American life." But they never again became real friends. Still, Howe thought her extraordinary. "I really liked her; when she cut me, it was painful...There was no one like her before. There is no one now."[44]

Alfred Kazin admitted an even more intense attachment to Hannah. He first met Hannah at the same party for Rabbi Baeck where Diane Trilling had had such an awful encounter with her. Kazin's recollections were entirely the opposite of Trilling's:

> *What luck, HA placed next to me at the dinner for Rabbi L.B., and I have sought her out*

> *several times since. Darkly handsome, beautifully interested in everything, this forty-year old German refugee with a strong accent and such intelligence—thinking positively cascades out of her in waves—that I was enthralled, by no means unerotically.*[45]

Soon part of her inner circle, Kazin introduced her to the New York Intellectuals. And he helped smooth her English usage in *The Origins of Totalitarianism,* paving the way for the book to be published by Harcourt, Brace & Company by sending the manuscript to Robert Giroux, who was then working for Harcourt. Hannah acknowledged his support by writing in the acknowledgments for the first edition "the great help of Alfred Kazin's friendship for book and author is beyond gratitude."

She and Kazin were close, especially in the 40s and 50s, sharing holidays, trips to Europe and New Year's Eve parties. Yet, the relationship had its moments of tension. On one occasion, Pearl Bell recalled, Hannah went with Kazin and his wife, Anne Birstein, to a lecture in New York.

> *She unceremoniously told [Anne] to go and sit in the gallery [upstairs] while she and Kazin will sit downstairs. Anne was furious. The next day, Kazin called Hannah to demand that she apologize to his wife. She put*

> *down the receiver and the friendship was as much as ended.*[46]

Although their friendship dissipated, Kazin claimed he kept her close to his heart for the rest of his life. In his 1978 memoir, he wrote, "[Hannah Arendt] became vital to my life. Much as I loved her and submitted patiently to an intellectual loneliness that came out as arrogance, it was for the direction of her thinking that I loved her..."[47] He repeated the sentiment with even greater intensity more than twenty years later: "I mentioned a lot of things I didn't like about her," he told Ettinger in an interview. "But in the end, I've never known anyone remotely like her. And I suppose in a very real sense, I really loved her."[48] This judgment gains poignancy since, as Kazin acknowledged painfully, Hannah had dropped any reference to his earlier assistance in later editions of *The Origins of Totalitarianism.*

After Heinrich Blücher's death, the poet W.H. Auden, who was gay, proposed to Hannah. A little later, another long-time friend, the prominent political scientist Hans Morgenthau, also offered marriage. Despite her loneliness and recognition that Morgenthau's was a serious proposition she rejected him too.

These men of her own generation were followed in the next by others who became her students and protégés across the many campuses where she taught in the very unconventional academic career she carved out for herself during her three and a half decades in America. Equally enamored by her intellect, yet frustrated by her complexity, many fell in and out of love, in one way or another, with this woman who broke every recognizable mold of femininity.

Given the demographics of most universities' departments of philosophy and theory at this time, many of these admirers were men; only in the early 1970s, while I was in graduate school, did the gender ratio among graduate university students in such departments begin to shift away from male dominance. Still, I began to feel a common bond between even these male admirers and me.

In the 1950s and 60s, when Hannah was invited to teach at several prominent American universities, the world of academia was overwhelmingly male. In her account of her own experiences in graduate school at Columbia University under the aura of men like Lionel Trilling, the feminist critic Carolyn Heilbrun described the times: women were not to be admitted to the "fellowship of learning. Men were what it was all about, men struggling for some assurance..." Those few women professors who were to be found

> *tended toward type. As we callow students saw it then, they were unmarried, hence unloved...Now, I can perceive that the wound*

those women displayed did indeed have to do with deprivation of their womanhood... They had become what I would later call honorary men; they presented themselves and their ideas in male attire.[49]

In this world, Hannah Arendt remained an anomaly. A pioneer among women, especially in the fields of philosophy and politics, she hated being recognized as the "first woman to do X," notoriously threatening to reject an offer from Princeton to appoint her as Full Professor because the university had emphasized her status as a "first woman" in its November 1958 announcement to the *New York Times*.[50] She didn't consider her sex an obstacle in any way. Nor did she attire or comport herself as an "honorary man."

In her reflections on Hannah's personality Helen Wolff described Hannah as having *Ausstrahlung*, a charismatic presence; she exuded "a passion of the mind." And that passion certainly bore an erotic force. Michael Denneny recalled the impact of her lectures in the early 1960s at the University of Chicago. At the time, Hannah was working through her yet unpublished work, *On Revolution*, and presented the book, chapter by chapter, in a great lecture hall filled with mesmerized students, mostly men

[N]o one had ever seen that degree of intellectual force...this was a mind at work like we

> *had seen very few...There were very many brilliant people at the University of Chicago...[but] Arendt...was a thinker...she actually thought...[T]hese abstract philosophical questions, she knew how they related to reality and life.*[51]

Yet Hannah communicated this electricity of thought in a particularly embodied way, giving her a seductive allure. "[I]t was very strange" Denneny continued,

> *because we used to joke about it. In her seventies* [sic] *this lady had very good legs...they were very shapely...You never forgot she was a woman...[T]here were other American academic women and they were radically different...[Hannah] was always womanly. She never tried...to be a non-woman.*[52]

Helen Wolff shared this impression of Hannah's womanliness. "She was very feminine in the sense of wanting to look her best, *trés soignée*, and particularly conscious of her fine legs, always shod by the famous Italian shoemaker, Ferragamo...She could be quite flirtatious if an attractive man was around, in a playful, non-committal way."[53]

As I plowed through these recollections I couldn't help noticing how very differently Hannah maneuvered through the Scylla of high intellectualism and the Carybdis of traditional gender roles, both of which stood like threatening monsters in the waters of academe, dangerous to all, but especially to women who dared not to drown. It seemed to me she'd hit on how to be seen as a woman without only being seen as a woman in every way that mattered to her.

After reading *Eichmann in Jerusalem* Gershom Sholem accused her of showing no trace of love for the Jewish people. In a letter to her Sholem said he regarded Hannah "wholly as a daughter of our people, and in no other way" and had expected something more sympathetic. Hannah replied that, as far as being a daughter of the Jewish people, she had

> *never pretended to be anything else or to be in any way other than I am, and I have never even felt tempted in that direction. It would be like saying I was a man and not a woman—that is to say, kind of insane... There is such a thing as a basic gratitude for everything that is as it is; for what has been given and was not, could not be, made.*[54]

But to Hannah demonstrating gratitude meant not passive acceptance but actively taking up her intrinsic and particular difference and inserting herself in the world as the "Who" she was. A woman-who-was-not-Woman.

Melvyn Hill, who later edited a collection of essays on her work, first met Hannah Arendt at the University of Chicago in 1962. A Jewish émigré from South Africa who had deserted the country over its apartheid policies, Hill applied for a graduate program with the Committee on Social Thought. Hannah Arendt was one of three people who interviewed him for admission.

> *I had no idea who she was...She didn't pursue any academic questions. The minute she heard I was from South Africa she wanted to know what was I doing here, how had I gotten here, what had my experiences been...and I immediately began to be able to talk about things that I hadn't spoken to anyone about for a number of reasons.*[55]

It wasn't easy to befriend Hannah Arendt, Hill explained. "[S]he was very demanding, she didn't abide fools lightly...For the lucky few who managed to engage in this kind of friendship, I think it became possibly one of the most important experiences in our lives."[56] Hill's friendship with Hannah continued into the 70s; she even came to Hill's wedding. She was, Hill admitted, a very complex person with divided loyalties, each equally compelling.

Yet, despite Hannah's complexity and vulnerability, and her deep commitment to privacy, Hill found certain aspects of her life difficult to accept. What disturbed him most was the Heidegger affair, which he took very personally. Learning about this relationship long after Hannah died, Hill became "quite grief-stricken," feeling the affair was "almost a betrayal. I felt there was something there that I couldn't reconcile myself. And in the end I simply had to admit that I didn't understand..."[57] The more Hill thought about the affair, exchanging psychological interpretations of Hannah with Ettinger, who had sent him drafts of her then unpublished manuscript about Hannah's affair with Heidegger—Hill being a psychoanalyst—the more ashamed he seemed to become.

> *Hannah was once the focus of my attention, for a long time. So you are asking me to go back in time in order to think about someone I once admired greatly, and perhaps loved. Now I am embarrassed by that infatuation, since I have come to learn who she was behind the mask of a learned scholar and profound thinker.*[58]

But there was one more turn in this story, one more defense Hill allowed himself, justifying his own abiding affection for this person he thought unacceptably divided against herself.

> *When all is said...I still remain faithful to her in my own way. Despite my retrospective anger, and the disappointment in discovering her weakness for a Nazi. As a person she was not who I wanted her to be, to warrant the love I felt for her. But as a thinker and writer*

> *she was probably one of the finest in our time. And her sense of humor was enough to plant the seeds of wisdom for a lifetime. And that I could most certainly love about her. She had spirit. Not* Geist.[59]

Ironic, I thought. Hill's explanation sounded uncannily similar to Alfred Kazin's identification of the source of his own abiding love for Hannah. She had a spirituality about her, Kazin had said, a kind of transcendence. And it struck me as even more ironic how, despite coming from different generations and cultures, both men's justifications of their loyalty to Hannah paralleled Hannah's own rationale for her continued affection for Heidegger. Despite his failings and even his duplicity, Heidegger taught her to think.

> *I know that he finds it intolerable that my name appears in public, that I write books, etc. All my life I've pulled the wool over his eyes, so to speak, always acted as if none of that existed and as if I couldn't count to three, unless it was in the interpretation of his own works... Then suddenly I felt this deception was becoming just so boring, and so I got a rap on the nose. I was very angry for a moment, but I'm not any longer. I feel instead that I somehow deserved what I got—that is, both for having deceived him and for suddenly having put an end to it.*[60]

Heidegger's defensive arrogance didn't prevent Hannah from continuing her friendship with him until the end of her life. Nor did Hannah's self-righteousness turn most of her closest admirers away. Including me.

In her later years, Hannah displayed a growing stubbornness. More insistent than ever on the correctness of her viewpoint, unwilling to bend either to fact or criticism, she became what Mary McCarthy, one of Hannah's closest friends, called a *Besserwisser* ("smart aleck"), using a term McCarthy had learned from talking with Elżbieta Ettinger. To illustrate the point, McCarthy recounted a story from a time she was traveling with Hannah in Germany.

> *We were walking on the grounds at Marbach [with the poet Ludwig Greve] and Hannah points to some tree and says* 'Das ist ein Nussbaum' [That is a walnut tree] *and 'No, no," I said. [Ludwig Greve was with us and he] knew...something about the...trees and he just said* 'Hannah, das ist kein Nussbaum' [Hannah, that is not a walnut tree] *and she shut up.*[61]

But then, McCarthy added "there was also this timidity...and shyness." Especially after Heinrich died, Hannah was incredibly lonely. "She didn't talk about her feelings...[S]he wrote me a little more than she talked...about missing him. She was very, very much alone after his death, terribly alone...I don't think she ever got over that."[62]

I began to think Hannah's mask of bravado might be covering a deepening sadness. For the most part, it was an effective cover. Few penetrated the wall of privacy behind which Hannah carefully guarded her vulnerability; she kept all but closest friends from glimpsing the well of fears and loneliness she felt as ever-present threats. And even those few were given only partial views, as if Hannah were distributing pieces of herself among them so that no one, except perhaps Heinrich, would be able to assemble the puzzle of who Hannah really was.

Helen Wolff remembered Hannah telling her

> *of one trait that one would not have associated with her on one's own—a great shyness...She never gave the impression of shyness though. She seemed so secure in her opinions, so rapid in her grasping of situations—but alerted by herself I noticed, when she gave a lecture at Goethe house, New York, that her hands trembled as she turned the pages of her script.*[63]

Wolff also understood, in an intimate way, the impact of being a refugee, a condition she shared with Hannah: they had both been in France when the Germans occupied Paris and were forced to live "on the run."

Hannah shared with Wolff details of her escape from Gurs and finding refuge in Montaubon where, once reunited with Heinrich, "far from giving in to anxiety, they explored the beautiful countryside [and] Hannah in her high-spirited way made of this anguishing experience a kind of 'gift of time.' "[64]

This refusal to be typecast into the role of Jewish victim extended into Hannah's efforts to seek post-war reparations from the German government for damages sustained by having her academic career cut short by forced emigration. When the case investigators inquired whether she hadn't also suffered long term psychological or physical damages from the Nazi era, which should be taken account in the settlement, Wolff recounted how Hannah "declared, laughing, that, no, she was perfectly healthy and always had been," a response that "stunned her interviewers, used to assertions of maximum damage, but not surprising to anyone familiar with Hannah's visceral truthfulness."[65]

The trouble was her "visceral truthfulness" contained messages difficult to reconcile with other revelations Hannah communicated. And, in some cases, friends ignored or weren't given access to certain "truths" about Hannah.

Lotte Kohler, who became Hannah's literary executor after McCarthy died, told Ettinger that Mary McCarthy "had loved Hannah and knew a lot about

Hannah, but certain...layers in her life she did not know. Because Hannah didn't really open all these facets to her...This being rooted in her Jewishness, without being Orthodox...or religious."[66]

Although McCarthy claimed to know being Jewish meant a lot to Hannah, her understanding was cut short of real comprehension. Perhaps the same could be said even of Hannah's family who grappled with the meaning Hannah attached to her own Jewish identity, struggling to claim her for their own conceptions of "Jewishness."

At Hannah's funeral a conflict erupted, reverberating long after the event in the memories of those who attended the ceremony. Hannah had named Lotte Kohler and Mary McCarthy as executors of her will. Since McCarthy was out of town at the time of Hannah's death, the task of planning the arrangements and informing friends and family fell to Lotte Kohler, whose name appeared on a little card in Hannah's apartment: "In case of emergency, call Lotte Kohler." Lotte arranged for services in the same funeral parlor where Heinrich's had been held five years earlier, and then called Mary and the Fuersts, Hannah's Israeli relatives, who all assembled as soon as possible. An argument ensued between McCarthy and the Fuersts about the Jewish rituals to be included in the ceremony. Eventually they reached a compromise. Jewish prayers were said then and at the cremation that followed.

Piecing together these observations of Hannah I started to understand the enormous difficulty facing anyone trying to render a portrait of Hannah in consistent, even-handed strokes. Her integrity became distorted if you approached her only from one angle. But who was Hannah to herself? Did she ever reflect on her complicated, certainly unusual, even contradictory relationships, disclose conflicted feelings to confidants or close friends, or leave any clues about personal struggles with the life of the heart in the mountains of documents she accumulated in her life? It began to seem entirely possible that writing helped Hannah achieve some degree of self-acceptance or at least reconciliation with those parts of herself others found incoherent or just plain mad. Writing, as Italo Calvino once said, is one way to become different from the way one has been.

In her collection of essays, *The End of the Novel of Love*, Vivian Gornick examined Hannah Arendt's affair with Martin Heidegger. The truly scandalous part of the whole affair was Hannah's renewed friendship with Heidegger long after his support of the Nazi party and his maltreatment of Jews had become indisputable facts. Hannah's failure in the matter of Martin Heidegger, Gornick contended, was the result of her never being able to grasp the power of repressed feeling; being sealed off from "all knowledge of her own inner conflicts" made her more at fault in the Heidegger affair than an ordinary woman, who makes a mistake but at least tries to understand why.

Yet, to me, this interpretation missed the mark.

The emotionally distancing language scholars are taught to use is partly a clever way to appear respectably removed from the subject. If you're a researcher studying violence, you're vaguely aware that behind your apparently dispassionate inquiry lurk emotional battles you're fighting yourself not to blow the whole place apart and the closer you get to the heart of the matter, the harder you work to put scholarly sounding words on the page.

So I wondered whether Hannah had begun to work through not only the Jewish Question but also her own relationship to womanhood and troubled affairs of the heart by writing *Rahel Varnhagen.* Had insights she'd gained in the process carried into self-reflection, belying Gornick's characterization of her as a woman walled off from her own conflicted self? And would being immersed in writing about Hannah have a similar effect on me?

"If you only knew how dangerous love would be for me," Hannah confessed in a letter she'd written to Heinrich Blücher, her beloved second husband, on one of the many occasions when circumstances forced them to live apart. For as long as she could remember "even as a kid" she'd known she could "only truly exist in love." And that frightened her; she was afraid being in love meant she would "simply get lost." But with Heinrich, she said, she was "no longer afraid." "For god's sake you are my four walls." And within that home in the world she felt blessed because she'd "managed to get both things, the 'love of my life,' and a oneness with myself."[67]

Reading her correspondence with Heinrich I realized something Hannah never admitted out loud. Being a woman made her feel vulnerable. Like Rahel, she'd fallen in love more than once with the "wrong" person; with men, who, though not exactly like Heidegger, were unable to love her fully on her own terms. She'd become afraid to risk love again.

Not infrequently in her letters to friends who found themselves in the throes of some difficult romantic entanglement, such as Mary McCarthy or Rosalie Colie, Hannah provided a caring shoulder to lean on. But she tempered her compassion with the sort of cautionary advice that made her appear invulnerable to similar temptations.

"Please don't fool yourself," she once wrote to McCarthy, "nobody ever was cured of anything, trait or habit, by a mere woman, though this is precisely what all girls think they can do. Either you are willing to take him 'as is' or you better leave well enough alone."[68] To which McCarthy responded,

> *The point of this love is its honesty, everything is offered, nothing is held back. It's total, like total war...I've...become aware of how prudent...I've always been myself, how many precautions I take against being wounded... What's the use of falling in love if you both remain inertly as-you-were...If he hopes for an inner change...the hope is part of the man as much as the habitual reactions. If you take him 'as is' you take the hope too.*[69]

But being wounded by love was exactly what Hannah feared, a fear she had in common with many women, yet admitted only to Heinrich. How she longed for connection; how afraid she was to get lost. With Heinrich, Hannah could live the truth she'd discovered writing Rahel's story: she was an ambiguous woman, a woman both like and unlike what everyone expected or wanted her to be.

Not that her relationship with Heinrich was without its own challenges.

Some time in 1948 Hannah discovered Heinrich had been carrying on an affair with Rose Feitelson, a very attractive woman in their inner circle of friends, who helped edit Hannah's manuscripts for English consistency. Hannah never felt jealousy, her oldest friend, Anne Mendelssohn Weil, told the biographer, Elisabeth Young-Bruehl. She accepted the affair: "[Heinrich is] not the prisoner of our marriage."[70] She found a way to forgive Heinrich's transgression, even continuing to employ Rose as an editor. Despite this affair, "she never felt abandoned...[There was] such a profound fraternity and camaraderie between [Heinrich and Hannah]"[71]

Several years later, while on a second extended post-war lecture tour of Europe that included work for the Jewish Cultural Reconstruction committee as well as several visits to Heidegger, Hannah wrote to Heinrich:

> *Yes, dearest, we have become part of each other and our steps tread in unison. And nothing can disturb this unison, even though life goes on. Those fools think that devotion means life coming to a standstill and getting bogged down in one of the two persons. They are cheated not just out of their shared life, but out of life itself. Someone should finally tell the world what marriage really is; if it only weren't so dangerous!*[72]

What did embarrass and anger her was learning later from another friend she'd known from her Paris days, Lotte Klenbort, that stories about the affair with

Rose were still making the rounds through various gossipy circles. Klenbort thought she was giving a "real friendship service" by telling Hannah people were still talking about it, but Hannah considered the publicity such a deep violation of her privacy that she cut herself off from the bearer of this news, with whom she otherwise had had a very close friendship.[73]

Yet, unknown to Hannah, though she may have suspected, there were other affairs and attempted affairs.

Charotte (Lotte) Beradt, who had been a lover of Heinrich's in Berlin before he met Hannah in exile in Paris, became involved with him again in the early 1950s, soon after he ended the affair with Rose and had begun teaching at Bard College in the Hudson Valley area of New York. Heinrich would return to New York City on Thursday night from Bard, spend the night with Beradt, coming home to Hannah the next day, without her ever knowing where he had been the night before, Lotte Kohler reported to Ettinger, adding that Heinrich had once even made a pass at her.[74] Recoiling from his advances, Kohler challenged him: "And Hannah, what about Hannah? And he said, well, that should be no worry, there's nothing between Hannah and me on a sexual level. But otherwise, yes." Heinrich claimed that he and Hannah hadn't had a sexual relationship for two or three years.[75] Whatever intimacy existed between them seemed cemented by a concept of loyalty transcending sexual fidelity. All this complicated my perception of Hannah's emotional life.

"I don't think I told you," Hannah wrote to Mary McCarthy not long after Heinrich's death in 1970

> *for ten long years I had been constantly afraid that just such a sudden death would happen. This fear frequently bordered on real panic. Where this fear was and the panic there is now sheer emptiness. Sometimes I think without this heaviness inside me I can no longer walk. And it is true, I feel like floating. If I think even a few months ahead I get dizzy.*[76]

McCarthy responded with understanding, up to a point.

> *Yes, I knew for ten years that you were afraid of that sudden death...It occurred to me...that you had lived with that death for so long that the actuality must be in some way a relaxation of tension for you...the absence of the familiar fear must be in some degree a relief—a poisoned one. I do not know how you will manage this.*[77]

The ten years leading up to Heinrich's death had been tumultuous for Hannah. In particular, the fallout from her publication of *Eichmann in Jerusalem* left her more and more isolated, increasingly dependent on those who remained loyal for helping her weather the storm. At the University of Chicago, where she taught soon after the book was published, Hannah frequently dined alone in the faculty club. "[S]he was lonely...Part of it was the *Eichmann* [controversy]. She got the cold shoulder from a huge number of the faculty...it was a heavily Jewish faculty..."[78]

After Heinrich's death, another student, Melvyn Hill, became a kind of confidant for Hannah. "After her husband died, she was actually, I had the feeling, quite lonely. And I'm ashamed to say I didn't realize it at the time simply because I had always seen her surrounded by friends and I hadn't realized how many of her friends had died..." Hannah called Hill more frequently, inviting him to meet her for dinner and to one of her famous New Year's Eve parties.

> *[I]n retrospect I realized there was a kind of appeal in her voice that wasn't there before. She was lonely, she wanted company...That showed me a different side of her altogether...she was quite vulnerable...[E]ven her comments about what was going on politically had a certain melancholy tinge to it that I hadn't heard before. To me, a certain optimism had left her.*[79]

To me, *Rahel Varnhagen* reads like a cautionary tale about the consequences of a woman's complicity with society's exacting price for earning the mantle of respectability simply by conforming to social expectations. Except Rahel was written from the outside and in a voice so omniscient you'd hardly suspect its author experienced some of the same things.

Even today a woman who wants respectability still must do (and not do) certain things and if she is an outcast, a pariah, the kind of woman who doesn't fit or resists the social roles and expectations carved out for her, she needs to find a way to survive. The more difficult path is to become a conscious pariah, an outsider aware of her position and hell bent on rebelling against it. The trouble is, without a network of other pariahs, this path too often leads to self-destruction or at least to despair. So instead she might try manipulating conventional choices available to women in her milieu, trying to hide something that makes her seem less desirable. She might try, like Rahel, to marry beyond her assigned status or otherwise pass for someone she's not, becoming what Hannah called a 'parvenu,' a stranger even to herself.

I know how easy it can be for a woman unhappy with society's restrictions to run away from herself, to cross the border into the land of self-deception. And how difficult it is to learn to live in gratitude. That's what I think Hannah learned from writing Rahel. And what I have learned from reading *Rahel Varnhagen* through the multifaceted prism of Hannah's own life.

{4}

A Woman of Her Own Invention

> *She had learned that love could guarantee the whole of a human life only occasionally, that such love came only as an unpredictable stroke of fortune.*
>
> Hannah Arendt *Rahel Varnhagen: The Life of a Jewess*

BY SLIPPING INTO RAHEL'S STORY HANNAH FOUND A METHOD, A WAY INTO AND OUT OF HER OWN LIFE'S HAUNTED "SHADOWS," PAST SHAMES AND ILLUSIONS, AND LEARNED TO CONFRONT HER OWN LONGING TO ESCAPE WHO SHE WAS. And so I have slipped into hers and inside that kaleidoscope looked at myself again, fragmented, rearranged, trying to make sense of what my life might mean, bringing memories into the space between us, into what Hannah called the public space of action in concert with others.

In the summer of 1992 I left Dylan, the man I now think of as "my last Heidegger." We had met a long time ago when both of us were in other relationships and didn't act on our initial attraction not so much out of virtue or guilt as that we never really had a good enough chance. Though we didn't admit it to each other, I think both of us must have suspected fate gave us the chance to meet again at exactly the right time for all the wrong reasons, just to see what we'd decide to do. We made our life together into a habit, strong enough to be almost too difficult to break.

Dylan was just returning from a European trip and I was going to the airport to meet him. I brought along my friend Françoise for moral support. Later, Dylan said he knew something was wrong as soon as he saw her.

The plane was delayed; my anxiety mounted.

"What if he tries to persuade me to stay?"

"Stay calm," Françoise counseled. "Do some Zen. You've made your decision. He can take care of himself."

"He suspects something. I just know it. Yesterday he called on his way to Heathrow. He was acting as if he'd found salvation; pledged undying love. All I could say was 'Have a safe journey'."

"He should get a clue. Anyway, everything is ready. Just make your announcement and don't let him say anything. And then leave. After we drive back from the airport I'll be waiting down the street for you. If you don't come out in twenty minutes, I'm coming to get you."

A few weeks before, I'd sublet an apartment, a tiny studio belonging to a Japanese graduate student visiting relatives in Tokyo for the summer. I would have preferred to leave the area entirely, but was slated to direct a summer seminar for schoolteachers on gender and authority, loosely based on the book I'd written the year before. No, the irony of my chosen subject wasn't lost on me.

Compared to the four-bedroom home I shared with Dylan, the apartment was Spartan. On either side of a large room were two small beds. The narrow kitchen consisted of the usual appliances and a wooden table with a pair of wobbly chairs. Nothing about it was attractive except the low price. But for the few weeks I needed transitional space, it would suffice. So I borrowed a truck and, before Dylan was due home, moved most of my books, my computer, my son Ari's bike and our clothes into the place.

On July 14th, the day before Dylan returned, Françoise and I celebrated my impending liberation by holding a Bastille Day garage sale in the alley next to my soon to be former home. We decorated posters with French flags and hung them around the neighborhood to advertise the event. I still have one folded in a box of mementoes.

Staging the sale was an innocuous adventure in vengeance, but it gave me great pleasure, especially unloading Dylan's old shirts and jackets for twenty-five cents apiece. After earning several hundred dollars selling junk we took ourselves to a fancy restaurant for a meal and good bottle of wine. Then I returned to the house to pack the rest of my things and stored them in boxes in my study.

I planned to move back to San Diego at the end of the summer. It was a sudden decision, even for me. But in the few weeks since the spring semester had ended everything in my life had changed. I'd fallen in love with a woman named Amy. That I was in love with a woman was less of a surprise to me than that I felt love at all. For most of the year before I felt either numb or filled with dread. Mostly, I just felt like a fake.

Then Amy appeared.

She came to my office the first night of that spring semester to add my class on women and politics. I said it was already full. She explained she'd graduated years before from a college in the east and wanted to take the course just because the subject interested her. Plus she had time. A Navy lieutenant and helicopter pilot temporarily stationed in San Diego, she had a research project in mind—about sexual harassment in the military—and figured the class would help her frame it. I found her incredibly attractive.

Tall and statuesque, she carried herself with a calm elegance belying her age—she was then not yet thirty. Her pixyish spiked hair, mismatched earrings, and devilishly erotic fringed leather jacket created a frisson, clearly marking off who she was from the khaki uniform she wore to work every day. In her warm eyes, the color of wild mushrooms, crinkling at the edges when she smiled, as she often does, I saw the glimmer of an old soul.

Daniel Mendelsohn has written that in men's desire for men there is repetition and a hunger for a return: "The mirror placed before the mirror, the infinite passage of sameness reproduced so many times that it creates the illusion of multiplicity and choice."[80] Perhaps the same could be said about women who love women. But that's not how it has been for me. No, what attracted me to Amy, what I fell in love with and will love without end, was her uniqueness, her utter singularity and inviting difference from me.

At first I held back, respecting the boundary between teacher and student. And that's odd to recall because I don't remember feeling deterred by the fact I was still living in a supposedly committed relationship. Then the class ended, the rules changed.

The last weekend that May I flew to San Diego for university commencement. It also happened there was a demonstration of student and faculty support for the department scheduled for the day before graduation. It was 1992 and the California budget crisis was so extreme the university president began cutting entire departments. My department, Women's Studies, was spared, which made a lot of other people very unhappy. But what really drew me to San Diego that weekend was Amy.

Amy and I had met for lunch the week before at a small Thai restaurant in midtown San Diego. Her idea. As we shared stories about our very different careers—she the military officer, me, diametrically opposed—something shifted, something opened. I felt like Rahel had once described, suddenly not wanting to "sigh through life almost unconsciously, like a duty."[81] I remember telling Amy I was coming back to San Diego the following week, a trip I hadn't planned at all. I mentioned the rally, hoping she'd take the hint.

Arriving on campus a little late that Friday afternoon, I positioned myself on the steps leading down to the assembly area, standing near the rear with a good view around the perimeter of the still gathering crowd. A friend came up to me and started talking but I was distracted, looking for that pixie hair, those leather fringes. I'd just about given up when I spotted her. She wasn't paying attention to the demonstration either. She was looking for me.

Mendelsohn again: "When two men have sex...[each] knows exactly what his partner is feeling and experiencing even as he himself has his own experience of exactly the opposite, the complementary act... Sex between men dissolves otherness into sameness." If the aim of sex is to know the other completely, he continues, "gay sex may be, in its own way, perfect, because total knowledge of the other's experience is, finally, possible."[82] Perhaps that's true. But he's missed something I think. Because the kind of sexual experience I had with Amy that night, and still have after all these years, put me in touch with something equally profound, something I'd never experienced, regardless of the gender of my partner.

When sex is grounded in trust you open to the other's experience. But no matter how much you know exactly what she's feeling, as if you no longer can tell whose body is whose, just when the boundary between you starts dissolving and you feel as if you're melting into her, just then you become intensely aware of an edge you're crossing, back and forth, back and forth, and this space between the two of you, this insistent pulsing line, this border, this paradoxical point where one person ends and another begins, this, this is the neighborhood of desire, the topography of longing and connection, the place where you know another, skin to skin, touch to touch. And you know her because she is not you and knowing she is not you allows you to love her.

I had to tell someone I'd fallen in love with a woman, someone who would understand and not ask me how that could happen. So I told my friend Lynda who also happens to be a lesbian. Lynda split her life between northern and southern California and traveled with me every week to San Diego from north to south. Three hours door to door, we had it down to a science. It was Lynda who helped my older son understand about Amy and me some weeks later.

"I'm so happy for you, KJ. But what are you going to do now?"

I hadn't thought that far ahead. Amy was leaving the next week for a short, three week "Det"—Navy lingo for ship's cruise—to Vancouver and then on to Seattle and all I knew was I wanted to meet her. Dylan would soon be away, his son would be with his ex-wife, and my younger son, Ari, had a weekend planned with some friends. I flew home and bought a ticket to Seattle.

But Amy had thought ahead. "I'll be happy to see you. But there can't be any physical intimacy between us if you're still with him."

"He's left on his trip."

"You know that's not what I mean."

"I'm coming to Seattle."

"Fine. But I meant what I said. If I don't insist on this rule, I'll get hurt."

We spent a long amorous weekend at a little B&B run by two women. It was early summer. I remember standing on the small porch outside our attic room in the afterglow of lovemaking, watching seaplanes taxiing for takeoff, rising up over Lake Union, looping wide toward Lake Washington and then arcing west over a corner of the Puget Sound and above Elliott Bay before turning back to the city center and, with Mt. Rainier in the distance, circling tight around the Space Needle until finally landing as light as a dragonfly on water. A flight pattern like an upside down heart in the sky.

"That's a Cessna 172," Amy said, pulling me closer. "Maybe I'll fly commercial planes when I get out of the military. Everyone assumes that's what every military pilot wants to do. I'm not sure. There's so much I want to do I haven't even discovered yet."

"Me too. I mean, not flying, but unchartered territories. That's where I'm headed. And I want you with me."

"I could never have refused you, you know."

"But I understood that. And that's why it was easy to agree to the terms."

The whole of the rest of my life suddenly presented itself in a single moment and an image of such beauty appeared with the gentlest of turns of colorful glass shards. And without renouncing my past, I no longer felt tethered. I could take my past with me into the present unfolding moment by moment. Years later, I would think about this time and recall Hannah's words to Heinrich Blücher: *For god's sake you are my four walls. I have managed to get both things, the 'love of my life,' and a oneness with myself.* For the first time in my life, I felt uncompromised in love.

How had I fooled myself for so long? Had I, like Rahel, taken a duplicitous route to get away from assuming responsibility? Like her, had I wagered it was possible to "entirely get away from what one truly is; away, far away, like a feeble little ship driven far off on a vast ocean by wind and tempest..."?[83]

One night, not long after I returned from Seattle, I lay alone in the northern California house I shared with Dylan and thought I heard the house groan like some long-suffering patient, as if its rooms were deteriorating organs, its walls the sagging flesh of a diseased body, seeking release. I had been living a festering sore of a lie. "And everything that I wished to purchase with such effort really has never existed for me."[84]

People who didn't know Dylan and me too well or were too much like us to notice the truth had always considered us a perfect couple. Two intellectuals, each with a young son, discovering an amorous connection exactly when they needed it most. How clever, how lucky they are! But as I lay there that night with the door opened to the little porch off the bedroom, the moon waning in the sky, I recalled how early we'd allowed jealousy and self-doubt to pool in our lives.

Even though sometimes he'd doubted his own professional standing, I'd been jealous of Dylan's more prestigious position and resented his apparent indifference to the problem of my working 500 miles from our home. And Dylan had been jealous of the fact that my son, Ari, lived with me all the time while he had to share his own son every other week with his ex-wife. Admitting none of this to me, he papered over his complicated feelings with ostentatious gifts and displays of affection, while I just as cleverly covered mine with my signature move—soldiering on to the point of self-abnegation and then diving deep into a well of self-pity.

I even pretended everything was fine when I left Ari in his care for three days a week and flew south to San Diego to teach. I didn't see what I didn't want to see. Every other week when his son was away Dylan's mood darkened in subtle ways. He took care of the essentials well enough—food, clothing and shelter were amply supplied. But his affection became cramped. It never occurred to me then that the reason wasn't because he lacked the ability to be more effusively caring. He was simply stuck in a melancholic longing for his son; grief, magnified by his own fear of abandonment, occupied almost every corridor of Dylan's heart.

It occurred to me now that when we'd moved from the small cottage where we first lived to this big house we gave all the boxed in anger and disappointment and grief too much room to grow in and old lies and recriminations we both had carried with us from lives past, but not forgotten, expanded and multiplied and rotted, like perverse loaves and fishes, filling every corner of every room until in that great, groaning brown clapboard house there was nowhere to hide from the fact that we were dangerously ill-suited.

I didn't want to admit I'd become immobilized by stubbornness, by a refusal to avoid feeling disgraced. As shameful as it felt to acknowledge the violence that had infected our relationship two summers earlier—an incident I'd taken great pains to downplay, and only much later came to appreciate as an ironic moment of saving grace—I thought I'd feel even more humiliated if I accepted any responsibility for my part in that drama.

No, it was easier to convince myself that living with someone at a common address, someone with whom I shared intellectual pursuits and familial obligations, was enough like love to keep me in place. Easier, that is, until I began to understand that living means even the strongest habits can be broken. And ought to be. Because when you admit you can't know the future any more than you can change the past, a sense of lightness, of light, enters your heart and you start to care more about where and who you are than where and who you've always been or might yet become.

The night Dylan returned from his trip was one of those hot San Francisco summer evenings, the air thick and steamy. We were driving across the Bay Bridge in silence. Françoise and I sat in the front, Dylan in the back. In the rear view mirror I watched him roll down the window and light a cigarette. I turned on the radio and we continued in silence. Arriving at the house, Françoise made some excuse for not coming in and then walked down the street and waited in her car. *If you don't come out in twenty minutes, I'm coming to get you.*

Dylan sat down at the kitchen table. I stood at the other end of the room, near the back door. He hadn't yet gone upstairs to discover the boxes I'd packed.

"Why don't you sit down?"

"I'd rather stand."

"What's the matter?"

"Nothing's the matter. I'm leaving you."

"What! Why?"

"*What! Why?*" I will always remember the expression on his face at that moment. He had the look of a man neither surprised nor hurt but feigning astonishment for the sake of appearance. I knew then he wanted me to leave as much as I wanted not to stay and that I could walk out the door and be gone from his life without incident.

"This is all a lie and you and I know it."

"But I've just come back. I've come back to get married. I tried to call to tell you that. Where were you?"

I thought, Why should I give him the relief of the truth? If I tell him he'll be able to hide behind the mask of the aggrieved lover and never even have to try accepting responsibility for his own mendacity.

Once in Paris, early in our relationship, we were staying in a romantic little hotel near St. Sulpice. As soon as we arrived we'd made love. Then, after calling one of his Parisian friends to meet us for dinner, Dylan went to take a shower, leaving his address book open on the bed. I glanced down and noticed a strange icon, like a little inverted triangle or an upside-down check mark, next to the name of the woman we were meeting for dinner. It so happened that her surname had the same initial as mine and on that same page, next to my own name, I found the same little squiggle and flipping through the pages saw it appear again and again.

When he came out of the shower I confronted him. He didn't deny the results of my research. He laughed. Yes, I had discovered his secret code. Wasn't that funny? He laughed again. "But, oh, my dear flower, that's all in the past." Nothing to worry about. She's just a friend. Just a friend.

The next year I returned to Paris to complete some research and Dylan joined me a week later on holiday. Days I spent in the *Biblioteque Nationale*, he entertained himself visiting old haunts and friends, including the woman we'd met that time for dinner.

One evening I was dressing for dinner in the bedroom of the apartment we had borrowed and Dylan called to me from the living room to please bring his cigarette lighter when I finished getting ready.

"Where is it?"

"In the front breast pocket of my blue jacket hanging behind the bedroom door."

I reached in and along with the lighter pulled out a small pile of condoms. We'd never used condoms.

"Here you are," I said, throwing the lighter onto the table. "And these were there too." The condoms landed in his lap.

And without even thinking, as if he had the excuse ready made, he said "I've had this old jacket for twenty years, my dear flower. I must have forgotten." *What! Why?* "Oh, no, you can't be thinking...don't be silly. There's nothing to worry about." *She's just a friend. Just a friend.*

But if I'd heard the hint of duplicity in his explanation, I didn't let on. I ignored it and, instead, continued to lie to myself. I lied to myself by believing him. Like Rahel, "I lied in order to obtain a reprieve for my life. I lied; I did not declare the demands of my heart, my proper deserts; I let myself be suffocated...I simulated, I dissimulated, I twisted and twisted and twisted."[85]

As this memory surfaced on my way out the door I allowed it to tether me a little longer to that part of resentment I wouldn't let go of yet, the part that kept me from forgiving, kept us both bound together for a while even after we'd parted and would continue to hold us back from getting on with who we were. Backing out the door, I clung desperately to resentment like some perverted security blanket until, much later, I remembered Hannah's portrayal of Rahel Varnhagen and suddenly found myself staring at the same ignoble fact Rahel finally confronted: that I had erred as much as the man, could be as mean and, in the end, was no less vulgar.[86]

One winter, not long after I'd suspected Dylan's infidelities might be habitual, we took another vacation to Europe and on the way home stayed for a night at a friend's house in London. It was a communal house and among its residents was a man I'd been attracted to many years earlier when I met him the first time. The attraction was mutual though neither of us acted on it. Not then.

That night, Dylan drank a lot and fell asleep fairly early in the guest room. I stayed up late talking in the kitchen with my friend. Old feelings surfaced. I confessed I was unhappy. I wanted someone to hold me and to hold someone who wanted to be held. And there he was, wanting the same things. Upstairs, in his bed, we whispered these things to each other. Then I took a bath and went to sleep in the guest room. Pretense, I learned, had been Rahel's habit and now it had become mine: "I did not want to let myself be stabbed; wretched cowardice; I wanted, unhappy creature, to protect the life of the heart."[87]

"I'm leaving you."

"What! Why?"

"It's too late."

In her biography, Hannah was critical of Rahel's masquerade, the way she tried to transform herself, hide who she was, imagining that "disguises, camouflage, changes of name could exert a tremendous transforming power"[88] and allow her to cover her Jewish identity "with a dress." Falling in love with Amy felt like coming out of hiding for me, but not in the obvious sense, not in the way most people talk about "exiting the closet." Because, you see, for me, heterosexuality was never a disguise behind which hid some more authentic lesbian core. I didn't have a problem loving men; my problem was the kind of woman I became with the kind of men (and women) I had, until then, chosen to love. And the kind of woman I became loving Amy wasn't because she was a woman too. That idea has always been odious to me because it reduces the complexity of love to an effect of one's gender.

With Amy I'd rediscovered a love of life and a oneness with myself; that was how coming out of hiding felt to me. Still, I now faced the challenge of confronting others' assumptions and realized another lesson to be drawn from Hannah's exploration of the life of Rahel: living well flows first from a fundamental gratitude for the givenness of life, not only a gratefulness for the present, but also for all the moments leading up to it.

In early August, my older son, who was then in college, came to California for his annual summer visit. He knew I had left Dylan. But I hadn't told him the whole story. We had planned a trip to western Sonoma County for the weekend after he arrived, and he was excited about camping along the Russian River and canoeing through the Redwoods with his brother and me. I was hoping for an opportunity to explain myself then.

My sons packed my old Honda Accord with sleeping bags and some equipment we'd borrowed from a friend—mine was stored for shipping to San Diego—and we set off early the next morning on the hour's drive, crossing the Bay Bridge and then the Golden Gate, heading north on Highway 101 toward Sebastopol to meet the rest of the seminar group at Burke's campground a little beyond Forestville. While we were driving, Ari played video games and Jed caught me up on the progress of his acting career. He had just finished two years' training and had landed a part in an off-off Broadway production.

Our conversation carried me into a reverie about another trip the three of us had taken a dozen years earlier when I'd driven alone with my sons across country in a beat up blue Volvo sedan, insisting on making the move in the car without my second husband, who was too disgruntled a passenger to take on long trips. It took ten days on that slow, move West to make it across the continent, ten days of stopping at battle memorials and fantasy towns, ten days of campsites and a few hotels and side trips to the Grand Canyon and the Painted Desert and Petrified Forest and into other worlds my older son invented, entertaining his baby brother while I listened to the Rolling Stones on an eight track tape deck and drove on and on into my yet unknown future that lay at the Pacific end of Interstate 8 and involved an unexpected turn in the road to the place now weighing on my mind.

When we arrived at the campsite the others were already setting up. We arranged our gear near a cluster of redwoods and went for a walk in the woods, returning a few hours later to help set out food for the barbeque. After eating we sat around the fire telling stories. When Ari fell asleep Jed and I moved to a picnic table a few yards away to continue talking. Every now and then I looked up at the cluster of stars triangulated around Vega, as if expecting to hear a bright melody from Orpheus's lyre playing such sweet tunes a mother could explain her sexual transformation to her adult son without anxiety.

"So, Mom, how's it going, what's new?"

Thank you Orpheus!

"Well, Jed, one thing that's new is I've fallen in love...with a woman."

"Are you serious?"

"Perfectly. Her name is Amy."

"Wow. What can I say? I'm, I'm...I never expected that answer to my question."

"I guess not. But, I thought you, of all people, would understand. You're an actor; you're with gay people all the time."

"Sure, I understand. But it's different. You're my mother... Does Ari know?"

"Yes, I've already told him."

"And what did he say?"

"He said he's used to this sort of thing, living in Berkeley."

Jed just looked at me for another few seconds and then put his arms around me. "Mom, as long as you're happy, I'm happy for you."

My friend Lynda lived in a large house atop the Berkeley hills and with her equally large heart offered to let my sons and me share her place after we returned from our trip. We arrived at Lynda's early the next evening and Jed spent time alone with Ari. I went up to Lynda's study to read. A little later, Jed knocked on the door.

"I just talked to Ari. Mom, I don't know, either he's completely out of touch or he's the Buddha."

"Why, what did he say?"

"I asked him if he had a problem with your being in love with a woman and all he said was 'No....do you?' "

A year after I moved back to San Diego I worked up the nerve to visit my father with Amy. I offered no explanation for the fact of her presence, not even sanitizing our living together, which Dad knew from talking with Ari, with that old reliable obfuscation, "She's my roommate." I called to say we were coming and we simply turned up one Sunday afternoon at his apartment in Brooklyn.

It was summer. We'd just driven down I-95 from Old Lyme, where we'd inspected the recently poured foundation for the house we were building on the property Amy bought a few years earlier, thinking she might like to move back east one day. From New York we were heading to Philadelphia, where she was stationed on the USS Forrestal as Catapult and Arresting Gear Officer giving her the harrowing job of making sure planes catapulted off and tail hooked on in one piece. She had lots of great Navy stories and since my Dad had been in the Navy, I was counting on her getting us through the visit.

My stepmother Caroline opened the door. Hugging her I looked over her shoulder and saw Dad already seated in his favorite chair at the far end of the dining table, waiting. Years ago, one arm of the chair had broken and he'd glued it back together but now, his debilitating illness progressing, he'd let the chair lapse back into its invalid state, as if the chair was just another part of his increasingly malfunctioning body. I leaned over to kiss him and then introduced Amy, who, taking off the USS Forrestal cap she'd worn especially for the occasion, shook his hand.

"Nice to finally meet you, Mr. Jones."

We were just in time for lunch and Amy helped me move the table away from the wall so we could all fit around it. When it was only Caroline and Dad they kept it pushed back for a wider path from the front door to the living room, which adjoined the so-called dining area. Years later, after Caroline's funeral, I went back to that apartment alone for one last look at the place where they'd lived for four decades and was stunned by how tiny it was and astonished all over again at how they'd managed to stay there as long as they had, first with my two stepsisters stuffed into an unimaginably small bedroom, then with just the two of them, until finally the place held Caroline alone.

Move? Why move? A nice breeze across the Narrows. A view of Coney Island in the distance. Fireworks over New York Bay in July. Good shopping on the Avenue. And all you had to do was look out the window every now to keep an eye on the family car parked in the street below. Who would move from a place as perfect as that?

We sat eating ham and cheese sandwiches and drinking diet Pepsi, Dad in his usual spot, me on the left with my back to the wall and Amy across from me, with Caroline scurrying to and from the kitchen with potato salad and pickles and chips until she settled into a seat next to Amy.

"The USS Forrestal had that big fire in 1967."

"That's right, Mr. Jones. One hundred thirty-four men lost their lives. We learned a lot about safety in that tragedy. No ordinance allowed on planes on the deck. And we're all trained in firefighting. The same mistakes wouldn't happen again. Kathy tells me you were in the Navy. I guess that's why you know so much."

"Long time ago. I was in the Bugle Corps. Enlisted during the war."

"He lied about his age to sign up," Caroline adds.

"I didn't know that, Dad."

"Got shipped out to the South Pacific. From D'ego (he always called San Diego D'ego). Never liked officers much."

"Why's that?" Amy asks, not missing a beat.

"Didn't respect 'em. When the shit hit the fan they couldn't tell their ass from their elbow." He laughs. "We were supposed to salute whenever we were wearing our hats. I tried to get away without wearing mine as often as possible."

"People have to earn respect, don't they?"

"Kathy tells me you fly helicopters."

"That's right. In San Diego I was flying H-46s."

"Those old workhorses from Vietnam? They're still flying them?"

"They've been around a while. Getting parts is harder to come by. I was Maintenance Officer on my last tour in San Diego."

"Hell of a job."

And so it went, Dad regaling Amy with stories from his Navy days and listening intently to hers. When his energy began to lag, I suggested it was time to get going. Then I gave him a hug and kissed him goodbye.

Amy reached out her hand. Dad didn't take it. Instead, briskly pushing back his chair, he extended his right arm and, as if he were standing at attention on some old battleship, snapped his hand to the corner of his imaginary cap and saluted the naval officer goodbye.

A week or so later, Amy mailed Dad a USS Forrestal cap with a set of Lieutenant's bars attached as a surprise. I found that hat about a dozen years later, long after he'd died, carefully stored in a box of Dad's things in the hall closet. His lovingly wrapped, carefully guarded, seal of approval.

I held that hat in my hand then and other lines from Hannah's writing came to mind, augmenting stories about my past, stories I'd woven out of remnants of memory, stories that would remain incomplete if I ever again allowed resentment, or any desire to escape responsibility for who I was or who I had decided to become, shape the narrative.

"*Who* somebody is or was we can know only by knowing the story of which he is himself the hero...everything else we know of him, including the work he may have produced and left behind, tells us only *what* he is or was."[89]

Not long ago a friend of mine who has known me for years asked me a question.

"There's something I've always wondered about," she said after two glasses of wine. "What made you fall in love with a woman? How did that happen?"

How did that happen? It's as simple and as complicated as this: I've been lucky, for more than twenty years, lucky. Lucky to have had an education, a career, a family, a whole network of social support. Lucky to fall in love, the same as any other human does and not like anyone else.

And this, and the rest of the story I will tell you, on no account would I now wished to have missed.

{ 5 }

Reading *Eichmann in Jerusalem* in My Father's House

The trouble with Eichmann was precisely that so many were like him, and that the many were neither perverted nor sadistic, that they were, and still are, terribly and terrifyingly normal.

Hannah Arendt, *Eichmann in Jerusalem*

WHEN I SET OUT TO WRITE ABOUT HANNAH ARENDT AND BEGAN TO REREAD HER KEY WORKS I SAVED *EICHMANN IN JERUSALEM* FOR LAST.

A report on the trial of Nazi deportation commander Adolf Eichmann, *Eichmann in Jerusalem* was her most controversial "public" work. Gaining her both notoriety and infamy, the book also became the cause of her greatest pain.

A haunting meditation on the eclipse of morality during the Third Reich, *Eichmann* remains deeply disturbing even today, decades after the sordid events it described have passed into memory. Over the report hangs the shadow of Hannah's complicated judgment of the scope of horrors we have come to call the Holocaust or *Shoah*, whose source she summarized in the unfortunate phrase, "the banality of evil." Among the more disturbing conclusions she reached were those about Eichmann himself. To her, he seemed to be more a clown than a monster. He wasn't evil, she said, he was "thoughtless," unable to reflect on the fact that what he was doing was wrong. As evidence she cited the following incident: Someone once suggested to Eichmann he join the S.S, to which Eichmann replied, Why not?

As if he were only a "leaf in the whirlwind of time," Eichmann appeared in Hannah's narrative like someone unable to distinguish between sending people to their deaths and doing his job. The real trouble, she wrote, wasn't just Eichmann but how many others were like him—terrifyingly normal, banal perpetrators of evil. What had happened, Hannah wondered, to make so many people thoughtless? "From the accumulated evidence one can only conclude that conscience as such had apparently got lost in Germany."

Hannah pulled no punches. She judged even members of the Jewish Council responsible, citing records documenting how Jewish officials cooperated with the Nazis by providing lists of those to be deported.

The banality of evil? Jews guilty? Her ideas were scandalous, many concluded. She may be Jewish, her fiercest critics said, but she was certainly soulless; she must be one of those self-hating anti-Semitic Jews.

The year *Eichmann* was published the Anti-Defamation League sent out a circular to all rabbis to preach against her on Rosh Hashanah. To this Hannah responded in a letter to her friend, the author Mary McCarthy, "What a risky business to tell the truth..." I wondered why had she taken the risk. And what it had cost her.

Then I read another letter Hannah had written to McCarthy and felt a shiver down my spine. Writing *Eichmann*, Hannah told her friend, had been curiously cathartic; it had cured her of certain emotional attachments clouding her judgment of her own past. "Ever since I [wrote the book], I feel light-hearted..."[90]

For weeks I tried to figure out what Hannah meant by saying writing *Eichmann* made her feel "light-hearted." At the time, I decided I didn't believe her. I'm not sure I want to even now. And yet, I've come to think reading *Eichmann* can help thinking about questions of responsibility and culpability in our own dark times.

I was reading *Eichmann in Jerusalem* the October of 1995 when my father took a turn for the worse. He'd been battling colon cancer for five years. Now he was dying, ending my daughterhood; and losing that status, perhaps even more than losing him, made me deeply afraid.

A punctilious, judgmental man with a drinker's obsession, he lived in Brooklyn his whole life, largely absent from my childhood, looming in it. The oldest of six surviving children he learned to play trumpet from the Vincentian fathers at St. Stanislaus Church in the polish section of Greenpoint and with his horn enlisted in the Navy, lying about his age, to get out of little Warsaw as fast as he could. When I was very little he took me every Sunday to the Knights of Columbus Hall to watch the marching band until my mother's impatience with unsurprising rhythms frustrated his hobby and our outings. Except for the occasional trip to Manhattan to see the model train show I don't remember us doing anything special again until, years later, he took me with him on weekly visits to the movies.

My erratic, high-heeled, sexy mother was a gambling kind of drinker and wouldn't settle for the predictability of a John Phillip Sousa when she could have the velvet-tongue of a Mel Tormé or the twangy seduction of a Hank Williams. Mom was a sucker for melodrama, for movies where Jimmy Cagney played the repentant mobster or Susan Hayward, another redhead, shouted: "I don't need you, I don't want you, you go find some scared little girl and tell her what a big, brave man you are." Dad took pleasure retreating from such histrionics into his model car collection or lining up the family shoes in the kitchen on Saturday and polishing them for hours. We had the best-shined shoes in Mill Basin. Their marriage lasted until I was nine when their attraction to out-doing each other's bad habits finally undid them.

Drinking was the one real thing my parents had in common and over time it became a kind of binding anti-bond, something keeping them together in their apartness. When they drank, they fought more, and more violently. On the surface, it was about money and sex and, in the early days, about having to live with my grandparents. But drunkenness glossed a deeper fury each must have felt at being tied to the other, bound to have and to hold forever the one person least likely to last.

For the first seven years of my life my parents and I lived together with my maternal grandparents in Mill Basin. The arrangement ended when my grandparents decided they wanted their own apartment and my parents couldn't afford the house on their own. After Dad left, Mom and I stayed in the apartment the three of us had moved to. That's when Mom started dating the policeman whose wife hung around our block one day waiting for my mother to get home from work just so she could call her 'whore' to her face.

"Do you know what your mother is, little girl?" she asked me as I walked home from fourth grade in my school uniform.

"Of course," I said, attempting to cut her of at the pass, "she's an operator at the Telephone Company."

"I don't mean what she does for a living. I mean what she is. She's a whore, a thief. She's trying to steal my husband and my little girl's Daddy. Would you like that, little girl? Would you like it if someone was trying to steal your Daddy?"

"My Daddy doesn't live here anymore," I said, expecting a shard, the tiniest crumb of sympathy.

"It's no wonder. With a whore like your mother for a wife, he must have been too ashamed to stay."

At the time, I didn't know what a whore was but it didn't matter because I didn't care what she called my mother. I just wanted her not to stand outside my apartment when I walked home from school and embarrass me in front of my new friends. My new friends were Jewish. Their mothers played Mahjong and cooked potato latkes and noodle kugel with raisins and cinnamon and one day would invite me, I could just tell, to their daughters' Bat Mitzvahs. It was embarrassing enough to be the lone Catholic in a Jewish neighborhood. I didn't need any loud-mouthed Italian woman standing with her snotty kid on my sidewalk interfering with my getting into the house fast so I could lose the uniform.

What I had figured out already was how to play the sympathy game. How early I learned that if you were good at it, you could turn the tables on your accusers and pretty soon people who'd complained about something you'd done would feel sorrier for you than they did for themselves.

What sources, I wonder, did I consult in my self-education? Most certainly, *The Lives of the Saints*, those martyred aficionados of the sympathy game. The nuns at school told us to look to them for our models. But of what? With so many arrows and spikes and crowns of thorns circumscribing every delicate part of the body, what else was I supposed to think besides putting the greater glorification of self-abjection in the service of personal fame?

Or maybe it was just all those Cagney movies I watched with Mom, the ones where some lousy rat of thief and murderer turns cowardly confronting the electric chair in the penultimate scene. You could feel the audience's sympathy rising because, after all, he is the hero and what's a little mayhem among friends.

Such were the central texts in my youthful moral education. Years later, after I'd studied chapter and verse in the world's major religions, I found nothing new. If you wanted dogma, the rules of engagement for the sympathy game, every system seemed to foreground the same thing—do this and not that to win salvation, to get a better job, to find love, to save your marriage, your kids, the whole damned planet. Do this and you can forget about thinking.

The Italian woman kept vigil and so Mom and I moved across Flatlands and into the bog of Canarsie, where we lived until I started high school and we rented a large second floor apartment in a rambling Victorian in Crown Heights. We stayed there two years until Mom married Jim and moved back to Mill Basin. I lived with them until college and, after freshman year, got married the first time. Meanwhile Dad met Caroline and made a new family with her and her children and for the next forty years lived in the tiny Shore Parkway apartment where he was now dying.

Such random and chaotic memories as these surfaced and it seemed perfectly ordinary to me that they did. After all, I told myself, I was going to visit my dying father. It was natural that the long sedimented past bubbled up. The night I arrived at Dad's apartment I jotted down a few notes and didn't look at them again until many years later when I thought about *Eichmann* again and remembered Hannah saying that what she had written allowed her to let go of her past. But, that night at my father's house, I couldn't even imagine letting go to be possible. You see, I was still devoted to dredging the past up, lock, stock and barrel, looking for any excuse, any reason at all to blame the artifacts for how awful they looked behind the exhibition glass in the museum.

My father and I had a difficult relationship. At least that's what I thought then. As to what he thought, he never told me directly. And because he was the parent who left, he had the benefit of absence and a brand new family to make the power of his silence and my belief in his wisdom grow out of proportion.

One day, a year or so after he'd left, we were riding on a bus back from one of our movie outings. It was unusual for us to be on public transportation. Dad loved his cars. And being in control of the driving. But, for some reason, that day we were on a bus. I don't know why being surrounded by a group of strangers allowed me to muscle up enough nerve, but suddenly I opened my mouth and blurted out what I'd been contemplating for months.

"Dad, why don't you come home?"

"Ask your mother."

"Can't you just try again?"

"Your mother doesn't want me back."

"How do you know that?"

"Ask her. I'd come back. But you have to ask her."

I believed what he said. And never asked my mother to explain.

But the real question I was asking was—don't you still love me?

Once, when I was twenty-two and studying political theory in Europe, I wrote Dad a letter asking why my parents divorced. I must have thought the years had softened him enough to offer an explanation. But all he wrote back was to say that was a long time ago and no use going over and spent the rest of the letter recounting news about his new family back in Brooklyn. There was one stepsister's new job and the other's pending marriage, and my stepmother's talent in the kitchen. No sympathy there, I figured. But that didn't stop me from trying.

I devised more clever ways to test him. One Sunday, I waited until the last minute to take the bus from my end of Brooklyn to his, knowing I'd be at least an hour late for dinner. I thought that if he was at the door laughing and pointing to his watch, I was golden. But if he said nothing for an hour or more, I'd crossed the line and at exactly the right moment would admit my mistake *mea culpa, mea culpa, mea maxima culpa*, accept penance, genuflect and be returned to the fold. But when he opened the door all he said was how happy he was to see my son wearing that blue sweater Caroline knitted for him and didn't Jed want to go out for a ride on his new brand new red Schwinn bike.

And while I was still in graduate school, I regaled Dad with quotations from Karl Marx, convinced the right turn of phrase would demonstrate my evident wisdom and uncanny ability, given that I'd grown up in a household without books, to master some of the most difficult works of Western philosophy. Oh, he was impressed all right; you could just tell by the way he walked out of the room.

But the greatest test of all was the year I asked my father to testify in the battle with my first husband for custody of our son.

Dad appeared every day for a week and when his turn came he took the witness stand, swearing on a stack of bibles that his grandson Jed was better off living with my boyfriend, Mike, and me than being moved anywhere else. Yes, he got to see him frequently enough. No, he didn't see anything wrong with his daughter's relationship or with how Mike treated Jed. By keeping what he really thought to himself I kept my son. But the truly amazing thing is I didn't understand then what he had done.

Only once, when we were arguing about politics and I mentioned Mike, did Dad break his silence on the subject. It was several years after the custody battle and by then I'd moved to Kentucky and married Mike.

"That lousy bastard thinks he's so smart, but he doesn't know a thing, he isn't worth even one hair on Caroline's head," he said, shaking his fist in my face. He'd never hit me as a child but it felt like he wanted to now.

"Edward, calm down," Caroline said. "It's not Kathleen's fault."

"He thinks he's too good for us. Where is he today? Again in the library? He makes me sick. He's too good for us? Well, we don't need him. Even when he's here all he does is sit in the corner and sulk."

"He's depressed, Dad," I said. "It's depression, not arrogance."

"He's a lazy Jew bastard, not worth a hair on my wife's head."

To use an American cultural metaphor for bigotry, my father made Archie Bunker, a narrow-minded character in the popular American television series, *All in the Family*, look mild. Whenever I visited I steeled myself for a litany of racial slurs and commentary about lazy Blacks and sloppy Russians. And, of course, of course, there were the Jews. The Jews.

But the strange thing about my father was his heart wasn't in it. When it came down to someone in particular, he recurred to the person, sacrificing the slur. He didn't do this in some facile way, as in "some of my best friends are...(fill in the minority blank)." Dad was no liberal. Instead, he described the person in a story with fullness and grace, stressing particular acts of kindness performed.

But he wouldn't go there when it came to Mike.

"Dirty bastard," he mumbled and went back to his beer. I rose from the table and left the apartment. But in that half-conscious way you feel a troubling thought emerge in a far corner of your brain, I suspect I knew even then why my father was furious.

Only much later did I understand my father's anger wasn't about Mike's being Jewish or even that I converted to Judaism myself after Mike and I'd married. "Well, at least there'll be some religion in the home," he quipped. Besides, he couldn't protest too much; he'd abandoned Catholicism for his wife's Lutheran beliefs, though, he was quick to point out, that switch wasn't as loaded as mine. No, what provoked his rage was that courtroom. It had challenged my father's sense of morality a little too close to the bone, depriving him of the occasion to say what he really thought. He didn't trust Mike but because my father loved me he had stood in court and sworn everything was fine. And I was so caught up in my own self-righteousness I didn't think to ask him how the whole process made him feel.

In those days I thought one only needed logic and a few hardy facts to reach conclusions about the egalitarian parameters of human dignity and mutual respect. I dismissed my father's inability to forget the category and see Mike as a person as one of Dad's many unacknowledged contradictions. Worse still, I considered my father thoughtless.

There was such smugness in my judgment because, of course, it hinged on my belief that I displayed no such moral weakness myself. It would be a long time before I tested my prejudices and confronted the difficult questions Hannah first raised in *Eichmann*. "Could the activity of thinking as such, the habit of examining whatever happens to come to pass or attract attention, regardless of results and specific contents, could this activity be among the conditions that make men abstain from evil-doing or even actually 'condition' them against it?" I needed to learn how to separate thinking from ideology.

But now my father was dying and I went to Brooklyn swimming in these memories. One late afternoon I sat vigil at his deathbed, watching my father's eyes flutter open and then close. I was thinking about the time and distance between us when he turned toward me and asked, as easily as if he were asking for a sip of water, if I would change his bedclothes. I stood up and put my arm around his back, raising him enough to take off his pajama shirt. It occurred to me he must have done the same for me when I was a child. Removing his thin cloth pants, I slid my arm underneath his knees lifting his bony legs high, as I had done to my sons when they were small, and taking the soiled diaper from below his buttocks, replaced it with a clean one, gently closing the top of it over his pelvis, sealing its edges above his fragile hips. His hips formed a perfect frame around his hollowed belly so that the whole of his torso took on the appearance of a porcelain bowl, transforming the tumor protruding its center into a pale pear, like some calcified delicacy encased in my father's translucent skin. As to the rest, I pretended to see nothing. Not the penis, not the grayed groin hair, not the feces, not the urine stained clothes.

At that moment I felt the father let his daughter go and as he let her go she let her anger at him for being the father who left and her anger at herself for being the never-good-enough daughter join and surface in the room and the father took it into his delirium describing snapshots from his youth and when the father parted company with the man I was only Kathy watching Edward Jones dying in the bed.

I let Edward go and buried him in a plot of land in a Staten Island cemetery where he rests now with his wife Caroline beside him and thought I put my daughterhood to rest. I stopped reading *Eichmann.* Except daughterhood isn't so easily put to rest. Neither is *Eichmann.*

A month after my father's death, a student of mine was murdered by her boyfriend. She'd been a strong woman, a self-defense instructor and director of the campus women's center. They'd met at the gym in the community college where they'd both been students before moving to San Diego. He dropped out of school soon after they arrived. It was a difficult relationship. Sometimes when they fought, her friends said, they pushed each other around. He began to do drugs but she wasn't afraid. She told him to get his act together and then threatened to leave. A few weeks later, after a crack binge, he strangled her and tried to make it look like someone else did it. He confessed a week after he was arrested.

That summer, when the trial began in San Diego, I picked up *Eichmann* again. "It would have been so much more comforting to believe Eichmann was a monster." But, I wondered, what was so comforting about monsters?

One day the killer took a seat in the witness stand. Raising his large hands to form a circle in the empty air in front of him he described how he put his hands around his girlfriend's throat and then repeated the action. I remember listening and thinking how handsome he was.

I tried hard but couldn't see any monster. Instead images of things I'd read about or remembered from my own life floated before me. And suddenly I felt I had once been at the scene of a crime, witnessed atrocities, helped hide evidence, and otherwise acted normal. I had in fact once been a victim of violence and lived to tell the story. I guess I still wanted monsters to blame. What a consolation monsters were; what a simple, elegant way not to see how easily anyone can do something awful.

Maybe we corral the familiar because it's all we really know. But I've come to think that knowing right from wrong isn't enough and that's a strange place for an intellectual to be. It means throwing out the facile formulae and comforting slogans and trying to think, as Hannah used to say, without a banister to guide you.

When I was a child I used to play a game. I'd lie down in the middle of the living room rug and stare at the ceiling. My perspective shifted. With the world upside down I floated, suspended above everything. Below me was empty and quiet. That's how it felt reading *Eichmann* again after my father died, after the student was murdered. The world upside down, empty and quiet. Without the monsters, it was so much harder to live.

At the end of the murder trial, the jury convicted the young man in the death of my student. One October night two months later he hanged himself in prison, leaving a note for his attorney. "Tell my mother I loved her; tell her I'm sorry," the note said. Perhaps he had become a monster to himself.

I began to sense what Hannah Arendt meant by feeling light-hearted. It wasn't gaiety but a lightness, a kind of roominess of heart she'd felt after releasing the demons. But I wasn't certain she'd been completely honest. Because in place of monsters she'd put something far more frightening.

What I got from reading *Eichmann* was seeing how important it is to refuse to accept righteousness as anyone's prerogative and this has been the most difficult lesson to take. For years, I believed outrage at the sight of injustice was self-evidently moral and aligned myself, rather arrogantly, on the side of the struggle against it. Condemning all social and political iniquities committed against life's hapless victims in the name of justice became autonomic for me. I had discovered how to play an advanced form of the sympathy game and hadn't counted on also discovering that I might have wound up on the moral side more by accident than self-conscious design.

Reading *Eichmann* at this time in my life had brought me to this— if I had been born at another time, in another place, I could have been Eichmann. The thought occurred to me not because of parallels between my life and his, shared causal factors that predict which humans will do what awful things to which others. No, it was the absence of parallels, the uniquely ordinary tale Hannah wove out of the facts of Eichmann's life that got me to think and I began to see I could no longer be certain I'd not only know the right thing to do but would do it.

Believe me, I tried to find an exit. At first, I thought, of course, I never would have perpetrated such atrocities. Then I found myself wishing that if I'd lived in the 1930s and 40s, I'd have been Danish or maybe Italian. But if I absolutely had to be German, then, angel of mercy, let me have been Sergeant Anton Schmidt.

Schmidt had been in charge of a German patrol in Poland and his job was to collect stray soldiers and return them to their units. In the course of his regular duties he befriended members of the Jewish underground and began supplying forged papers and trucks in which Jews escaped. For five months he persisted, until he was arrested and executed in 1942. I wanted to believe I'd have been Anton Schmidt. But, the thing is, I couldn't be sure.

I couldn't be sure that if they asked me for the names of neighbors, I wouldn't cooperate to protect my job, my family, myself, or if they asked me to prove my Aryan descent I wouldn't get out the appropriate pedigree. And if they invited me to head a project that would ensure the greater glory of nation and bring honor to the highest powers I might have accepted the offer and then, once charged with high crimes, might have advanced to the highest level of the sympathy game and said I had done it because after so many disappointments in a vale of misfortune I had finally gotten the chance to do something I was called on to do and therefore was not guilty in the sense of the indictment.

I began to think the Eichmanns among us exist not because of where they were born or because of what gods they worship and certainly not because there's a little Eichmann in everyone. They exist because the world has changed and there are no longer any simple formulae distinguishing right from wrong to turn to when we're confronted with something unexpected. We have to decide all on our own what we should do and what we might have to risk doing it.

Thinking demands a burdensome kind of vigilant, imaginative observation of the world. And maybe that's why many people prefer to avoid it. I'm no exception; too often I've sought a simple rule to apply to a complex situation, instead of engaging the difficult practice of talking with myself, actively investigating choices I face before deciding what to do. If I try to respond to a challenging or unanticipated situation neither out of habit or custom, nor in obedience to a "command of either divine or human origin, but on what I [decide] with regard to myself"[91] I'm brought face to face with an apparently simple but inherently complicated question: will I be able to live with myself if I do this instead of that?

How had Eichmann been able to decide it was not only acceptable but also imperative to send millions to horrific deaths? Had some rabid anti-Semitism driven him to his murderous conclusion? Hannah never doubted Eichmann's anti-Semitism. But she also didn't think anti-Semitism alone explained why he'd done what he'd been told to do. Nor did she accept Eichmann's excuse that he was just following orders. In fact, Hannah observed, Eichmann took pride in reporting at the trial how, near the end of the war, he'd defied Himmler's order to interrupt the extermination process. Eichmann only followed the orders of the Nazi state and the source of all orders in that state was Hitler and Hitler alone.

Eichmann's thoughtlessness—his inability to think from the point of view of anyone else, his obedience to whatever principles the will of the *Führer* declared to be necessary to the cause—meant that although he knew what he was doing he had become incapable of thinking for himself whether what he was doing was wrong. And this thoughtlessness became the hallmark of what Hannah meant by the "fearsome, word-and-thought defying *banality of evil*."[92]

Many people still find abhorrent Hannah's claim that Eichmann, the man, was no monster. Everyone knows murder is wrong; certainly, then, murdering millions without a guilty conscience must be the classic example of monstrous behavior. Or madness. Surely only a monster or a madman could commit such heinous deeds. And that's an understandable reaction. Most of us hold fast to a well-guarded belief that rules and standards used to tell right from wrong, rules we assume to be universal, cannot be easily discarded. Not I, we believers in our own inherent goodness insist; I would never comply with such an order. But Hannah wouldn't let anyone rest on such a convenient way to avoid having to think for herself. "The trouble with Eichmann," she wrote

> *was precisely so many were like him, and that the many were neither perverted nor sadistic, they were, and still are, terribly and terrifyingly normal. From the viewpoint of our legal institutions and our moral standards of judgment, this normality was much more terrifying than all the atrocities put together, for it implied...that this new type of crimi-*

> *nal...commits his crimes under circumstances that make it well-nigh impossible for him to know or to feel that he is doing wrong.*[93]

The idea that "an average, 'normal' person, neither feeble-minded nor indoctrinated nor cynical, could be perfectly incapable of telling right from wrong" defies any ordinary understanding of good and evil. And yet, Hannah observed, "without much notice, all [these rules governing right and wrong] collapsed almost overnight...What happened? Did we finally awake from a dream?"[94] How had it become so easy for so many to behave like Eichmann and participate in carrying out these atrocities?

Hannah explained it this way: the Nazi state had generated a "totality of...moral collapse...in respectable European society—not only in Germany but in almost all countries, not only among the persecutors *but also among the victims.*"[95] And at that sentence, many people throw her book across the room in disgust, perhaps missing the other point she made: not everyone complied with the system.

But Hannah's writing has made me wonder why we need to believe a solid wall separates the performers of horrible acts from the rest of us? And what holds that wall in place?

"When I think back to the last two decades since the end of the last war," she wrote in the mid-1960s, "I have the feeling that this moral issue has lain dormant because it was concealed by something about which it is indeed much more difficult to speak and with which it is almost impossible to come to terms—the horror itself in its naked monstrosity."[96] Trying to think the unthinkable—the horror of state-ordered, socially co-ordinated manufacturing of corpses in the twentieth century, or of other genocides in previous centuries and in this one—can take one's breath away. Not even time's healing power seems to bring relief.

> *[T]his past has grown worse as the years have gone by so that we are sometimes tempted to think, this will never be over as long as we are not all dead...This past has turned out to be 'unmastered' by everybody, not only the German nation.* [97]

Yet Hannah insisted on confronting those concealed moral issues even though they looked like "side issues...compared with the horror."[98] She pushed past the speechless horror to grapple with the moral implications of the "ubiquitous complicity"[99] surrounding the Holocaust. Because not grappling with those implications would allow Eichmann to gain what the monk Thomas Merton, deeply influenced by reading *Eichmann in Jerusalem*, would have considered a "posthumous long life," making us all, like it or not, "vulnerable to complicity in deeds of destruction."[100]

And what a long life Eichmann already has had. Can't we finally defeat that man in the glass booth?

Hope lies behind that question and the answer stares me right in the face: Once the monsters are gone, only we humans are left.

I don't know about you, but that makes me feel light-hearted.

{ 6 }

Beginning Again: My Most Beautiful Monster

All sorrows can be born if you put them into a story or tell a story about them.
Isak Dinesen quoted by Hannah Arendt in *The Human Condition*

ONE BRIGHT JUNE, I VISITED THE ORACLE AT DELPHI, STOPPING ON THE ROAD TO THE RUINS TO RENT A ROOM IN A BARE WHITE STUCCO HOUSE ON A HILL OVERLOOKING THE CORINTHIAN SEA, SPARKLING BLUE IN THE DISTANCE. The room was spare, furnished only with a bed, one chair and a small table with a ceramic lamp that cast a circle of light barely wide enough for reading. The road to

Delphi had been dusty and long and I needed a shower. I took my towel and soap to the bath down the hall.

The water was the temperature of melting ice, so I managed only a quick rinse and went back to the room to wash my hair in the sink. Filling the basin I bent over it, sweeping my long hair forward. Dipping a small glass into the pooled water, I wetted my hair, dabbing shampoo into it, slowly gathering the dangling strands into a soapy ball and then rinsing until my hair squeaked clean. I reached for a towel, twisting it into a turban around my head, and that simple gesture unexpectedly returned to me the long forgotten sensation of my mother's hands, her musky smell wafting into the room when a light sea breeze fluttered the curtains.

Each of us is born into a world already made that can persist without us. Sometimes the world's indifference to us bears so heavily down we begin to move fatalistically toward an edge, forgetting we'd once entered the world as a creature unambiguously new. We forget how our birth interrupted life's inexorable coursing toward its own end, signaling possibility. We forget that though we must die, we "are not born in order to die but in order to begin."[101] But if somewhere in a faint corner of our heart a corpuscle of memory breaks through, it might release us from the torpor of forgetfulness so we can begin again. "The miracle that saves the world...is...natality...the action we are capable of by...being born."[102]

That night, almost three decades ago now, clouds troubled the Delphic moon and I dreamt of my mother.

In the dream I walked down an alleyway between two rows of red brick houses. Passing old Chevrolets and Buicks parked in sloping driveways, I opened a gate into a long neglected garden. Someone was cooking; the air smelled of laurel and thyme and roasting lamb. Through the kitchen window, I saw a woman, my mother, smile and beckon to me.

"It's a long time since you've come to see me," she said. "Have you been hiding?"

"I didn't think you wanted me. So I stayed away," I replied. "You're cooking?"

"Surprised? But I always feed you when you're hungry. And you're hungry now, aren't you?"

No, that wasn't the dream.

In the dream, my mother walked down an alleyway between two rows of red brick houses. Passing old Chevrolets and Buicks parked in sloping driveways, she opened a gate into a long neglected garden. Someone was cooking; the air smelled of laurel and thyme and roasting lamb. Through the kitchen window, she saw a woman, her daughter, smile and beckon to her.

"It's a long time since you've come to see me," I said. "Have you been hiding?"

"I didn't think you wanted me. So I stayed away," she replied. "You're cooking?"

"Surprised? But I always feed you when you're hungry. And you're hungry now, aren't you?"

And I opened the door to my mother and began to remember how hard I had worked to create my most beautiful monster.

My mother left me when I was still young, but old enough to know what she had done and to refuse to accept her decision. Willfully and with calculated precision, she decided to drink herself to death.

I resented her for being so intent and mercilessly focused on dying. So I erased all those things about her I had ever loved and into the blank space of her absence poured every awful thing I remembered or imagined she had done.

Filling the hole in my heart with allegations of her many betrayals, I regaled all who would bear witness to my pitiable life with tales of her calculated abandonment. As for her ingenuous sensuality, her vivacity, her refusal to conform to anyone's ideal of a mother, I failed to mention these traits in stories I told and instead paraded her memory in public outlined in scarlet letters, never once admitting how much I had benefitted from her cavalier parenting or acknowledging the pleasure I derived from her pain.

But the morning after my dream in Delphi, I followed a road to the earth's center and there, touching that navel, opened the door to my mother again. Behind her swayed a procession of Sibyls, those riddling prophetesses sired by death's coupling with desire. Daughter in a long line of daughters guarding Gaia's shrine, my mother walked toward the throne.

My mother's hands; the cords of all link back to the earth's navel.

From Hannah I learned to think about history differently. I used to track back from the present to my life's past, searching for traces of what Hannah Arendt once called the "subterranean stream" of the elements of my origins. Believing then in causality, I treated the past as the inveterate predictor of the present, "as though everything that in fact happened could not have happened otherwise."[103] Then reading Hannah and living with the memories it provoked I began to question my belief in causality and confront the fact that such a belief, rigidly adhered to, meant refusing to bear the burden of my past and the responsibility that past had placed on me.

Of course, I knew Hannah had in mind the terrible weight the most momentous events of the twentieth century—the emergence of totalitarianism and the catastrophe of the Holocaust—had put upon the shoulders of modern humanity. In the aftermath of these events, she said, we face new difficulties: "the bitter realization that nothing has been promised to us, no Messianic Age, no classless society, no paradise after death."[104] The twentieth century marked humanity's "coming of age" and its first "disastrous result...is that modern man has come to resent everything given, even his own existence—to resent the very fact that he is not the creator of the universe and himself. In this fundamental resentment he refuses to see rhyme or reason in the given world."[105] But couldn't this also be the case for the way anyone thinks about her personal life? And wouldn't it also affect how she saw herself in the world—as someone beset upon by external events, like "a leaf in the whirlwind of time?" After all, who'd hold a leaf responsible for landing by chance in some place and starting a fire?

Maybe resentment had driven me to push my mother away. Not literally, of course, but by using her as a convenient excuse to complain about or to hide behind whenever anything disappointing happened to me. *If you only knew how difficult my childhood had been.* I'd been known to say something like that more than once. Maybe I resented having been born at all.

So, besides bearing the burden of major events of the last century, encountering my own, more private history and shouldering events of my past demanded an equal "coming of age" and bone-chilling confrontation with reality. Without denying what happened, or submitting to its weight as though nothing could have been any different, I would have to give up the blinders of fatalism and abandon the illusion of guaranteed redemption. Nothing would be left then to protect me from responsibility for my own part in the story.

Of course it was entirely possible for me to continue to dwell in resentment of the past. It had become a habit. It must have taken root with that first tinge of hostility I felt at not having had the ability to choose the time and place of my own birth and if I held onto that feeling, it would build and build becoming an almost unbridled force of refusal to see rhyme or reason in the given world, leading me to treat any limit to making myself the center of the universe as only another obstacle to overcome, even believing, perhaps only secretly at first, that everything was possible. Resentful of the given world, I could deny its givenness.

Resentment is the default position of the thoughtless. The alternative is gratitude "for the few elementary things that are invariably given us, such as life itself, the existence of man and the world."[106] Resentment is relatively easy to acquire but gratitude is much harder to cultivate.

To dwell in gratitude means to act in acceptance of the circumstances of my lineage. These circumstances describe where my story began and catalogue the events that have shaped the context of my life as it has continued. "Whatever touches or enters into a sustained relationship with human life immediately assumes the character of a condition of human existence...Whatever enters the human world of its own accord or is drawn into by human effort becomes part of the human condition."[107] Although circumstances conditioned my activities and framed the choices I made, they didn't determine what I did or where I went. "The conditions of human existence...never condition us absolutely."[108]

The more I thought about it, the more the fact that I was not the automatic by-product of my beginnings became truly frightening; in fact, it was much more frightening than the opposite and perhaps more frequently entertained idea that I had not chosen to be the person I appeared to be but was merely the unwilled result of my past, dragged into enacting a role, or playing a part, or behaving in ways that biology or fate or some other external force pre-determined. Oh, to be a leaf in the whirlwind of time, blown from moment to moment, bossed around by time's currents, unburdened of thought.

Gratitude is the opposite of passivity because passivity is the unconscious reception of everything that happens, has happened or might happen. Contentment comes from cultivating active acceptance of the chance

I was given to make some mark in the world within the endowment of time, however brief or long, I have to live in it. "[S]uch gratitude expects nothing except, in the words of Faulkner—'one's own one anonymous chance to perform something passionate and brave and austere not just in but into man's enduring chronicle...in gratitude for the gift of [one's] time in it.' "[109] And gratitude implies even more. "[G]ratitude for life having been given at all is the spring of remembrance, for a life is cherished even in misery: 'Now you are miserable and still you do not want to die for no other reason but that you want to be.' What ultimately stills the fear of death is not hope or desire, but remembrance and gratitude."[110]

I would like to dwell in gratitude. I would like to remember.

Dad must have met Mom some time around 1947. I never learned exactly how or where they first encountered each other. Parents being so easily mythologized as not to require an actual past, I crafted several versions of their story.

Knowing my mother loved sailors, sometimes I imagine my parents meeting at a USO event like the ones in the early 50s my mother took me to with her mother on Sunday trips to the Armory in Manhattan, excursions sponsored by the Ladies' Auxiliary of the

Catholic War Veterans, which both my mother and grandmother had joined. Besides my mother's obvious enjoyment at serving food and drinks to the sailors and dancing with every one of them, I remember little about those events except that they were held in a large, brightly lit room lined with young men sporting rakish blue woolen uniforms with white striped pants that fit tight across the rear and draped over shiny black shoes, shinier than my father achieved during his Saturday routine polishing the family's shoes in our kitchen.

As a young woman my mother spent many evenings with her girlfriends dancing to the big band sounds of Tommy Dorsey at the Copacabana. Could be Dad first saw her there. Having played horn in the Navy band as a young man, he'd have gone to the Copa to listen to the trumpets.

But whenever I look at my sexy mother in the *Daily News* photograph where she is posed in Prospect Park on the afternoon of her eighteenth birthday, coyly sliding the hem of her skirt up the full length of her thigh, pretending to adjust the seams in her hose, I imagine my father seeing her for the first time that day and realizing immediately that what he needed was a *soupçon* of Irish hussy to spice up the mixture of his diligent Polish and serviceable Welsh family stew.

Of course, it was entirely possible my parents met changing trains on the elevated subway platform that used to carry the BMT across Brooklyn. Each of them would have been heading to work—she to the phone company in Sheepshead Bay and he to his job as a clerk in an ad agency in Manhattan. As usual, they were moving in opposite directions. But maybe they stopped long enough to glance across the tracks and, noticing each other, thought, Why not?

> *[T]he world is full of stories, events and occurrences and strange happenings, which wait only to be told...[O]nly if you can imagine what has happened anyhow, repeat it in the imagination, will you see the stories, and only if you have the patience to tell and retell them...will you be able to tell them well.*[111]

The truth is, most likely they met in some bar.

Dad was a man of indefatigable routine and predictable outing. Mom's style tended toward the peripatetic. What they had in common was drinking. Like two broken clocks they must have discovered themselves in the same place at least once on the same day and taken advantage of the coincidence to start a relationship.

But however it happened, one fact I know for certain—I arrived nine months after the wedding.

Every May on their anniversary I take out their wedding album and each time I focus on a different detail. This time it's Mom's ankle-strapped stilettos peeking out from below the hem of her ivory satin dress. She's holding her head high as she walks down the aisle on my father's arm. She's slimmer than I remember her. What intrigues me most is my parents are smiling.

For the first half of the 1950s we all lived together with Mom's parents in a red brick two-story house on East 63rd Street in Brooklyn. In those days, it seemed to me an enormous structure, much larger than the one I stand in front of the day after I return from Delphi. But it's the right house; I know it. Because there, down the alley, is the window of the room that once was my bedroom, tucked in between my parents' room at the back of the house and my grandparents' in the front.

The winter I turned five Gramps, my grandfather, set up a table in a corner of their bedroom and placed on it a wooden dollhouse he'd built, outfitted it with miniaturized furniture resembling our own. I watched him craft each piece in his workshop in our basement, noting how carefully he returned each tool to the exact spot he'd outlined on the wall in its shape. He planed and sanded the wood for a small table fit for the corner of one room in the dollhouse, a room the tiny version of my grandparents' room, and told me he'd make a tiny dollhouse exactly like the one he was now building to sit on that tiny table and then I imagined inside that tiny dollhouse an even tinier table with another dollhouse sitting atop and my mind raced on and on into an infinity of ever smaller versions of my world until reaching a spot I couldn't see but thought must exist, the tiniest spot of all where everything once must have begun.

The cords of all link back to the earth's navel. I come from a long line of Sibyls.

One evening that same winter our family physician, Dr. Berman, appeared on our front porch and I ran into the kitchen to hide; I'd been afraid of him ever since the day, two years before, when my body forgot how to swallow.

That day my body rebelled, I'd been sitting with my grandfather having tea or, rather, a cup of milk with a few drops of brewed tea to color it the slightest hint of beige. I remember raising the cup to my mouth to sip. But when I tried to swallow liquid poured from my nose. So I tried again, but my throat jammed shut, rerouting the potion again through my nostrils. Dr. Berman was immediately summoned and when he arrived I demonstrated my trick for him. Without hesitation he bundled me into his arms and whisked me off the hospital.

"No use lying to you," Dr. Berman told my parents, calling them later from the hospital. "She's got bulbar polio; paralyzes the throat. Only thing to do is keep her here...and wait."

Six-seven-eight-nine...I was down for the count, surrounded by an entourage of nurses and doctors.

Gramps would have none of it. In glory-be-to-God choruses he made an Irish wager—"No more drink if you spare her; on my mother's life, I swear it." *I'll take you home again, Kathleen.* Two months later, he did. And never touched a drop of drink again.

"You can come out now," my mother called to me. "The doctor's not here to see you today." It was Nana he'd come to examine. My forty-five year old grandmother, thin as a rail, but a smoker, had been complaining of pains in her chest.

"She's had an attack," my mother said. "She needs to rest."

"What kind of attack?" I asked, nervously helping my mother set up a small cot and bedside table in the living room where the couch used to be.

"An attack of the heart," she said. "She'll be fine." Then, for no apparent reason, she asked me if I wanted a puppy.

"You mean it? A puppy?" I'd been nagging her for months. I'd been given a small turtle for a pet, the kind they used to sell at the circus, but which now, so my older son tells me, are among the world's most endangered species, made nearly extinct by trafficking. For a week the turtle contented itself, waddling in and out of the shallow pan lined with small rocks and twigs I'd salvaged from the vacant lot down the street. Then one day, both turtle and pan disappeared.

"Where's Charlie?" I asked my mother, staring at the space on the kitchen floor between the oven and the pantry where Charlie had been lodged.

"It died," she said. "Got caught in the mouse trap."

Right away I decided a larger animal might be a more sustainable pet and promptly started my campaign for a dog.

"Yes, I mean it," Mother nodded. I got so excited I forgot all about Nana's attack for a while.

For a month, every day after Kindergarten I ran upstairs to my room, the puppy scampering behind me, and retrieved the bag full of plastic medical implements I'd received the Christmas before and then tiptoed quietly back downstairs to where the patient lay. If Nana was awake, I took her temperature and pulse, adding the results to the chart Dr. Berman had given me to record the fluctuations of her misbehaving heart.

"I'm going to be a doctor, Nana. I'll invent a cure for attacked hearts."

She smiled turning her wan blue eyes toward me, squeezing my hand.

"Are your feeling better now, Nana?" She nodded.

"Do you want me to read to you, Nana?" Another nod. I picked up my favorite book and repeated the story of Madeline and all the little girls in a line, which Nana had read to me on those nights I groped down the hall from my room to hers, escaping the sounds of my parents' fighting.

> *In an old house in Paris that was covered in vines, lived twelve little girls in two straight lines. In two straight lines, they broke their bread. And brushed their teeth, and went to bed. They left the house at half past nine. In two straight lines, in rain or shine. The smallest one was Madeline.*[112]

Stories, Nana told me, helped hearts beat into balance again; so I aimed the magical words right at her heart.

All sorrows can be borne if you put them into a story or tell a story about them.

Every day Dr. Berman came to hook Nana up to his portable electrocardiograph machine and as he read the printout I studied the lines on his face, hoping for some sign that Nana was healed. He remained expressionless for weeks. Then, one particular Saturday his eyes sparkled.

"We've done it," he said in generous delight. "Her heart is perfectly fine."

A week later Dad moved the couch back into the living room and took the cot back to the basement, where it stayed for two more years until the house was sold and my grandparents moved to their own apartment, two bus lines away. And a week after the living room was reassembled my dog disappeared.

No one ever told me why the house had to be sold and it occurs to me now I never really knew if my parents ever had owned it. But somehow it was taken away and I needed someone to blame for its loss; my mother was the easiest, available target. She'd moved us out of the house, I assumed, to be rid of her parents. And the dog. It turned out I was wrong on both counts.

As much as I wanted the arrangement of living with my grandparents to last forever, my parents must have longed for some privacy. Whether to fight or to drink or have sex, or cook their own meals, or maybe even learn how to love each other again, they must have wanted a home of their own, some private place in the world to hide in. And probably so did my grandparents.

My parents found an apartment to rent near my school. On weekdays, my grandmother picked me up from school and took me to her place on Lenox Avenue where I waited until Mom returned from work to take me home. It began to feel as if I had two sets of parents; shuttling between them became a kind of adventure.

In my grandparents' neighborhood I made a new set of friends whose families seemed almost as odd as mine. There was Moira, who lived with her adoptive mother, a nurse who regaled us with stories of her charges on Kings County Hospital's mental ward, her gout-ridden father, an older brother named Billy, who was a motorcycle mechanic and displaced Playboy of the Western World, with whom I promptly fell in love, and a maiden and miserly aunt, who occupied the odiferous basement of the house, along with mountains of newspapers and a menagerie of cats pissing incessantly in every corner. And there was Ellen, without brother or sister but whose parents fought about her father's drinking almost as much as mine battled through theirs. And finally, my side-kick, Susan, who lived next door to my grandparents' three-room, second-floor apartment in a house that her family actually owned, complete with upright piano, a caramel-colored cocker spaniel, a little brother we could tease, and a perpetually aproned and bespectacled stay-at-home mother, the only one of the three of us who had a family sociologists of that era would have called normal.

In those days, whether out of ignorance of the real dangers or a genuinely lesser risk from predators on the young, parents gave urban children, even young girls, a wider latitude to roam as long as they stayed in a group. So after school the four of us girls would amble down Nostrand Avenue and enter the Winthrop Street Playground, where we ruled the monkey bars with the acuity and vision of circus-trained acrobats. On Saturdays we wandered as far as the wide acres of Prospect Park and along its paths we trekked like intrepid explorers in a yet undiscovered paradise.

If we were feeling less adventuresome, we'd walk around the corner to play stickball or potsy on grids we chalked in Technicolor exactly in front of Mrs. Fiori's house on 34th street, just because she'd said we shouldn't. And when, as she inevitably did, Mrs. Fiori screamed at us that her husband, Frank, worked nights and had to sleep days and couldn't stand such a racket, we'd sashay forth, all four of us, hands on hips, and I'd blurt out a well-rehearsed taunt:

"What, do you think you own the street? The street belongs to the borough of Brooklyn, the county of Kings; anyone can play here. That's the law."

One Halloween Ellen, Moira, Susan and I donned Moira's sister's bridesmaids' gowns. In gauzy skirts of frothy pink and aquamarine we bounded around the blocks we had permission to maneuver, clopping along, clickety-clack, in rhinestone-studded, high heels we'd discovered in the back of the closet. Hoarding scores of Mars Bars and bags of candied corn and apples jammed with pennies, we hauled our loot around in sacks fashioned out of tattered pillowcases.

On the whole, we were polite. But woe to those who weren't home; they were met with the wrath of the fearless foursome. With socks stuffed with powdery chalk we marked the houses of the cheap and unfriendly for the ghouls and goblins to find. At the stroke of midnight all the souls of all the dead would be released from Holy Cross cemetery and search the chilly streets for the condemned neighbors, promptly sinking their chattering skeletal teeth into the flesh of the unregenerate and faithless. Or so we imagined.

Later that Halloween night, I returned home to my parents arguing from the respective corners of their marriage, fists and bottles flying. But their battles mattered less to me now that I had my grandparents to go to.

Weekends Mom and Dad took me with them to Bart's or Ralph's, their favorite neighborhood watering holes, and on Sundays we drove to Gilmore's Bar and Grill near my grandparents' apartment, joining them in a large black and white tiled dining room at the back where the cook served roast beef dinner with all the fixings.

You might think that spending a good chunk of my childhood in bars with my parents was damaging. (Believe me, once I learned it was supposed to have caused me great pain I played up that angle for sympathy.) But, to tell you the truth, it wasn't so bad.

In those days, the neighborhood bar was a family hangout; merely one point on the perimeter of all the other sacred and secular enterprises encircling my childhood, which included the parish church and school, Woolworth's—or the five and dime, as we used to call it—the local bakery, an A&P food market, the soda fountain, the corner gas station, the Gil Hodges bowling alley, the beauty parlor and the bar. Dads who were mechanics or shipping clerks, truck drivers or salesmen and Moms who were secretaries or nurses came into Bart's after work for a quick beer or a shot of whiskey before walking the two blocks home to their semi-detached houses where three to six kids from each family, except mine, could be found playing stick-ball or jumping rope in the street before supper.

On Saturday evenings, mixed shuffleboard teams competed for pitchers of beer and small plastic trophies. Winners' names were displayed on a blackboard near the front door; my mother's featured prominently among them. We kids sank quarters into the juke box and played Patsy Cline or Elvis Presley and ate hamburgers and drank cokes at small tables covered with red and white checkerboard cloths, desperately longing for summer when our Dads would form baseball teams and don spiffy uniforms emblazoned with the bar's logo to compete with rival bars in the neighborhood world series, which was always followed by an end-of-season barbeque.

We knew most of each other's secrets—which Dads had had affairs with which Moms, which Moms had gotten beaten or yelled at over dinner, which brothers were the altar boy the parish priest most liked to see at Mass, which older sisters had gone "all the way." Trading secrets made everything seem normal; it was a child's way to build a private space in which to share pain.

Still, what frightened me then wasn't my parents' drinking or even their fights—though those could be harrowing—as much as the possibility they might divorce.

Divorce, we had learned from the nuns at school, was the sort of sin from which no one recovered. You could confess to adultery and be given penance; you could beat your wife, say you were sorry and be forgiven. Even murderers could receive absolution for their crimes. But, no matter what happened, no Catholic was meant to divorce. Excommunication and certain damnation awaited those who ignored the heavenly fact of marital permanence. Knowing that made me worry about the fate of my parents' souls more than the physical consequences of their fury and so every night I prayed to God to keep my parents together, embattled but married forever.

I was nine the summer my Dad began to take suspiciously extended business trips, strange excursions, given his sedentary and lackluster job as an advertising sales agent for RH Donnelly. That same summer Mom spent hours on the phone with unknown callers who'd hang up on me whenever they heard my kid's voice.

Thereafter I was sent most weekends to visit Aunts Florrie and Mae, my grandfather's sisters, who lived in a small spinster apartment in a brick-faced six story building on East 16th Street. On those July evenings the orange sun lingered low in the steamy sky long enough for an evening walk down Cortelyou Road with cousin Ursula, Florrie's daughter, who was close to my mother's age. Ursula took me to Woolworth's on Flatbush Avenue where the summer special was a swinging string of bright balloons, each one more tempting than the next. Cloistered inside every balloon was a tiny paper, a sacred talisman announcing a prize.

If I picked a winner, for a penny I would be rewarded with a banana split sundae, heaping scoops of coffee and vanilla and chocolate ice cream swimming haplessly in a pool of muddy fudge, dressed in hats of whipped cream. Atop the whole mess stood a cherry, electric red. But if it cost more than the quarter I had, I'd lost, and would content myself wandering up and down the wooden aisles of display cases filled with cheap toys and trinkets.

Stacked in neat piles separated by green glass dividers I'd find a treasure trove of office supplies, cream colored pads decorated with daisies on the front cover and boxes of yellow Adirondack pencils waiting to be sharpened, and pink erasers and paper clips and plastic cases for carrying pens in your pocket. And I'd imagine myself to be a scribe sitting quietly at an oak desk, tapping my pencil lightly on the leather-bound blotter, waiting for the right word to float into my reverie and glide me on glorious syllables to the next comma in the strange sentence that was my life. Past the metal carousel of sewing notions laden with Bakelite buttons and snaps stitched onto cards of glossy white paper I'd meander, making my way to the perfumes where I'd fall again into a trance, dreaming about what a woman who'd wear "Evening in Paris," or "Tweed," or "Moon Drops" might be like for a mother. Surely nothing like mine.

After a while, Dad came home less frequently. Then, not at all.

Dad's departure generated my first real major moral quandary—either God hadn't heard my prayers and therefore was not ubiquitous, as Sister Mary Aloysius had said, or he'd caused the evil of my parents' damnation. And what kind of God would do that? Had

God simply stood idly by and allowed my parents to separate? But if that was true then he wasn't all good. Whichever way I thought about it confronted me with a dilemma: should I reject God or my parents? Here, for the first time, I was presented with the disappointment of holding fast to any ideology. I didn't know what else to do except pray harder.

Sacrificing all candy and soda that Lent, I waited for The Big Sign, something like the stigmata. My hands and feet remaining stubbornly intact, the closer it got to Good Friday the more forlorn I became. Holy Thursday I went to stay with Aunt Mae and Aunt Florrie.

After dinner, I locked myself in the bathroom, pretending to bathe. Stripped down to my panties I knelt on the cold tile floor and pleaded for an answer to my prayers. But when I looked down my hands still weren't bleeding. On Easter Sunday I took communion, chewing especially hard on the host.

"Body of Christ, I hope it hurts."

Dad didn't move back, which left me at least part of the time in the care of my wayward mother.

Mom was never detoured onto the pathway of alternative activities by the prospect of my being at home. She simply changed the rules of her domestic management, suspending the curfew on my TV watching. While she played all night poker with "the boys" from

Bart's, I'd watch Jimmy Cagney in *Angels with Dirty Faces* or maybe Humphrey Bogart in *The Maltese Falcon.* If it was a Cagney, Mom would sit next to me a few minutes and moon over him. "He's my favorite; a little guy, he takes crap from no one."

Mom's cousin Faith came down to New York from New Haven frequently to party with her. Faith had thick black tresses, big breasts and ruby lips that made her look like Jane Russell. She was almost as wild as my mother. When Faith and Mom hit the town they were a knockout duo.

One particular visit, Mom and Faith spent all day drinking and playing poker with a bunch from Bart's. When I got home from a school basketball game, they were still at it. I watched the card game for a while, then went into the living room and turned on the Million Dollar Movie as loud as I could. Hours later, the group had dwindled to Mom and Faith and two guys. Mom stuck her head in the living room doorway and said it was time for bed. She and Faith and the guys wandered down the hall to Mom's bedroom "for some adult talk." I went to sleep.

Around midnight the springs on the twin beds in my mother's room began to squeak contrapuntally and I snuck out of my room, tiptoeing across the creaky floor to peek through her bedroom door's keyhole. There was my mother, incandescently naked, one hand gripping a man's stiff organ and rubbing herself with the other while she watched Faith gyrating on the twin bed beside her, getting done in a very non-missionary position. Then they switched. I held my breath and kept watching and would have continued except I was afraid to get caught when they stopped.

A year or so after the spring of his departure, my father hatched the brilliant idea to take me to the movies on what had become his weekly visits. Uncomfortable with wordy intimacies, he resorted to this ritual as a way to fill the awkward space between us. Arriving precisely at 5:15 p.m. every Friday night in his always meticulously shined gun metal gray Chevrolet sedan, he'd greet me with a single beep of the horn and I'd emerge from our East 57th Street "garden apartment"—a misnomer of the highest conceit—without either of us having to endure his laboring through another conversation with my mother.

Dad was a man of habit, not studied insight. He never consulted the local listings in the paper. No matter what they were playing, we always went for the double bill either at the Marine on Flatbush Avenue or the Brook around the corner on Flatlands. I preferred the Brook because of Mrs. K, the little old woman—she was probably all of fifty—who staffed the ladies room on the second floor.

"Hello again Mr. Jones. Hello, Little Miss. You're gonna like this one, it's a winner. But the second one's sort of a drag. You can come see me if you get bored with it, honey."

We'd settle in the loge section of the darkening theatre, fifth row from the railing, always on the left. While the lights dimmed, I'd watch the arabesques of smoke from Dad's *Lucky Strikes* float in the air, dancing like blue ghost-sisters, and wonder where Mrs. K was. Within five minutes, she'd be standing on the burgundy-carpeted steps. Leaning her large frame into the brass banister, she'd reach into her uniform pocket and pull out a mentholated cigarette. Once she'd lit it and inhaled deeply, she'd sigh and fold her arms across her broad chest. And she'd stay in that position, comforting me by the sheer fact of her existence, until five minutes before the film ended when she'd resume her watch in the brown leather lounge chair just inside the vestibule of the ladies rest room. Yes, the mere habitual fact of her being there allowed me to relax into the rhythms of Dad's silent visits enough to watch the movies.

In those days before PG, R, or X had entered the parental lexicon, Dad's predilection for routine launched my education in human behavior in ways he never intended but didn't interrupt. One particular night, there appeared on the screen the chameleon face of Joanne Woodward in *The Three Faces of Eve.*

"Honey," she said, "there are a lot of things you never seen me do before. That's no sign I don't do 'em."

I couldn't believe my ears. Here, finally, was the sign I was looking for: my mother, talking to me through the face of Eve Black. Nothing in my catechism had ever brought such clarity to the situation of my mother. Because that's what she seemed to me then: a situation in need of a story.

Joanne Woodward let out a wild Eve Black cackle and put her head down on the bar, only to raise it the next moment reincarnated as the shocked and stupefied Eve White.

So that was it. The mother who cooked me spaghetti and meatballs from her Italian friend's recipe copied so carefully into a tattered brown journal, or brought me with her to her office at the telephone company in Sheepshead Bay some Saturdays and let me assemble a stationary store's worth of paper and pencils and clips so I could play *Daily News* reporter while she caught up with her office work, that was the Eve White part of my mother. But the mother who played marathons of shuffleboard at Bart's, or took me to Coney Island and parked me on the merry-go-round, giving Mr. Salzstein, who managed the menagerie of carved carnival-colored wooden horses, enough quarters to keep me there for at least an hour while she crossed the street to ride the Cyclone roller coaster again and again, by herself or with some sailor she'd have met in line, that part must have been Eve Black. And so was the mother I saw that night in the bedroom with Faith and those men.

I couldn't wait for the next Friday night movie, certain I'd discover more celluloid clues explaining my mother's unpredictable mothering.

A succession of musicals, big splashy Technicolor dreams full of pathos and desire, played in revival one summer and my father and I went to see every one. *Carousel, Oklahoma, The King and I, South Pacific*—I remember them vividly. I learned how my mother could be swept off her feet by someone in a surrey with the fringe on top, even in the middle of New York; that chance could hit her up side the head and make her fall off the track of her life until she picked herself up, dusted herself off, and started all over again. And how she was searching for Ezio Pinzo or Yul Brenner, for any prince charming she could conjure out of Canarsie, anyone who would make up a new life for us, far away from the bowels of Brooklyn, preferably in some remote and mythical land where mere women married rich, French-whispering plantation owners or entranced kings.

And we'd all live happily ever after.

But we didn't.

The real lesson I had yet to learn, the lesson my mother's death finally taught me, was the one I read years later in Hannah's essay on Isak Dinesen, describing what Dinesen had garnered from her own youthful follies: "while you can tell stories or write poems about life, you cannot make life poetic, live it as though it were a work of art...Life itself is neither essence nor elixir, and if you treat it as such it will only play its tricks on you."[113]

Thinking back to those movies, I realize they meant more to me than I'd understood then. They gave me not just clues to the mystery of my mother's behavior, but ideas for a fiction I wanted us to live and also for the one I would later try to conform my own life to.

We moved four times in the years between my 10th and 16th birthdays and in the summer of '65 settled into a large second floor apartment in a rambling Victorian house on Fenimore Street in Crown Heights. My mother compensated for the latest dislocation by giving me two rooms of my own: a study as well as a bedroom.

In my study I could lock the door against the daily drama of my own vertiginous life and escape into plot outlines I crafted, undisturbed. Under the languid lemon light of a goose-necked lamp, I'd sit at my grandfather's old walnut slant top desk and scribble for hours until the phone would ring and my mother would announce her departure for the evening.

That year Mom was hell bent on populating her love life with boyfriends who reminded her of Jimmy Cagney. For a while, she only dated men named Jim. At least it was easy to remember their names. One Jimmy the Rebel ambled into Bart's Bar and Grill in Mill Basin on a warm Sunday afternoon when my mother and her friend were setting the record for most points scored in the shuffleboard tournament.

"Beers for the ladies," a gruff voice called out from the corner stool at the end of the bar opposite to where I was sitting, reading my new *Teen* magazine and sharing a pint of Breyer's coffee ice cream with Jake, the bartender, who'd given me a dollar to relieve my boredom and his sweet tooth with a visit to the candy store on the corner. Mom turned her auburn tresses and blue-green eyes in the direction of the voice. Sizing him up immediately as a fortyish James Dean wannabe with a Cagney twist to his smile, she seized the opportunity to ante up. See you and raise you, her poker face said.

"I'll take mine with a whisky chaser, Jake."

"Sure thing, Gerry; the Rebel's paying."

And that was it. Jimmy the Rebel sashayed into the middle of our lives and for a year besotted my mother.

One fall evening I saw the Rebel's blue boat of a Cadillac turning the corner. Cruising down our street he parked in front of our house and swung his Texas boots out to stand at the curb. Then, preparing to mount the steps of our porch, he preened in the side view mirror, slicking back his sandy hair and licking his lips. He leaned long on the buzzer until Mom poked her head out the window and said she'd be down right away. When he saw me standing next to her he waved.

"Hello, little darlin'. You look mighty fine. I see you got on that bracelet I gave you. Got a date?"

"Yeah, do you?"

"You know I do, sweet thing. Your mama and I gonna paint the town red. Want to come?" He didn't mean it but it never occurred to me to call his bluff and say, yes, sure, take me with you. Anyway, I had a date, and, unbelievable as it sounds, his name was Jimmy.

"No thanks, I've got better things to do."

"That Clark kid, huh? He's sorta cute. You like him fine, dontcha? His Daddy used to think my Gerry was fine too. But I set him to right about that, didn't I?"

"I have no idea what you're talking about."

"Sure you do, peaches, you know exactly what I'm talking about. I know you do."

And I did. My mother told me everything. A few months before there had been a terrible fight at the bar and the Rebel made it clear to some other man ogling my mother that he should "stay away from my woman." Mom told me this story proudly. Two men were fighting over her, the beloved object of desire.

The funny thing was Mom never really hid her sexuality from me. She just couldn't talk about sex. Once, soon after the Faith-and-Mom in the bedroom night, I asked her to explain the facts of life and she blushed. This was years before anything approaching sex education found its way into the school curriculum, leaving the burden of reproductive instruction unequivocally on parents' shoulders. The Sunday following our aborted conversation, Mom sat me down on the couch after Mass and started reading to me from *Facts for the Catholic Girl*, a euphemistic and anti-erotic pamphlet she'd picked up from the leaflets at the back of the church. But when she got to the page depicting a man and a woman sitting in bed she simply said "We'll finish this later."

That evening, after she'd gone out for the night, I rummaged in her drawer looking for the pamphlet so I could read the rest myself. What I found instead was a Xeroxed copy of a pornographic story that provided many more details for the parts she couldn't find words to describe. Mom instructed best by anecdote and example.

"I don't know what you're talking about," I yelled at the Rebel. "I never know what you're talking about because you're never talking about anything that makes sense," and slammed the window down and went to my room and waited until they'd left to go out on my date.

A hunter's moon hung low in the sky as my Jimmy walked me home from the movies that night. We'd seen *Dr. Zhivago* and I was in a dreamy state, mournful over Lara and Zhivago's doomed love. We held hands. This is it, I thought. Tonight we'll go all the way. But as we neared my house, the front door opened and a man ran out with another man running down the street after him.

"You'd better go now," I said and climbed the stairs to our apartment and stood in the hallway for some minutes.

Except for a low moan, the apartment was quiet. As I entered the living room, twisted carpet and tumbled bottles announced the scene of a battle. Down the hall, my mother emerged from her room, adjusting torn clothes and nursing her swollen eye with an ice pack.

"Christ, Mom, are you all right?"

"I'm O.K. A little worse for the wear."

"The Rebel?"

She nodded.

"Mom, you've got to break it off."

"I did. I told the Rebel I didn't want to see him anymore. I've met someone else. His name is Jim. He was here too. When the Rebel started yelling and belting me, Jim went after him and chased him down the street."

A few months later, the Rebel disappeared into his savage destiny. Mom married the other Jim the following spring, wearing a gray dress trimmed in white linen lace, the one I buried her in four years later, the few years it took her to kill herself, slowly, deliberately, and, I now believe, without malice on a steady diet of Seagram's and water.

Jim, it turned out, was another drinker. I'm sure he loved my mother, the same way one alcoholic loves another, to the bottom of one bottle and into the next. I spent that first year of their marriage trying to convince my mother Jim wouldn't leave her. If he left, she'd become my responsibility.

"I'll be back in a few minutes; just going for cigarettes," Jim would announce.

"He says he's going out to get cigarettes," she'd say, as if Jim wasn't in the room, "but he's lying; he's meeting his girlfriend."

"I'm coming right back, I said."

"Mom, he says he's coming right back."

"He won't be back; he'll be gone forever."

And then, of course, he'd be gone for hours. Not with another woman, just down the corner at Bart's, where my mother would eventually join him to drown her fears.

I gave up trying to convince her not to worry and, a year later, got married myself. I suppose I married at such a young age to get away from my mother. But as much as this was true, I was also following her lead. Part of me wanted to be exactly like her, to light out for the territory, licentious and free.

A year after my marriage, little more than a year before she died, Mom moved with Jim into an apartment three floors below mine.

In her treatise on the human condition, Hannah Arendt wrote about privacy. "The only efficient way to guarantee the darkness of what needs to be hidden against the light of publicity is...a privately owned place to hide in...From the beginning of history to our own time...the bodily part of human existence needed to be hidden."[114] Hannah thought some things should be shown and some hidden. But who decides which ones, I wondered? What had my mother been trying to show me by moving the site of her self-destruction right under my nose?

One day I ran into her on the street, some months after my first son was born. Seeing my mother in broad daylight, I could no longer avoid the fact that her once curly auburn hair had matted and faded to grey; her still young, freckled face had become blotched and swollen. Her skin was yellowed; her eyes sunken and far away. Why was she deliberately showing me she was poisoning herself? At the time, I couldn't understand. All I really wanted to do then was turn away. But I made some feeble attempt to help.

"Have you been to the doctor?"

"Yes, he said he'd help me find the right treatment." I looked at Jim standing next to her. He rolled his eyes, turned his head and started whistling as if to say I'll believe that when I see it.

"Mom, you're not getting better. Aren't you eating?"

"Sure, sure, of course. Stop worrying."

"I want you here for Jed's birthday."

"Where else would I be?"

The next Tuesday I invited cousin Ursula to lunch, wanting someone else to bear witness to Mom's deterioration and perhaps share the blame. Mom played with Jed in the living room while I went into the bedroom to get a sweater. When I came back she had fainted and Ursula was trying to revive her.

"I just got a little dizzy," she said. "It must be the medicine I'm taking."

For a while I tried to cajole Mom back to health. Then I gave up.

A month later I found Mom passed out in her apartment. Jim drove us to the doctor's office on Long

Island while Mom rested her head on my shoulder. She turned toward me once and smiled. I left her at the hospital and never saw her alive again.

For a long time after, for decades, I pretended my mother hadn't willed her own future or tried to show me what that future might look like if I kept tagging along for the ride. It wasn't until far along my thinking journey with Hannah that I allowed my mother a certain dignity for the life she'd chosen and only then could begin to feel gratitude for the life I'd been given—the first time at my birth and again when she died and once more when my mother's hands reached out to pull me back from the edge.

My mother's hands wrapped around my head. The cords of all link back to the earth's navel.

My mother's generation hadn't fully formed the questions that led women of mine to revolt against being reduced to handmaidens of bodily existence sequestered away in the private sphere of the home. Yet, from the time she left high school she held a job and thought of her work as a career, certainly much more than the "career" of homemaker the culture's dominant messages encouraged her to find fulfilling no matter how temperamentally ill-suited she was for that job.

My mother existed in a lacuna, in some uncharted, anxious space between her generation and mine, until whatever irreconcilable difference she had been able to self-medicate away between the woman she was and the woman she was supposed to be became so overwhelming she decided to retreat from the world altogether and withdrew into a space that wasn't even private, living out the self-degrading last months of her life hiding in plain sight of me, as if she'd wanted to teach me one last lesson, one I refused to learn until long after her death.

I come from a long line of Sibyls.

My favorite, my most beautiful monster, I know why I harbored you the longest: you were the monster I used to feel sorriest for myself.

Getting pity is a clever way to avoid responsibility. But cleverer still is figuring out how to continue to get pity even while pretending to be indispensable. If you pretend to be someone without whom the whole world would collapse and only later, and at exactly the right moment, reveal that you aren't, why, then the greatest pity awaits you. But you must appear capable, become expert at seeming irreplaceable; you must be talented enough so most people won't see how desperately you need attention, yet not too resourceful or no one ever will try to save you. Because what you really want is the right person at exactly the right moment to think, poor thing, and come to your rescue.

Ah, pity, where is thy sting?

The darker side of pity, whether pity is asked for or given, is the unacknowledged investment pity has in suffering continuing. Pity does not "look upon fortune and misfortune, the strong and the weak, with an equal eye;" it depends on misfortune and has a "vested interest in the existence of the unhappy."[115] Self-pity is bound by the same glorification of suffering; in this case, the suffering is one's own.

I pretended I could take care of everything. I went to great lengths to prove my credentials by finding other suffering people to rescue. Oh, but I wasn't looking for anyone like my poor excuse for a mother. You must understand. I was finished with that. After all, I am a professor, an educated woman with a Ph.D.

Such illusions comforted me until I reached forty; the same age Mom was when she died. "Wisdom is a virtue of old age, and it seems to come only to those who, when young, were neither wise nor prudent."[116]

In my fortieth year, my older son Jed entered his third year of college. I was still living in Berkeley with Dylan and my younger son, Ari. As I said, he was a cultured man, refined, with good taste. We had all the trappings of middle class normalcy—loads of scholarly books on our shelves, a big four-bedroom clapboard house on the Berkeley flats, where we entertained celebrated friends at elaborate, well-attended dinner parties. So what if he drank too much or that sometimes I drank too much with him. I became comfortable enough to say I loved him and, in time, that made him comfortable enough to say he loved me.

One summer night after Dylan fell asleep in the living room I went upstairs to bed. A few hours later, he stumbled into the bedroom and when he started to snore I snuck out to sleep on the couch in the study. I was still dreaming when the first blow hit the back of my head. By the second and third ones my dream exploded.

"Stop, stop, you're hurting me."

But the punches kept coming and I began to feel weightless, as if I was floating outside my own body. Outside looking in, what was happening to that woman on the couch no longer much mattered. Her body could lie there forever and I wouldn't care. I wouldn't have to care; I would be free from all caring. But an arm with a will of its own reached out and a hand grabbed the man's hair and pulled him off. And that's when I saw her: In that man's face I saw my most beautiful monster. That same auburn hair, those same puffy, sad eyes, begging for release: *Let me go, let me go.* And my mind grasped what my arm already knew: I did not want to die an early death like my mother.

Whenever I think back to that night, I think about how I am lucky it happened. No, not lucky, really. Because I wanted it to happen. I willed my mother to visit and she appeared in Dylan like a warning: *I am only the monster you have made by hiding from my death. Cling to me and you will remain duty-bound, forever. Let me go and find some other way into your own life.*

How comfortable I had been all the years holding onto her; how difficult it would be to live without my most beautiful monster. But how freeing if I learned to live with the necessity of having the mother I had. "[T]he price for absolute freedom from necessity is, in a sense, life itself, or rather the substitution of vicarious life for real life." To live as if one could be free from necessity is to live life like a story and not live life itself.

My mother never wanted to be rescued. And I didn't want to save her. When she died I kept her close by resenting her for leaving, turning her into my monstrous obsession.

And so now I must tell you the rest of the story.

I was awake when my mother left me. And, oh, how I wanted to keep her, and, oh, how I pushed her away.

I am sixteen again, waiting for her to come home to our apartment. I hear her spiked heals ricocheting down the elm-lined avenues, their syncopation calling me to duty. Clip/clip. Clop/Clop. Clip/clip. She climbs the stairs to our apartment, fumbling for her keys. Clop/Clop. I open the door. She makes it to the sofa, giggling. She's funny when she's drunk, but I try not to laugh. I'm tired and sort of embarrassed. A friend is spending the night and I don't want her to see my mother like this.

"Why are you so late," I say, pretending to chastise her. But my mother laughs and laughs and slips off the sofa.

"I was trying to call you and you and you...didn't answer. You were looking at me..." She wags her finger at me in mock reprimand. "You were looking at me, weren't you? Naughty, naughty," she says with a tsk, tsk, tsk through her teeth. She still had all her teeth then. Four years later, she had them all pulled out.

"I was in my room," I lie, taking her hand, pulling her back onto the sofa. I remove her shoes and slide off her stockings. She has the most beautiful legs.

"Hey, I'm not finished with that, don't take it away." I am trying to take off her sweater.

"That's not yours; leave it alone and I might give you some." She buttons the sweater and tries to stand.

"Mom, where are you going?"

"To work. I have to finish a project."

"You have to sleep first." I push her back on the sofa and consider leaving her there. Then I remember my friend.

"Peek-a-boo," she says as I pull her blouse over her head.

"I see you," I say. And then, I can't help it, I'm laughing. Because her slip is on backwards, her hair is a mess, her lipstick is smeared and she smells like a saloon, but, dammit, she's a riot, my mother.

I get her up from the couch. Arranging her left arm around my shoulder and my right arm around her waist to steady her, I walk her down the hall toward her room. She starts singing: "Redhead, Redhead, everybody loves Redhead." I put her to bed and go back to my room.

"Is everything ok?" my friend asks.

"Sure," I say, pretending she hasn't heard the commotion. I want to tell her it's just my redhead, my feisty, unbounded, slapstick-of-a-drunk mother and if you're my friend you'll get used to it. "Let's finish our homework," I say.

Clip/clop.

I watched Mom's favorite movie the night she died: *Angels with Dirty Faces.* Jimmy Cagney playing Rocky Sullivan, a kid from Hell's Kitchen. He's a tough guy on the lam in his old neighborhood, the admired hero of the kids living there now. He falls into an easy pace exchanging trade secrets about his life as a scofflaw. Then he's caught by the cops and sent back to prison, condemned for his crimes. But his old pal, Jerry Connolly (Pat O'Brien), now a priest ministering to the wayward youth of New York, begs him to turn yellow when he takes that walk down death row. Do it for the kids, he says; don't let them think yours is the only way. Rocky has his pride; says he won't go without his reputation intact. They strap him into the chair. And just before the clamps close around his wrists, he starts bawling like a baby.

And I cried too at the sight of my mother on the screen, now as Rocky Sullivan, letting me go in the moment of her death so I could learn to live in the world without her. And what a blessing the world gave her then, honoring her moonstruck madness and the fact that she'd lived at all the only way she could: both too fast and too slow ever to make it past forty.

Scientists have offered a plausible explanation of how we were born, while poetical thinkers like Hannah have answered best the question of why. Her explanation is paradoxical. In *The Origins of Totalitarianism*, written in what she called the shadows of the "society of the dying," the system of concentration camps which transformed people into "ghastly marionettes with human faces" reliably marching toward their own death,[117] she reached the following conclusion: Our birth happens for no determinate reason or purpose, except to give each one of us an opportunity to live and leave behind tracks for others to trace. Interrupting life's business-as-usual, birth interjects a kind of surprise twist to what seemed like the end of a story.

Something new becomes possible; new stories can now be told.

Hannah's studies taught her that totalitarian regimes try to annihilate spontaneity itself. By regulating birth and death, whether through prohibition or requirement, such systems use science and ideology to manufacture both monsters and saints and erase what is human from the face of the earth. In the end, terror succeeds by cutting "the moral person off from the individualist escape and in making the decisions of conscience absolutely questionable and equivocal."

Out of this strange narrative, Hannah created a political theory. She put what she called "the human condition of natality" at its conceptual center, making birth, the fact that we are born, the foundation of politics. In the yawning gulf between what had been, and what could be, between past and future, Hannah wrote about the risks anyone can take with the one chance she's been given to become herself.

A few years ago, I picked out a shell from a pile as a prompt for a prose poem. As I looked at this shell my mother appeared again in my mind's eye.

Ruby Lips

In my hand I hold a tiny shell, a small place, an island. On its minuscule landscape I see the layered history of a volcano, the whole of a world whirled round itself. Waves of vil-

lages ripple at its foot, spilling out of time. Millimeters higher lies the settled green forest, content on its thick roots to canopy together parrot and salamander and fern, containing a riot of mossy green girdled in saffron. And there, look there, lonely, near the top, boulders of once wild lava grasp the edge of the world as if they were pieces of the moon, humbled, dropped down to earth. Gaping, at the peak, a gabbing mouth, ruby-lipped, never closing, marks the rough entry to the earth's core. This island is an angry mound. Why shouldn't it be? Discovered, settled, when all along its desire was only to survive, high and wide in the world, forever.

Like a lipsticked, high-heeled island, from one end to the other my mother was a lonely display. Wide hips swaying, she'd sashay into the room until the room, embarrassed by its own limitations, broadened to greet her. "They call me 'Red,'" she'd announce. A one-word volcano about to explode. An angry mound. And why shouldn't she be? Discovered, settled, when all along her desire was only to survive, high and wide in the world, forever.

I hold this island, my mother, in my hand and wonder if perhaps the will to dislodge the world from itself might cease.

My mother left me, but she was no monster. She left this life in her own time and by her own rules. I understand now: it was the only way she knew to become herself.

{7}

Imagining Hannah

I do not believe there is any thought process possible without personal experience. Every thought is an afterthought...a reflection on some matter or event.

Hannah Arendt, "*What Remains? The Language Remains*"

THE LAST FIFTEEN YEARS OF HER LIFE, HANNAH ARENDT LIVED IN NEW YORK IN THE TWELFTH FLOOR RIVERSIDE DRIVE APARTMENT SHE SHARED WITH HER HUSBAND, HEINRICH BLÜCHER, UNTIL HIS DEATH IN 1970 WHEN SHE WAS LEFT IN THE SAME SPACE WITHOUT HIM. There, facing a wide window overlooking the Hudson River, her back to the metal filing cabinets holding the records of her life, she wrote many of her books, including *Eichmann in Jerusalem*, *Between Past and Future,* and *Men in*

Dark Times. Found in the typewriter on her desk at the time of her death in 1975 were pages from the final sections of her unfinished manuscript, *The Life of the Mind.*

Arranged in folders in the cabinets behind her, Hannah stored souvenirs of her origin and exile. In one section, she filed her birth certificate, her passports and other identity papers, along with legal documents and family records. Into this same folder she later added her poems and a personal essay ("The Shadows") she had written as a university student. Other files held copies of essays, lecture notes, reviews, and personal letters.

For decades, she saved thousands of documents, willing them to the Library of Congress, and to that stone and metal memory bank I traveled one very hot summer a few years ago. I went not searching for more facts but for contact with traces of Hannah.

Scientists tell us touch is the oldest sense, followed closely by smell. But what makes touch unique among all the senses is its singular ability to connect our bodies to others and to the things those others have worn or held or admired or carried into the world. If I can't touch someone, I can still touch what she has touched, feeling the object in my hand become warm again, as if alive. The inter-subjective sense par excellence, touch may be the most essentially worldly of senses and infinitely more reliable than sight. Seeing what they want or fear, eyes are suggestible, Kathryn Harrison once wrote. "But I've never known touch to deceive."[118]

Every morning for a week, in the muggy heat of the Washington summer, I walk from Union Station to the Madison Building and enter the Manuscript Reading Room of the Library of Congress. This particular summer, the country is on high security alert and the city feels as if it is under siege.

Walking up barricaded streets past the Senate building, past a phalanx of police patrolling the perimeter of the domed Capitol, past the Supreme Court, imposing and dazzlingly white and now bordered by sentries securing the steps, I wonder what Hannah would have said about the blockades and searches and metal security detectors and color-coded alarms, all the trappings of homeland security fencing in the democratic spaces she so prized.

"[F]reedom of movement...is...the substance and meaning of all things political. In this sense, politics and freedom are identical, and wherever this freedom does not exist, there is no political space in the true sense."[119]

Of course Hannah knew politics could also be an arena of conflict and interest. Yet, her vision of the political was, most of all, of a space for the sheer joy and gratification that came from being in company with one's peers, in a place intended for action, alive to the possibility of beginning something new. But today it's raining hard, as if these advanced security measures embarrass the weather itself into becoming a convenient excuse for the failure of public assembly. There's no joy here today.

Times before in Washington, whether demonstrating for the expansion of rights for African-Americans, for workers and women, or gays and lesbians, how alive the arriving crowd felt to me. On the train from New York, sometimes there were more demonstrators than commuters and I'd begin to believe all over again we really could change the world through the force of mere assembly. And as we swelled into hundreds of thousands of people spilling into the capitol's streets from all directions, I'd hold back just a little to marvel at the moving play of clever costumes and signs and in the camaraderie of songs and jokes being traded among people who didn't know one another and would probably never meet again, citizenship seemed to me a force, palpable and erotic, created not from ties of land or blood but out of desire, the sheer desire to be among so many unique others, each one connected to the next and, through those connections, making real something unprecedented and wonderful. It felt good to be there then. But now, walking along these barricades, nothing feels the same.

The main reading room of the Library of Congress is housed in the impressively large, domed Jefferson building. I take a seat in a small alcove to the left of the entrance and begin scrolling through finding aids for the collection of Hannah's papers, gazing up from time to time to read the inscription on the ceiling, visible from my reading table: "Of law there can be no less acknowledged than that her voice is the harmony of the world." A grand thought, as long as the law is founded in justice, as long as it doesn't speak in the voice of the Nuremberg Laws or embody the will of the *Führer*.

Hannah's records—some 25,000 items stored in 95 containers—are organized into the same groupings she originally arranged: family albums, medical records, birth, death, and divorce papers, Hannah's passports and US naturalization papers are in all one box. Personal and professional correspondence occupy another twenty, files of her lectures and teaching notes a further ten, and *Eichmann* and its aftermath, ten more. Drafts of *Between Past and Future*, *Men in Dark Times*, and *On Revolution* fill one box each and there are notes for an unfinished manuscript on Karl Marx in another. I don't know where to begin.

Finally identifying what seems most important to my tactile research project, I leave the Jefferson building and walk one long block away to the Madison Building, where the actual documents are housed.

Passing through security, I put my things in a locker, bring the permitted paper and pencils for note-taking and settle in front of a computer only to discover it's been reserved for researchers of Supreme Court Justice Harry Blackmun's papers. So I move to another of the four screens set aside for scholars utilizing digitized files and there I remain, transfixed for hours, making notes, printing documents.

A labor of love has gone into the transferring and numbering of these records into digital files. But if you have ever read documents on a computer screen for more than a few hours you know your eyes start to burn and your back begins to ache and even the fleshy pad where the bottom of your palm meets the table goes numb from holding the mechanical mouse while scrolling through yards and yards of documents. All this makes reading difficult enough. Add to that Hannah's habit of typing replies to letters she'd received on the back of the originals, and the task becomes even more formidable.

Hannah used to insert a carbon in between a received letter and a blank sheet of paper on which she would have a secretary type her reply, imprinting a copy of what she'd written on the reverse side of the original letter. Since, in her years in America, she used very thin, almost translucent paper, sometimes one side of the letter "bled" through to the other. The result is a weird dance of words, moving forwards and backwards at the same time on the page, like a conversation between two people constantly interrupting each other. There is more than a little confrontation with both friend and enemy in the reams of correspondence saved in these files.

As the images of the contents of Box 1 appear, I read a series of letters between Hannah and her stepsister, Eva Beerwald. The ones they exchanged in 1948 about events in the last days of Hannah's mother's life are especially poignant.

In her Arendt biography, Elisabeth Young-Bruehl described the difficult relationship Hannah had with her mother, Martha. Sensing almost from the beginning that Hannah was not very much like other young girls her age, Martha encouraged her daughter's independence, yet still remonstrated her in subtle ways whenever Hannah's resistance to conventionality became what she considered too difficult to handle. A precocious, moody, somewhat sickly child, Hannah found ever more inventive ways to frustrate her mother's efforts to make her conform. Feeling confined by more traditional notions about how a "normal" female should act, Hannah became what she once described, referring to Rahel, as "a woman of her own invention."

As an adolescent, Hannah claimed to have felt strange, out of place, *unheimlich*, as she called it. Whether it was her father's death when she was only seven that launched her mood swings between cheerfulness and despondency or having to become her mother's companion while remaining her daughter, I imagine Hannah engaged in a rebellion of sorts against this burden of precocious responsibility. "But then the gas ovens came," she once remarked ruefully to Heinrich; daughterly duty trumped independence.

After they emigrated to America, Hannah, Heinrich and Martha lived together—in separate rooms, one floor apart—in an upper west side boarding house where they first found residence in New York. Martha never quite adjusted to life in the U.S. Unsettled, disoriented, and unable to speak English, she relied more and more heavily on her daughter for solace from the "homelessness" and "statelessness" she must have felt. But this daughter was already making her way in a new language as an increasingly public and publicly recognized writer and no doubt felt her mother holding her back.

In the summer of 1948, Martha decided to return to Europe. It could have been only her own discomfort that drove Martha away, but I began to wonder whether somehow she understood the conflicts her daughter was experiencing and wanted to alleviate the resultant pain. Whatever the reason, "*Mutt*," as Hannah called her, set sail on the Queen Mary to live in England with her stepdaughter, Eva Beerwald. At some point during the voyage, Martha developed chest pains and had to be hospitalized as soon as she disembarked at Southampton.

> *23rd July 1948*
>
> *Dear Hannah:*
>
> *Yesterday I had your telegram. I expect you had mine today. Since Tuesday,* Mutt *has been unconscious and it is hard to tell whether she is still suffering when the effect of the drugs...leaves off...I only hope the heart will not last much longer as there is no hope for improvement...If this reaches you still in time for an answer I'd like to know whether* Mutt *and you would prefer cremation. There is a crematorium here in Southampton.*[120]

On July 27, another telegram arrived from Eva: "Mother died sleeping last night Arranging cremation Affectionately= Eva="

Hannah received notification of her mother's death while she was vacationing alone in New Hampshire after working especially hard on the manuscript of her monumental new work, *The Origins of Totalitarianism.* Reading the telegram from Eva, she admitted in a letter to Heinrich, filled her with mixed emotions; she felt "both unhappy and relieved at the same time." Thinking how often she had given in to her mother's demands for conventionality and to be taken care of made her feel as if "all this was the biggest mistake of my life." She could neither turn down all her mother's requests, nor fulfill them because what was being demanded of her was so radical "it would have been a radicalism of destruction for me and all my instincts."[121] She wanted Heinrich to understand she knew he had borne the burden of these demands as much as, if not more than, she. "I really couldn't change anything," she continued, "I didn't even consciously deceive you because I was always resolute about one thing, mainly never to have mother move in. But then the gas ovens came..."[122]

Heinrich wrote back immediately, explaining he had known the situation was impossible. "You did your best," he wrote, adding that "she [Martha] would never have had enough, for when one has the passive love of a sponge, one always feels dry..." Had it been his own mother, he continued, he might have found himself in a similar predicament. Except that his mother's "craziness" had made him suspicious of her love "from the start—which was obviously quite wrong, but...kept me from ending up in your situation." Whatever Hannah had offered to console him during those years of living with Martha had been enough help "to the extent that I could be helped...Hitler and Stalin did more than saddle your mother on us."[123]

Except he didn't end the letter there; his anger at Hannah's mother, bottled up for so many years, spilled out onto the page. "But what really infuriated me was the way she constantly sucked your blood, and her total lack of respect for your incredible accomplishments. And on top of everything, she was the one...who handled you thoughtlessly, as if you were a man." And then, perhaps thinking those words too harsh, he pulled back a little, acknowledging that Martha must have had genuine feelings of love for Hannah, although, he added, those feelings "ultimately dissolved in a flood of insipid sentimentalism."[124]

"[A]s if you were a man." Was Heinrich's expressed rage, I wondered, a defense against the affront to his own sense of masculinity and fears of inadequacy that *Mutt* certainly had played upon, especially in the earlier years, complaining about Heinrich's inability to find steady enough work to support them all. It was, after all, Hannah who learned English first, landing more regular employment while still pursuing her scholarship. And through the years, even after Heinrich was employed at Bard College, it was Hannah's notoriety that gave the couple a degree of economic security, albeit not to any luxurious extent. And it couldn't have been easy for a man of his generation, no matter how progressive a thinker, to be around the burgeoning circles of admirers giving his wife the respect and admiration more often reserved for men. More people than *Mutt* seemed ready to treat Hannah "like a man," something Hannah herself never seemed worried about. If anything, it was her mother's insistence that she behave "like a woman" that would have incensed Hannah.

Maybe it's unfair to be overly critical of Heinrich's response. After all, Hannah needed someone she loved and respected deeply to say what she had done for her mother was enough. It must have been especially important to have Heinrich forgive her for burdening him with her mother for so long, regardless of what circumstances created the arrangement. No doubt Heinrich's response reassured her. And yet, something else in this exchange made me wince.

I know what it feels like when a mother dies almost as soon as the daughter no longer insists she should stay. There is sadness; there is also relief. Paroxysms of guilt deepen the pain felt at becoming unburdened in this particular way. And though she doesn't want to admit it, there really is only one person whose forgiveness could mitigate that daughter's guilt. The trouble is, she is no longer there. And the fact of death's finality makes her angry all over again—at the mother for leaving, at herself for wanting her gone. Ever more deeply the daughter stuffs that anger down, where it festers until she finds a way to forgive and be forgiven.

In *The Mother Knot*, her elegiac memoir about her own mother, Kathryn Harrison maps such anger's contours with great clarity and intensity. On her deathbed, Harrison's mother calls her to her side. " 'After I'm dead," she whispered, "you're going to be very angry with me.'...I recognized her words as a gift, but I couldn't perceive its magnitude...Even my mother's implicit request for forgiveness, her admission that when my anger arrived it would be righteous...hadn't been enough to convince me it was safe to feel it."[125] Nor did she yet know how to forgive.

Eighteen years would pass before Harrison, unearthing her buried mother, carries through plans to have her cremated in the hopes that this might bring her the release she so desperately needs. Traveling to a beach on the Long Island coast of New York, she wills herself "to feel and remember—to possess—as much as I could of this day." Then, she walks into the sea. "When the waves reached the middle of my thighs, enough of me immersed that I could claim to be in the sea with her, I turned the bag over and poured my mother out...A woman, my mother, her dress dragged by the current. Departing at last, because at last I was allowing her to go."[126]

Although her own mother was nothing like Harrison's, Hannah probably sensed her mother's demands for conformity would have to remain unmet if Hannah was to become her own person. But a wellspring of fear might also have lain below Hannah's conflicted feelings about her mother's death. No matter how much Heinrich's words may have comforted her, Hannah would have to find her own way to resolve the mixed feelings I could read between the lines of her apologetic letter to Heinrich.

For a long time I stare at that telegram announcing Martha's death. Feeling closer than ever to this dead friend of mine, I realize what I want most to touch are Hannah's personal things: the notebook Martha used to record Hannah's young life and Hannah's collection of passports. I make an appointment to meet with the archivist the next day to argue my case. After initial resistance, she agrees to let me see the originals.

That night it's impossible to sleep. I keep imagining Hannah holding that telegram in her hand, feeling as if her life is about to begin and then thinking she must be the most horrible daughter for feeling that way. She takes the telegram out from time to time and reads it again, as if the telegram itself embodies her conflicted emotions.

These artifacts, these carefully guarded, left behind things from Hannah's life are the art works of a life, a collection of beautiful and rarified objects offering "a premonition of immortality...of something immortal achieved by mortal hands...tangibly present, to shine and to be seen, to sound and to be heard, to speak and to be read."[127] To be seen, to be heard, to be read, and, yes, also to be touched, singeing the body with the heat of remembrance of the life they emerged from, though long past, still also present.

"Above all," writes Diane Ackerman, "touch teaches us that life has depth and contour; it makes our sense of the world and ourself three-dimensional."[128] And, I believe, it makes other people, even those no longer present, become three-dimensional too. I suppose that's why I needed a tactile connection to Hannah: instead of the iconic, inaccessible Hannah, I wanted a Hannah more completely human.

I spend the next day at the library seated at a table on the other side of the reading room. Before me, on a metal trolley, rest four boxes of files. Crossing dimensions of time, my arm reaches into the past while the rest of me remains, however precariously, in the present. My hand brushes against a small leather object and I lift it out of its cardboard coffin, suddenly trembling at holding the same book Hannah's mother held in her hand for the first time a century earlier, the leather-jacketed journal in which Martha penned a mother's reflections about the earliest events in a daughter's life. The trace of Martha's touch lingering on its surface, I caress the book's faded red cover for several long moments until, skin to skin, it becomes incandescent.

Another memory floats back to me. A decade earlier I had been researching archives from the Paris Commune of 1871 at the International Institute of Social History in Amsterdam, where I'd gone with my friend, Françoise, to explore a collection of papers and artifacts for some essays we were writing about nineteenth century French women's activism. The archives weren't terribly well organized and one day, as I reached into a folder, my hand rubbed against some scratchy fabric. Pulling the material out to look closer at its tag, I noticed its peculiar shape and color and gasped at recognizing the green canvas satchel with the red emblem as the one Louise Michele had carried around barricaded Paris and taken with her to prison. The dead come to life; dust bursts into flames. Still holding that satchel, I glanced around the room. But in that great silent hall not one head turned to greet the assembling ghosts. Not then, nor a decade later, as I disinterred another woman's remains buried long ago in library vaults in another city.

Unser Kind, Our Child.

"Johanna Arendt was born on a Sunday evening at quarter past nine, on October 14, 1906. The birth took twenty-two hours and went normally. The child weighed 3,695 grams [8 lbs 4 oz.] at birth."

At a very young age, Johanna, seemed active and cheerful, precociously attentive and keenly observant, a wizard with language who already possessed "a burning interest in books and letters." But when she was two, loneliness and illness began to conspire against her. Her father contracted syphilis in his youth and while Hannah was very young, he suffered a recurrence, slowly deteriorating into insanity. Hospitalized in 1911, Paul Arendt died two years later, when Hannah was seven.

"[R]emembrance reveals the meaning in the form of a story."[129]

In these fragments of story a mother scribbled on the pages of a small book appeared themes and episodes familiar to me, patterns in childhood's disorienting cycles that condition the shape of a life. Through them, I imagine Hannah taking up residence in another house, the house of word and story, making sense of the world disintegrating around her.

Below Hannah's room, in the parlor, her mother Martha plays the piano, surrounding her ill father, Paul, with sonorous Schumann sonatas or the lilting cadences of Brahms. Paul's moans mix into a musical buzz vibrating the floorboards, tingling Hannah's bare feet while she reads alone in her room. What Hannah most loves is reading or listening to stories and when her father is home and healthy, she sits with him for hours repeating from memory tales she'd learned at school, mixing them into her own peculiar chorus of adventures, casting herself in the dual roles of vulnerable maiden and conquering hero. As Paul's health deteriorates his patience wanes and soon he finds Hannah's chatter difficult to listen to, interrupting her fable by abruptly turning away.

Most weekends now she spends with her grandparents and on Sundays goes walking with her grandfather Max through the linden and lilac-filled park. Grandpa Max tells Hannah stories. Cloaked in fabled affections, she feels shielded from sorrow for a while.

But then Grandpa Max gets sick too. So sick that Hannah is unable to visit him and for many spring weeks after school all she wants to do is sit at her window and listen to the sounds in the street.

"Hannah, close the window, what are your doing? You'll catch cold."

"I'm trying to remember."

"Remember what?"

"Grandpa's voice. Do you think it sounds more like rain or rustling leaves? Or maybe the clip-clopping of horses' hooves?" Clip-clop. Clip-clop.

One day, Hannah sees dozens of people come into the house, men carrying large vases of flowers and women bearing linen-wrapped baskets filled with breads and cheeses. And then, rising slowly up through the ceiling, Hannah hears the chords of Bach's requiem. Soon Hannah watches everyone following Mama and Grandma Klara out the front door, forming a procession winding all the way down *Tiergartenstrasse*. Excited, Hannah waves to her mother and smiles. Mama nods and turns away.

"Mama!" Hannah cries. Her mother told her Grandpa Max would soon be going where no one could see him. If this was the day, then why was everyone following him? Would they all, including Mama, stay away now too?

"Mama!" Too far down the street to hear her now, her mother keeps walking. Hannah rushes downstairs to follow and discovers the neighbor who has stayed behind to care for her. "It's alright, *Liebchen*, Mama will soon return."

"But where has she gone with Grandma Klara and the others? Why can't I go with her?"

"It's your grandfather, little one. He has gone to his resting place. And they are paying their respects."

"Can't I go too? I can help him rest."

That night Hannah dreams of her grandfather. In the dream he is cutting up cloth and giving small pieces to Hannah. "Keep these things in your pockets, Hannah, and you will never be lost. Now go; go on by yourself." In the dream, Hannah laughs while she follows the same path she always took with Grandpa Max. Along the way Hannah ties bits of cloth on low hanging branches until she arrives at their favorite bench and lies down to sleep. In the dream she isn't afraid when she wakes up at night in the park and has to follow the trail home by herself. Just like Grandpa Max said, she can find her way by herself. But then she awakes from the dream and is crying. Because no one saw what she did in the dream. She is all alone.

"Do you know how many leaves there are on *Tiergartenstrasse*?" Hannah asks her mother later that same year, in October, a few days after her seventh birthday. "Two hundred and five," says Hannah, hoping her mother will stop playing the piano and read to her instead. But when her mother turns toward her Hannah notices a kind of sadness clouding the lonely temple of her mother's face.

"Hannah, I have something to tell you. It's your father...how he has suffered...and now he is gone."

"I know Mama; he has gone to the hospital."

"No, Hannah. Gone; gone where no one can see him. Like Grandpa Max."

"Why are you sad, Mama?" Hannah asks, remembering her father and how they played cards and laughed, but also how strange he looked the last time Hannah saw him. He wasn't wearing his glasses and wouldn't even smile at her tricks and made her so mad she wished he would leave.

Sometimes Hannah feels as if she has two fathers, the kind, quiet one who lets her sit on his lap and touch all the pictures in his books, and the other one, the mean one, who calls her a nuisance and would rather listen to music than to her stories. And she isn't at all certain which one of them has gone away. Then, because her mother looks so tired and because Hannah doesn't know what else to say she repeats what she'd heard the rabbi say just before singing *Kol Nidre*.

"But, Mama, remember, this happens."

The next summer Hannah and her mother are supposed to go to the seaside. But by April Hannah's mother has decided to take a trip by herself, leaving Hannah behind with Grandma Klara, her father's mother. Hannah doesn't like Grandma Klara. She doesn't know any stories and makes Hannah sleep alone in another room at the end of a long hall and won't let her hold any of Grandpa Max's papers or books, not even to look at the pictures, and doesn't believe Hannah knows how to read or can count to more than a hundred. But when Hannah tells all this to her mother, Martha just closes her eyes

"Mama needs a rest, Hannah. And Grandma Klara does love you and takes care of you. Be a good girl; come here now and kiss Mama goodbye."

It seems like forever before Hannah's mother returns but when she does Hannah is so happy to see her she crawls into her lap and covers her face with kisses. And then Hannah says, loud enough for Grandma Klara to hear, "And now can we go to the seaside, Mama? I want to see Grandma Fanny and play with my cousins."

August 1914 brings horrible news that spins the world around in a terrific fright and instead of a summer filled with games and happy stories, Hannah and her mother rush back to their house in Königsberg and a few days later pack for Berlin.

"But Papa's books!" Hannah cries when she sees her mother bundling only two small suitcases of clothes.

"We must leave them."

"Why? And what about the piano?"

"Hush, Hannah, we must hurry. Aunt Margarethe will have everything you need."

"I don't care; I want my own things," Hannah cries.

I'll do it to quiet her, Martha thinks as she wraps up a few of Paul's books, holding back tears.

At the station near the center of town Hannah sees hundreds of soldiers and farmers and whole families traveling with all their belongings stuffed into small parcels and bags.

"I don't want to go on the train," Hannah cries, shivering. "It's too crowded." Her mother thinks Hannah must be coming down with a cold.

But it isn't fever that's stricken Hannah. When they return to *Tiergartenstrasse*, Hannah is sick. And afraid. Afraid of leaving, afraid of being left. Will she ever manage to love and not get lost?

Twenty-five years pass before Hannah confesses these earliest fears in a letter to her second husband, Heinrich. "You see dearest, I always knew, even as a kid, that I can only truly exist in love. And this is why I was so frightened that I might simply get lost. And so I made myself independent. And about the love of others who branded me as coldhearted, I always thought: If you only new how dangerous love would be for me."

Wondering what her attraction to and fear of love meant to Hannah, I ask myself what lessons I might yet discover and take these questions with me to a flat in London, where I have gone to piece my fragments together. And there, in a room one floor below ground level, I sit writing at a desk in front of a window facing a wall and watch budding vines climb their lemon-green tendrils up white painted bricks while a small chirping bird, a wren, builds a nest. In this dank basement I smell the earthy hint of spring and taste regeneration's residue in the not yet ripened supermarket strawberries arrayed in a bowl nearby. And because, before and behind me, across thousands of miles and eons of time, someone collected souvenirs of her origins and exile, I can touch, in those layers of life's comings and goings, ages of beginnings and endings so that, in whatever time I have left on this earth, I might tell a story, a tale that could survive this ever-changing movement of life.

{8}

Love and Forgiveness: My Heideggers I

The path you showed me is longer and more difficult than I thought. It requires a long life in its entirety.

Hannah Arendt to Martin Heidegger, April 22, 1928

A LEAF IN THE WHIRLWIND OF TIME. The more I thought about Hannah's characterization of Adolf Eichmann the more I realized how easily I had settled into the habit of thinking about my own past as nothing more than a set of events determining my present, as if one's life was fully fashioned at its beginning, as if only time and circumstance were needed to create the equation that produced a person as its inevitable result.

The truth was, I didn't believe in destiny. And I'd long ago given up any traditional idea of God. So why had I spent most of my intellectual life enthralled to some version of fatalism? What had made it so painful to admit my limitations or accept responsibility for what had been mine to control?

Saying I was the daughter of Edward Jones and Geraldine Brennan named the place of my beginning, the neighborhood of my origins, a spot in time, the space of a moment when, like everyone else, I started into the world. Being born of Edward and Geraldine announced the chance I'd been given. But that chance, with all the peculiar circumstances and conditions surrounding its occurrence, and what I made of it were two different things. My meditations on Hannah helped me recognize the importance of acknowledging the difference and begin to comprehend just how much such an acknowledgment can cost.

My thinking journey had led to some extraordinary places. Reading *Eichmann* made me think about monsters and the hold I'd let them have in my life. But now I found myself wondering about those beings at the other end of that spectrum—those larger than life heroes or saints, whether real or imaginary, into whose hands one might first deliver her heart.

He was thirty-five and married when they met. She was a young woman, seventeen years his junior. He was the professor, a nervous, handsome, yet needy intellectual giant, architect of transcendental thoughtscapes. She was the student, a precocious, elegant, yet vulnerable scholar prone to moodiness and solitary reflection. They began a love affair that lasted five years, until the world shifted more than a little and events, at once personal and political, drove her into exile and him into what she called an ignominious little "mouse hole" a refuge of arrogant isolation from which he never fully emerged. In 1933, she, a Jew, fled Germany. That same year, he joined the National Socialist Party becoming *Rektor* of the University of Freiburg and wreaking havoc on many Jewish lives until he resigned the following year, likely the result of Nazi party leaders' dissatisfaction with the degree of his passion for the cause. Then, twenty years after the affair ended, something pulled her toward him again and she rekindled their friendship, which lasted twenty-five years more, until her death.

Hannah Arendt and Martin Heidegger.

The fact of their long-lasting friendship made many people, including me, wonder how it was possible for Hannah to reconcile with this same deceitful Heidegger—the one who once called Heidegger The Fox—rekindling a friendship many years after their radical estrangement.

A veritable army of commentators has mulled over that question, arriving at answers either indicting Hannah for being naïve, self-contradictory, a latent German nationalist, or, even worse, for being a self-hating Jew. Yet as I pondered this perplexity I came slowly to recognize the long, complicated process enabling the kind of reconciliation, including to her own vulnerabilities and flaws, Hannah worked hard to achieve, and in the dynamics of her love affair with Heidegger began to glimpse the ironic source of what had launched her on that journey.

Some time in late 1995 I came across a story in *The New York Times* about the controversy caused by Elżbieta Ettinger's book about Hannah and Martin's affair. The romance itself wasn't news; Hannah's biographer, Elizabeth Young-Bruehl, had first reported it more than a decade earlier. But Ettinger's characterization of Hannah caught my attention.

Ettinger portrayed Hannah Arendt as an emotionally dependent, adulatory pawn of Martin Heidegger, a hapless victim of a syndrome one might call Great Man-itis. She'd thought Hannah's obsession with Heidegger drove her to the point, rather foolishly in Ettinger's opinion, of forgiving Heidegger his Nazi affiliations. Explaining Arendt's misguided behavior was simple, Ettinger once said in an interview: "Love is irrational. There is nothing we can do about it." It turns out Ettinger's interest in the Heidegger affair had been motivated by similar questions and, for complicated and largely personal reasons, tracking Hannah's fascination with Heidegger developed into her obsession.

Born in Łódź, Poland in 1924, Ettinger had been forced into the Warsaw ghetto in 1940 along with many members of her family. Just before the ghetto's final uprising and destruction, she managed to escape and lived on the run under a false identity for several years. Much later, she began a relationship with Manfred Lachs, her much older Warsaw University professor, with whom she had a child in 1962. Fearing political reprisals for having turned down a job offer in Poland's National Security Office, in 1967 she left Poland with her young daughter and, supported by a fellowship from Radcliffe College's Institute for Independent Study, came to the United States, living and teaching in the Cambridge area, including a long career with MIT's Humanities Department, where she was on the faculty from 1973 until retiring in 1997.[130]

Ettinger hadn't initially jumped at the opportunity to write about Hannah, as she explained to Melvyn Hill, a student of Arendt's whom she interviewed:

> *I probably told you that the reason I turned down (at first) my British editor's proposal to write this bio—an act of self-defense I sup-*

> *pose—was my loathing of German Jews. But now I'm in. I don't regret but feel very alone.*[131]

But once she'd become more deeply involved with her research, she decided her book could fill a void: Despite the publication of *For Love of the World*, Elizabeth Young-Bruehl's biography of Arendt, Ettinger thought its portrait of Hannah remained incomplete. As she wrote in her proposal for a National Endowment for the Humanities fellowship:

> *What distinguishe[s] my biography...is my emphasis on Arendt's personal life & experiences. Ms. Young-Bruehl correctly defined hers as a 'philosophical biography.' In my view Arendt's personal experiences, above all else, informed her thought. These include a heavily burdened childhood; her Jewishness, a source of constant conflict; the love affair with Martin Heidegger, a manipulative, exploitive man; the status of a refugee & a stateless person, life in another language; the state of a Jew, torn between the German culture, a proudly accepted heritage & the German nation.*[132]

What gave her the perspective to write a more personal account of Arendt's life and work, Ettinger noted, was the fact that she shared

> *with Arendt some experiences which permit me to understand her better than many others who do not, and who, therefore, can write about her from the 'outside' only, not from the 'inside' as I can; my life has been changed forever by the Nazis, as was hers; I chose exile (though 30 years later) as did she, and approximately at the same age, the mid-thirties; I am cut off from the Polish culture in which I was born, raised, and educated as she was from the German; I write, as did she, in a foreign tongue, and as did Arendt live a 'life in translation'.*[133]

Left out of this account was another fact Ettinger acknowledged in letters to close friends and acquaintances—she had had her own experience with a humiliating Heidegger kind of love. "I understand better than you do, & other people as well," she wrote to Melvyn Hill in 1993 after sending him drafts of her work-in-progress,

> *[Hannah's] unrequited love for Heid[egger], simply because there was such a man in my life. Pathological liar, opportunist & the father of Maia, my daughter...Just as Hannah did, no matter how he hurt & humiliated me, I always came for more. It took me several decades to understand that this man was a sado-masochist, that he resented himself be-*

> *cause he was a Jew & spilled resentment at anyone who came near him (not many people did)—above all Maia & I.*[134]

In 1988, Ettinger began contacting many of Arendt's still-living friends, students, acquaintances, and others who could share personal stories about her. That May, Ettinger communicated with Mary McCarthy through McCarthy's editor and explained her interest in a letter thanking McCarthy for agreeing to be interviewed:

> *My first encounter with Hannah Arendt was on the pages of* Le Monde *in a review of the French translation of my novel...The reviewer's remark 'accusing' me of following Hannah Arendt in her exposure of the collaboration of the Jews with the Germans naturally sent me straight to Hannah Arendt. She remained an important presence in my life ever since.*[135]

Mary McCarthy agreed there was room for another biography of Hannah. "So does Lotte [Kohler]," she added. "We both think that. Why do we think it? I think it's the same in both cases, though I probably shouldn't speak for her. I think the Young-Bruehl book is awful...I don't think I've ever read it through, to tell the truth."[136] McCarthy introduced Ettinger to Lotte Kohler and that connection opened the door to an ever-widening circle of resources, including access to the yet unpublished and mostly unknown correspondence between Arendt and Heidegger.

Reading through Ettinger's archives I began to think her account of the Heidegger affair, and particularly her representation of Hannah as someone forever duped by Heidegger's wiliness, was partly a retrospective damnation of Maia's father, Manfred Lachs. Like Hannah's affair with Heidegger, Ettinger had met Lachs when she was his student and considerably younger than he. The relationship became increasingly bitter and tumultuous; acrimony between them continued even decades after Ettinger left Poland.

But something else about Ettinger's growing fixation on the affair intrigued me. I began to think her condemnation of Hannah's continued attachment to Heidegger provided Ettinger with a thinly veiled means of self-laceration, a confession, never made public, of ever having become such a man's prey. Was she trying to assuage her own guilt by posthumously condemning Hannah, I wondered? But if that had been, in part, the motivation, Ettinger nonetheless insisted on one important difference between herself and her subject. At least she had had the good sense to overcome such a dangerous attachment and thereby salvaged her integrity. Hannah, on the other hand, continued publicly defending Heidegger up to the time of her own death. And that, in Ettinger's view, bordered on the immoral.

What troubled me most was the over-simplification of Hannah's character that emerged in the pages of Ettinger's slim volume about the affair. The Hannah portrayed there was an emotionally stunted character, unreflective not only in her younger years, but even into maturity. More than that, Ettinger represented this Hannah as someone incapable of clear judgment.

> *[I]t is safe to assume that only with the passage of time and the wisdom of hindsight could Arendt fully understand the intention behind Heidegger's convoluted arguments [about why Hannah should leave Marburg and study elsewhere]. And when she did, her letters disclose, she felt belittled, manipulated, cheated. Yet this would change little in her behavior toward Heidegger.*[137]

To Ettinger, Arendt's public loyalty to Heidegger was an almost unforgivable sin. Prodding everyone she interviewed to explain this mysteriously undying love a Jew could have for a Nazi, Ettinger began to formulate a psycho-cultural explanation for the affair. Heidegger's power over Hannah may have been in part the result of his purposeful manipulation of the aura of mystique surrounding him—the man Karl Loewith, another student of Heidegger's dubbed 'the little magician from Messkirch'. Yet, Ettinger faulted Hannah for an intrinsic psychological vulnerability, amplified by a desperate attachment to German culture, making Hannah ripe for worshipful submission. In the end, Ettinger argued, Heidegger became the symbolic means for Hannah to achieve a sense of "intellectual belonging and cultural acceptance," which she, like "other young German-Jewish intellectuals sought in German philosophy." And that tradition, Ettinger claimed, had led directly and inevitably to Nazism; it became "a substitute for religion, and [its] philosophers the embodiment of Germanness and of the *Geist.*"[138]

Hannah's continuing loyalty to Heidegger represented to Ettinger an unconscious and ominous desire to solve the 'problem' of being a German Jew by choosing allegiance to the German over the Jewish part of her. "Heidegger fulfilled for Hannah the dream of generations of German Jews, going back to such pioneers of assimilation as Rahel Varnhagen."[139] Through him, Ettinger contended—and others she interrogated sometimes confirmed her opinion—Hannah could retain her attachment to Germany. But because love for Germany meant love for a country containing, in Ettinger's view, the "only people who could have done what they did," this proved a dangerous, even murderous attachment. When, in 1969, Hannah wrote her notorious tribute to Heidegger, downplaying his support for the Third Reich and, according to Ettinger, "display[ing] the same unquestioning generosity, loyalty, and love she had shown since the beginning,"[140] Hannah's loyalty took what Ettinger assessed to be a self-destructive, self-hating, yet predictable turn. Predictable, that is, because of her Germanness.

At stake, then, in Ettinger's telling the Arendt/Heidegger story was settling an even older score. Again and again in interviews with Hannah's friends and enemies Ettinger surfaced the ancient conflict, even enmity, between *Ostjuden*, Jews from the Eastern parts of Europe, and *Yekkes*, Jews of German origin, making the relationship between Arendt and Heidegger assume epic proportions.

"You know, sometimes I think she was a German nationalist," she admitted to the psychologist David Jaroff. "Really. I'm not going to write about it, but...it was something very, very deep in her, her love of the German language, which is so typical of Germans, who maintain that there is no other language in which you can talk philosophy..."[141] This explanation seemed especially appealing to Hannah's foes.

After reading Ettinger's short monograph about the affair, Saul Bellow, no fan of Hannah's, applauded her work. He'd only known of the Heidegger affair as a rumor. But Ettinger's confirmation of it, and the specific way she characterized Hannah in her book, gave it a reality for which he told Ettinger he hadn't been entirely prepared. But that didn't stop him from adding this salacious bit of information to an already long list of reasons for disliking Hannah. How to characterize the affair, he wondered?

The typology he'd hit upon was revealing in many ways. You could almost hear Bellow laughing. It was a kind of "Prussian love affair," he continued in a letter to Ettinger, meaning an erotic master/slave relationship. Hannah may have wanted to be seen as a Jewess of exceptional intelligence and *Geist* and admitted to the pantheon of German high culture, but for Heidegger, Bellow concluded, she was simply a Jew. And then he closed the letter with a gesture of solidarity toward Ettinger, offering to discuss anything that puzzled her about his assessment over a pot of "*Ostjudische* tea."[142]

Yet the more I thought about it, the less Ettinger's representation of Hannah told the whole story. Thinking about Hannah's love affair with Heidegger made me feel deep down in my bones what Hannah meant when she said the most terrifying thing is trying to think without any ideological "banisters" or morally certain supports to guide you.

I've had my own Heideggers. Different from, yet like enough to the original to enable me to comprehend how Hannah's lingering attachment to Heidegger might have taken her on a more tortuous route to her own sense of integrity than the road Ettinger had taken on the same journey.

My first Heidegger coached debate at a Catholic girls' high school in Brooklyn where I spent four long years surrounded by nuns, saturated in Latin. He was nineteen and tall and handsome in a boyish way when we first met. I remember how the close-cropped cut of his hair made his large ears stand at attention. Self-assured beyond his years, he seemed to have a studied wariness about him. His wide lips bunched into a smirk whenever he made some slapstick joke. And when he was lost in thought, he squinted and slouched, assuming the look and posture of *The Thinker.*

He appeared in our classroom one fall afternoon in 1962, shortly after school ended that day. He chose us, he said, because we were at the top of the heap. In an academic system with seven levels, we were supposed to be "college-bound." Sitting on the top of the desk in front of mine, he leaned forward, as if looking past me. With his right hand pitched like a fleshy tent, he loosened a slightly stained red paisley tie with his left and unbuttoned the collar of his white Oxford cloth shirt. I noticed the nails on his thick fingers were chewed short. Had I read Machiavelli by then I might have recognized the twinkle of a fox's eye in the regal pose of his leonine head.

"Do you know how to explain the balance of payments?"

The group of us twenty-five girls just stared, perplexed and silent.

"How about the concept of free trade?"

A few tittered.

"Have you heard of the EEC? GATT? The IMF?" His right hand tightening into a fist, he used his middle finger to pound on my desk as he pronounced each letter of that litany of acronyms whose meaning I learned later and remembered longer than Latin.

"Do you know what a syllogism is or how to structure an inference?"

He looked right at me.

"Do you know what a syllogism is?"

"No," I said. His lips swelled into a smile as he swung his legs off the back of the desk and walked toward the blackboard.

"Are all men mortal?" He asked. Turning his question into a declarative sentence he wrote on the board: All men are mortal.

"I guess you could say that." I stuttered.

"For the sake of argument," he added, and scribbled another sentence: John is a man.

"Therefore?" he bellowed, implying I shouldn't have had to wait for the prompt.

"You're mortal," I blurted out, more out of shock than conviction.

"Perfect. See, you do know. And you'll learn how to use that head of yours for winning arguments when you join the debate society," he said, tapping the top of my skull. "You do want to join The Society, don't you?

"Is that a question?"

I didn't know what debate was but John made it sound adventurous and I wanted adventure. So I followed this charismatic young man, six years my senior, who scribbled in my high school yearbook at the end of my first year, "To my little 'genius,' stick with it this year and next year you'll see plenty of action. Endurance—that's all you'll need."

And, oh, how I believed. He'd been a champion himself in the Catholic boys' high school where, I later learned, he'd debated away his own demons. He'd been a star. He told me I would be a winner. He said I'd endure. Nothing, nothing would stop me. After all, if I had The Society, what else did I need?

The Society. That's what he called us. To everyone on the outside, we were known simply as "John's girls." We must have seemed an odd bunch: some twenty adolescent girls and John. When I think about it now, I'm surprised no one raised even an eyebrow when a handsome young man, only a few years older than we were, demanded and received complete devotion from a couple dozen young Catholic girls. No one questioned his motives. And to tell you the truth, I think we all had our own reasons for keeping it that way.

One afternoon I stood in the hallway on the first floor of the brick high school building staring at the glass cabinets outside the principal's office filled with glittering cups bearing the names of debate tournament winners on metal plaques mounted on faux wooden platforms. Some day, I thought, my name will be among them and when I have that kind of recognition, something approaching fame, I'll be different from the hundreds of other tartan-skirted and green flannel-vested girls roaming the halls of my high school. There and then I resolved to become a winner no matter what it took. You'd think a good Catholic girl like me might have realized that the other side of pity is pride, which cometh before a fall.

We were a tight group, operating like any award-winning sports' team. Every school day afternoon and most weekends, we met with John at one of the girl's houses, usually Rhonda's, to discuss the topic we'd been assigned for a year—Resolved that a Latin American Free Trade Association should be created; Resolved that there should be Total and Complete Disarmament. Simple subjects like that.

Seated on worn couches at one end of the wood-paneled finished basement, a senior girl would be partnered with a new recruit, teaching her the basics of how to analyze that year's policy topic while in another corner John would be listening to the varsity debaters, Sallie and Janet, deliver the first affirmative's canned speech. Over and over they'd rehearse until each could recite scripted lines of attack in a perfect pitch that made the whole thing sound convincing yet unstudied. Sometimes John corrected Sallie's posture or Janet's cadence or diction. But what he didn't do was lavish praise.

In that basement, with the comforting, yet oddly disconcerting aroma of garlic and onions wafting down from Rhonda's mother's kitchen in anticipation of Rhonda's father's arrival home from his job, I learned how to tear opponents apart, how to give and take withering criticism, how to cross-question the opposing team into contradicting themselves—in short, how to argue like a man. The juxtaposition of those predictably gendered routines being enacted in the kitchen above us with our subterranean transgressions of those same regimens convinced me to make The Society my normal.

But what added to the attraction for me was that John was also a believer in the saying, slightly modified, that all work and no play made Jane a dull girl. He planned trips to the Metropolitan Museum and the Museum of Modern Art, folk music concerts, Shakespeare in the park. On Sundays, if the weather was good, there were picnics at Rockaway beach near the home he shared with his mother and sisters. And every August, the whole team journeyed to Tanglewood in the Catskills to hear Seiji Ozawa conduct the Boston Symphony orchestra playing Tchaikovsky and Beethoven and Rimsky-Korsakov. And if you were like me and didn't know where Tanglewood was or had never heard a live symphony, well, all the more reason to stick with the team. John opened a world for me I didn't know existed, much less dreamed I'd ever have a chance to make mine.

Except for my school texts, there were no books in my home and, after my father left, not even a newspaper. I remember my grandparents subscribed to *The Readers' Digest* and used to get a bound volume of abridged books sent to them several times a year. These were stored on a wooden plank placed over the radiator in my grandparents' kitchen and there I read shortened versions of *Anne of the Green Gables, Jane Eyre,* and other assorted Victoriana. Or at least those were the titles I most clearly recall, stories about some forlorn lass finally meeting a Prince Charming, who releases her from the poverty of her future for the presumptively more gratifying turn at spending the rest of her life caring for him.

Given my background, it came as a shock to be treated as someone with a brain requiring continual stimulation and use. And if the stimulation of my brain became the way to my heart, it seemed a small price to pay.

That may be why, when I remember those afternoon team meetings, I see my younger self again willingly becoming an acolyte among a group of girls, each one dutifully completing whatever task she's been given, as if filling 3 x 5 index cards with documentation culled from magazines and books and placing these in topical and chronological order in large metal filing drawers to be lugged by the varsity team from tournament to tournament, up and down the eastern seaboard, or outlining arguments from thesis to conclusion in the far left column of one page of a large, spiral-bound pad of art paper, long side at the top, always folded into eight segments, one for each of the eight parts of a debate, as if any of these efforts would be enough to ensure election to the inner circle of those granted the fullness of John's attention and, ultimately, his approbation.

We all wanted his approval. But I think even then, while I combed records of previous debates for mistakes to be summarized, reviewed and avoided, practiced speeches prepared to John's exacting standards until they were polished and perfectly delivered, complete with the appropriate introductory hook, and otherwise fashioned myself to his liking, even then I knew the direction my apprenticeship would take me.

Organize, Analyze, Fraternize. That became The Society's mantra. What it meant wasn't as simple as it sounds. Organize meant "organizing evidence." In other words, stealing books from the Grand Army Plaza library, clearing the stacks of the most coveted sources to prevent other teams finding them. (We always returned them at the end of the debate year). Fraternize meant flirting with rivals, especially the boys of Regis High, acting like Mata Haris infiltrating enemy camp to discover information about their next planned attack. Analyze seemed more straightforward. It meant taking apart every argument and counterargument on any subject, learning how to build and tear down the whole world with the postulates of logic, never caring where the ethics of any premise might lead. After all, in an adversarial system, winning becomes its own justification.

And there was one more tactic, except I don't remember what we called it. In fact, I don't even remember participating in the process at all. But my friend, Karen, says she was dragooned into the role of its chief practitioner the year my debate partner and I made it to nationals.

We made up evidence.

First, we learned to abstract a quote out of context, cutting it off strategically, before the qualifying phrase. No big deal; everyone in debate did that. (Notice the rationale). Then we practiced more clever methods of mendacity, simply turning out declarative statements with authorial aplomb about the impact of free trade on the balance of payments or the likelihood of a nuclear attack and legitimating them with an appropriate citation drawn from some obscure, "organized" source. You could reason that if winning was what mattered most it was only logical to lie.

In retrospect, it seems a minor infraction. Except for the fact that lying violated the principles of our Catholic education. Maybe that was why, even at the time, I chose to ignore the deception. Or perhaps my youthful socialization at the movies aided my endeavor to reconcile opposites. More likely, my avoidance merely masked the inherently difficult practice of actually living with contradictions.

Logic gave me what I wanted. Logic let me float past the shoals of Catholic morality, far away from the place where my mother's binges and affairs had been catalogued among the sins of the damned by priests and nuns and self-righteous others who never admitted their own vulnerability. Eyes fixed on the stars, rudder steady, I steered toward the island of situation, where my mother's excesses could be seen as efforts to free herself from the conspiracy of forces designed to keep her in one place. And so, it turns out, could mine.

Logic let me lead a double life. In the one, I remained the dutiful Catholic daughter, daily at prayer, a dedicated academic achiever. I studied hard, never missed a debate meeting or Sunday mass. In the other, I fashioned myself into a bohemian artist, a famous modern dancer yearning for careless romance. I did my homework and confessed my sins and secretly admired my mother. Had anyone confronted me with the paradox at the core of my life, I could have argued both sides.

Then a teacher at the neighborhood ballet school where I'd studied for ten years arranged an interview for me at Performing Arts High School and I began a campaign to convince my mother to let me audition and transfer there in the fall. It was impulsive, motivated as much by a desire to see if I could get in as actually wanting to go there. I also wanted to test John's reaction when I told him I was quitting the team.

"You can't quit."

"What do you mean I can't quit?"

"You've made a commitment. To the Society."

"I've changed my mind."

"Haven't you learned anything about team spirit? The team comes before everything."

"But this is my chance at an artistic career; it's what I've always wanted."

"You're a debater, not a dancer."

"You've never seen me dance."

"I've seen you debate."

"John, I'm quitting."

"You'll be back."

A week before the audition, John called my home. Whatever he said to my mother couldn't have been as important as the mere fact that he phoned. That impressed her.

"He's charming," she said as I took the phone from her to say I hadn't changed my mind.

"Hey Bones," he said, calling me his pet name for me, "we've missed you. Have you been keeping up with your research? Have you practiced your speeches? There's still a spot on the team for you if you come to this Saturday's meeting."

"I'm busy. I can't make it."

"Too busy to go to the Cherry Blossom Tournament at Georgetown?"

"Cherry Blossom? I thought you said that was only for juniors and seniors?"

"Exceptions prove the rule, remember?"

"Am I an exception?"

"Come back to the team and we'll see."

Could it have been his solicitation that hooked me? He could certainly be persuasive. He still is. But that doesn't explain why I never went for the audition or why I gave up all my other friends and activities and returned to debate.

I suppose I could say I made the smarter move, took the more intellectual path. Even though I had dreamed of becoming a Rockette or dancing with Martha Graham, I knew I had a brain and wanted to use it. But the truth is more complicated than that. I colluded in the process and traded a good part of my youth for the chance at a bigger prize: to belong to something secret and forbidden with absolute, unwavering dedication. In retrospect, I'd say the audition was a cover.

It's my junior year, one night two years after I returned to the team. I am in John's car, an old blue Chevrolet station wagon with faux wooden panels. The inside is littered with index cards and soda cans and other useless bits of debate paraphernalia. I am sitting in the front seat, turned toward him, clutching my books, my back pressed hard against the door, head bowed. I am holding my breath. He has driven me home last, after the team meeting.

"Can you drive me home last?" I had asked. "I need to talk to you about something."

We are parked outside my house. The engine is running. It is late. "What's the matter?" he says after five minutes have passed in silence. Then he turns the engine off. I look at my darkened house and say, almost carelessly "My mother is out, or already in bed." I wonder if I should get out of the car.

"Go on, you can tell me."

I lean back against the seat and take another deep breath and look up at the tattered upholstery lining the roof of the car. I count five tears in the fabric.

"You know you can tell me anything."

That's what he always says. But can I really tell him this?

"Say it," he says.

"In The Society, we have no secrets," I say.

"No, I mean say what you want to say to me."

"I..."

"Tell me."

He stretches his arm across the back of the seat and touches my shoulder, rubbing gently. The gesture feels weirdly inviting. I cannot look at him, but I begin to speak.

"I...like you."

"I like you too."

"No, I mean, I like you."

"Kathy, look at me. I like you too."

And that's how it begins. With a few simple words and a look separating me once and for all from the others.

Maybe it would be easier for everyone if I painted myself as the innocent puppet, accusing him of having all the power, being the one completely and clearly in control. There are times when I still want to revert to this version of the story. It makes so much sense. After all, he was my teacher and I was his student. End of story. Except there's always more to a story like that.

That first night we were alone in his car we told each other the saddest versions of our sad, sad stories. He was sixteen when his father, a sickly, alcoholic lawyer, died, leaving behind a mountain of debt and three children for his widowed mother to support on her meager schoolteacher's salary. I told him about my family. I suppose we each knew well enough how to play the sympathy game.

Years later, when I thought about Hannah and Heidegger's affair, I remembered that night in John's car and understood what Hannah might have felt. That she took a chance, that she gave Heidegger a look, began to make more and more sense.

"There exists a teacher; perhaps one can learn to think..." That was how she described her first experience of Heidegger. I can imagine her, at eighteen, walking into that wood paneled seminar room in Marburg one autumn day in 1924 and seeing at the front of the room a handsome, pensive figure, a man in whom she felt aliveness itself become present in thought. To a passionate thinker, what could be more seductive than that?

She must have studied how his features cut a sharp and sullen profile whenever he turned his head toward the window, as he often did, searching for the right word, the exact phrase. Tilting his chin into his chest, the fingers of his left hand resting near his lips, he spoke hesitatingly until she heard his words swell into an elliptical poem she once said conjured Thought itself into Being and made the dead speak altogether differently about the past.

I see her listening to him, as if in a trance, until his voice trails off and the sudden rough scraping of chairs and shuffling of boots breaks the spell. She stands to leave the room. Outside someone whispers: Had anyone understood a word? Yes, she must think, she did, she did. But she says nothing, knowing already she will meet him, passion for passion.

That winter, in February, he writes her the first of a series of solicitous, yet seductive, letters. "Dear Miss Arendt...." It begins formally enough, yet the honeyed, caressing prose makes evident his desire to befriend her, his need to care for her more than he should. "I must come see you this evening and speak to your heart."[143]

The forbidden beckons. Maybe she responds with mixed emotions, wandering the streets, impetuously at first, imagining chance might intercede and bring him to her like a gift she could accept without seeming to want it too much. Later, in the quiet of the seminar, perhaps she watches him more closely. Could a look signal willingness? In his letter to her, twenty-five years later, he confesses to have felt her gaze "leap toward him on the lectern."[144]

A few days after the first letter, another arrives.

> *Dear Hannah.... Why is love rich beyond all other possible human experiences and a sweet burden to those seized in its grasp?...Love transforms gratitude into loyalty to our selves and unconditional faith in the other. That is how love steadily intensifies its innermost secret...The other's presence suddenly breaks into our life—no soul can come to terms with that.*[145]

And so, they begin.

Alone in her attic room in Marburg, her mind on fire with a magical intensity, an inner, captured purpose, Hannah watches winter snows melt into spring lilacs. Sometimes she receives a few close friends. When they visit she celebrates and laughs as if nothing unusual has happened. But, for most of that year, she draws the curtains of privacy around her and waits, living in shadows, until he summons her and she goes to meet him.

> *How wonderful that you are coming. My lectures are on the 20th and 21st in the State Library (Friedrichsplatz) at 8:15...After the lecture I will—as I now do every day—take leave of my acquaintances and hosts and get on the No. 1 tram to Wilhelmshöhe, the last stop—perhaps you can—discreetly—take the next tram. Then I'll take you home...Your Martin.*[146]

> *Do you want to come and see me this Sunday evening?...Come around 9 o'clock! If a lamp is lit in my room, though, I will have been detained by a meeting...*[147]

Available whenever he wanted her, she arrives at the appointed hour in the designated spot—sometimes a bench in the park, occasionally a hotel in Kassel or some other small German town. They talk. Yes, his philosophical monologues mesmerize her; his cultured tastes in literature and music join her own. But there is something else. She feels something opening in her. Though his longed-for recognition ravishes and frightens her, making her feel sometimes like a silly girl, she has to admit she also feels a kind of power; she feels powerful submitting to him. If he is more reserved, more bridled in their wordless intimacies than she wants him to be, she takes his aloofness to mean that she is both beholder and beholden and with that knowledge draws closer to him and drifts further away from her more watchful self.

He has done this before with others. Yes, she knows that. But she believes him when he tells her their relationship is different; that she is different. "You come straight from the center of your existence to be close to me, and you have become a force that will influence my life forever."[148] He has never known a mind like hers. Maybe he has found a mind like his own; maybe he has made her mind his own. When he is with her he isn't thinking. Yet, strange to say, he is able to think more clearly because of her, with her. "...I am coming to my work with a great deal of energy. You have a part in that."[149]

Perhaps he desires her for what she can give him, neither admitting how much he needs what she gives, nor understanding how strong she has become in the giving. But, slowly, he sees a change overcome her, and tells her the joy he takes in her strength.

> *We have an effect only insofar as we are capable of giving—whether the gift is accepted immediately, or at all, is a matter of little consequence. And we have only as much right to exist as we are able to care about. For we can give only what we ask of ourselves. And it is the depth with which I myself can seek my own Being that determines*

> *the nature of my Being toward others. And that love is—that is its gratifying legacy to existence, that it can be. And that is what the new peace spreading across your face is like, the reflection not of a free-floating bliss—but of the steadfastness and goodness in which you are wholly you.*[150]

She attends his lectures in the spring and summer of 1925 and they continue the affair, their connection deepened by secrecy. Martin tells her "I am with you wherever you go, and in your dreams. I am happy about how kind you are, how you are maturing, and how strong you are becoming."[151] At the end of the term he goes to his retreat in Todtnauberg and finds his way into work with greater energy. He writes Hannah that he has

> *stumbled on new things that are occupying me for the time being...I have already forgotten what the world looks like, and I will feel like a mountain man going down to the city for the first time...You must sense it in every line, beloved, that there is a storm brewing in me—I just have to see to it that I come to grips with it in the right way.*[152]

The storm brewing is more than he can manage, more than she can bear. His damned isolation, his forgetting the world and her in it! Does he think she will always be patient? She won't. She will make her own way. Then he'll know what longing feels like. She writes him about her decision—she is leaving Marburg, leaving him.

In 1926, Hannah Arendt left Marburg as much because of her own difficulty balancing secrets as because Martin Heidegger insisted she was better off continuing her studies elsewhere—an argument she found self-serving. Yet the affair continued another two years, even after her engagement to Gunther Stern.

It's easy to say the affair would have ended anyway. Aside from how he behaved toward her, his later membership in the Nazi party, his refusal to allow Jewish students to receive their degrees, his efforts to block the appointment of Jews to academic positions, his speeches supporting National Socialism—all these would have driven her away. When she confronted him about this, his defense was pitifully thin.

But what's harder to grasp is why the end of the affair broke neither her love for him nor her attachment to his passions. "Do not forget me," she wrote him on the day of her marriage to Stern in 1929, "and do not forget how much and how deeply I know that our love has become the blessing of my life. This knowledge cannot be shaken, not even today, when, as a way out of my restlessness, I have found a home and a sense of belonging with someone about whom you might understand it least of all."[153]

Yes, I can imagine how she fell in love with Heidegger. It was like falling in love with the forbidden. But the real question is: why did she forgive him? Only many years later would I understand Hannah had taken the path she'd once celebrated in her interpretation of Lessing's *Nathan the Wise*. Like Nathan, her continued relationship with Heidegger expressed her readiness to "sacrifice truth to friendship." "Lessing's greatness, " Hannah said, "does not merely consist in a theoretical insight that there cannot be a single truth within the human world but in his gladness that it does not exist and that...the unending discourse among men will never cease so long as there are men at all."[154]

When, in Hamburg in 1959, Hannah gave her acceptance speech for the award of the Lessing Prize she conducted a thought experiment with her German audience.

> *Suppose that a race could indeed be shown, by indubitable scientific evidence, to be inferior; would that justify its extinction? But the answer to this question is still too easy, because we can invoke the 'Thou shalt not kill'...But in terms of a way of thinking governed by neither legal nor moral nor religious strictures—and Lessing's thought was as untrammeled...as that—the question would have to be posed thus: Would any such*

> *[racist] doctrine, however convincingly proved, be worth the sacrifice of so much as a single friendship between two men?*[155]

A way of thinking governed by no strictures: in German, *Selbstdenken.* Thinking for oneself. Thinking with no banisters to guide you. This was her approach to political judgments. And it was how she found her way back to her friendship with Heidegger.

John and I invented a private language, scribbling secrets on slips of paper, which we passed each other under cover of Society business like so many purloined letters. In those *billets doux* we arranged when and how to find our way back to that same barren Brooklyn corner where we'd first confessed our attraction for each other.

It's been nearly fifty years since that Brooklyn moment and still I can find my way back in my mind's eye as if it were yesterday. And when I visit in my imagination I have Hannah to remind me there is no single truth to describe a moment or what it has meant over the years or might yet come to mean as age eases us closer to the impossibility of ever being able again to touch what it once was: a beginning, an unpredictable beginning with an uncertain end.

Every night, after the speeches were practiced and the evidence for the next tournament was organized, he drove everyone home. Since I lived closest to the route to his neighborhood, I was always the last one dropped off.

Around the corner from my house near a cluster of trees we'd park to talk and hold hands and kiss; nothing more than a little fondling at first. But I was my mother's child. Sex intrigued me. One night, alone in his car, we rode down Ocean Parkway toward Sheepshead Bay, then out along the Belt Parkway, slowing toward the last exit in Brooklyn. We parked at a viewpoint next to the highway, right before the road split toward the bridge, and walked towards the tall reeds rattling near the bay's edge. Small waves rustled the grass near the water, calming me into the slope of his shoulder and while he held me I watched the sky kiss the earth until everything felt connected, heaven to firmament.

"My mother isn't home tonight," I said. "It's cold here. Why don't we go to my house for a while?"

Sometimes we stayed at my house, sometimes his; sometimes we went to a hotel. For more than a year we kept our affair secret until something made us want to tell.

First we told one of my friends on the team whose mother's second-floor apartment we used for our meetings. After everyone left, she let us turn it into our private retreat. Then, we took one of the nuns at the school into our confidence. As if to legitimate our transgression, she blessed the affair. And, of course, we told my mother. "I knew it, I knew it," she said. "When is the wedding?"

In my junior year, after my debate partner, Terry and I beat the Regis High boys in the last round to win the Cherry Blossom tournament, a representative from George Washington University cornered us and offered us full scholarships on the spot if we would come to GW to debate for four years. I was flattered, of course. Instead, when I graduated, I stayed in New York to attend another school in the Bronx where I'd also gotten a scholarship. By this time, John and I were engaged and our wedding was planned for the following summer.

Terry and I rented a four-room apartment on Decatur Avenue. The day I left home my mother gave me a business envelope sized accordion-pleated cardboard file just like the one she used to "organize bills". On the face of it, embossed in gold letters, it read "Cancelled Checks."

I used to watch my mother sit on the side of her bed, balancing her budget each month by moving money from one section of the file to another. If she'd dwindled the funds for food by a few too many bets at the track or nights out with her girlfriends, she'd add money into "food" from the one marked "rent" and put a marker, a torn shred of paper from one of the stenographer's pads she'd pilfered from phone company supplies, with the words "I.O.U $10" scribbled on it to remind herself to replenish funds before the rent was due. And if "rent" got too low, it could always be topped up from "savings." I still have this file in my desk drawer and, for a long time, I used it for exactly the same purpose, until one day, long after I'd finished my doctorate, paying for my education with the insurance money mother left me when she died, I covered the old labels with new tags that read "immunization records", "used passports", "social security cards", "birth certificates", and "important papers" and into this last section placed the small funeral home prayer cards memorializing the dates of my parents' and grandparents' deaths.

In the first semester of college I took a required course on religion and the Jesuit priest who taught that class assigned us William Barrett's *Irrational Man.* On that book's first page I read the following: "The story is told (by Kierkegaard) of the absent-minded man so abstracted from his own life that he hardly knows he exists until, one fine day, he wakes up to find himself dead." I didn't want to wake up dead and so began to study philosophy and poetry and in between reading Kierkegaard and Rimbaud sandwiched a job collecting bad debts for an encyclopedia company on Lexington Avenue so I could pay my own bills. Three evenings a week I harassed consumers who had defaulted on payments.

The company trained its collectors to proceed cautiously from moral suasion—"You signed a contract; it's your obligation to pay"—to threatening legal action. I was supposed to record the effects of my conversations on an index card and tally the evening's achievements in dollars potentially recovered. But my heart wasn't in it. Nor did Bob or Jim, my colleagues in collection, have more attachment to the work. Instead, we ordered in pizza and discussed how Kierkegaard might handle the existential dilemma of being paid more than the minimum wage to persuade the poor to turn over whatever discretionary income they had for a set of books already obsolete by the time they arrived.

Bob was reading Marx at the time and he convinced us to stand on the side of the oppressed, reasoning that using a few unseemly maneuvers to cover our tracks, such as lying about how many calls we'd made, was the price paid for solidarity. Anyway, it seemed a whole lot less ethically troubling than actual harassment. It reminded me of making up evidence; you said what you had to say so the right side could win.

Most Wednesdays, after I finished work, John picked me up outside the Grolier building entrance on the east side of Lexington Avenue and headed his car south toward the entrance to the FDR Drive and then onto the Brooklyn Bridge toward the Belt Parkway into Brooklyn or continued over the Riis Park Bridge into Rockaway. This particular Wednesday we were having dinner with my mother.

Mom had baked a chicken, a safe enough option until she decided to stuff it. She had prepared the ingredients, but then forgot to put the mixture inside the chicken. When she discovered her error she simply threw the concoction into a baking dish and shoved it into the oven, which wouldn't have been such a bad idea, except she forgot that too. We all had a good laugh when Jim, Mom's second husband, brought the resultant brown brick to the table. Later that night in the car on the way home, John announced he would send me to cooking school after we are married.

"My mother means well."

"I know that; it's just that I expect my wife to entertain better than that."

"Entertain? The only people we hang out with are the debaters."

"Yes, well, we have other friends, like Brian."

"Brian lives with his mother."

"It doesn't matter, that's what I want you to do. Besides, let's not argue. I bought you something special."

He handed me a box and I opened it to find a pair of dove grey leather shoes, sensual pumps, the exact design and color of the ones I coveted but couldn't afford to buy. I slipped them on and looked down at my feet and suddenly felt nauseous.

"I can't take them."

"Aren't they the ones you wanted?"

"Yes, they're beautiful. I just can't take them. It doesn't feel right."

"But they're a gift."

"I don't want them. It's a mistake."

Some time later that fall I began taking dance classes again. I hadn't been in a studio since the end of my first year of high school. Moving my body through space makes me feel free, so free that one day while I am dancing I even forget I am engaged. By the time I meet Eddie in literature class, I believe I am not supposed to marry John after all.

Eddie was a short, stocky guy from upstate New York who played rugby, read a lot of literature and listened to the Beatles and jazz; the opposite of John in every imaginable way. One October night, I go to Eddie's apartment for a party. I get home to discover John has called me four times.

"He wanted to know where you were," Terry says when I come home after midnight. "I said you'd call him when you got back from the library."

"Where were you? You know I always call you at the same time on Thursdays," he says as soon as he answers the phone.

"I was at the library."

"This late on a Thursday?"

"I figured we could talk another night."

"I'm driving up there tomorrow. We'll go back to my place for the weekend." I don't want to go, not for the weekend or ever again. I want to be with Eddie and Kierkegaard. I want to figure out who I am.

"But I have to study."

"So do I; we'll study together." He was preparing for his doctoral exams.

We are on the FDR Drive passing under the UN when I tell John I don't want to get married.

"You can't be serious."

"I should finish college first."

"You'll finish college. But we're getting married in August. That's what we planned. And you'll transfer to Brooklyn College next fall. We can't afford tuition, even with your scholarship."

"I like where I am."

"You made a promise." He's shouting now, pounding his fist on the dashboard. "A commitment means you can't just change your mind." He pounds again, denting the dashboard. I slide away from him.

"Why are you hurting me, Kathy? Don't you love me?"

I'd seen John cry. He is a man who knows how to use emotion to win an argument. But this time is different. This time I can tell I have hurt him and in that moment, I feel the balance between us shift.

"Yes, I love you," I say, touching his shoulder. "You know I do."

I give up my apartment and move back to Brooklyn to prepare for the wedding. Every day I have classes I take a bus, two subways and another bus up to the Bronx campus to finish my freshman year. I avoid Eddie.

One July night, a month before the wedding, we are making out on my mother's couch. John seems distracted.

"Kathy we can't do this."

"What's the matter? My mother's not home."

"I mean the wedding."

How embarrassing, I think. He doesn't mean it; he's just scared.

"But we've already sent out the invitations," I say. "We have to get married."

"What if I'm drafted?"

Those were the Vietnam days before the draft lottery. Almost everyone I knew had found some excuse, whether borrowed or bought, to get out of the draft. Or moved to Canada. I knew Canada was out.

"You can get an exemption by getting married; you'll be the sole household support. Besides, you can argue conscientious objection."

And this is the pattern we fall into, arguing each other into a marriage, never acknowledging that what each of us hears behind the other's hesitation is fear, the deep-rooted kind that brings two vulnerable, lonely people together only to find ways to hurt one another again and drive them further apart.

Maybe that was why, after we married, John continued The Society. He seemed more devoted to it than ever. Or maybe the team just became more successful.

Almost every weekend, John and the debaters went on a trip. Upstate New York, Pennsylvania, Washington, D.C. At first, I went along too. Except I didn't really have a place with them any more. I had become "the wife." But no matter how hard I tried I cannot get comfortable in that cramped room called "our married life."

In my mind now the four years of our marriage appear like a series of still life pictures. Here is the furniture in our living room—a mustard colored Swedish modern sectional covered in some cheap, itchy fabric. Here I am cooking spaghetti for The Society meeting in our apartment. This one captures a lemon meringue pie in its mid-air slide to the floor because, when John held it up to display proudly the first time my mother comes for dinner, it hadn't yet gelled. In this one I am home alone, watching on the bedroom TV as Sirhan Sirhan assassinates Robert Kennedy in the kitchen of the Ambassador Hotel in Los Angeles; I am crying, not yet aware I am pregnant with my first son.

Here we all are—John, the debaters, and me—traveling to Tanglewood later that summer, stopping along the road because I am four months' pregnant and must take, according to John, a mandatory five minutes' walk every hour. And here, the summer after that, we are driving home on the Merritt Parkway listening to Neil Armstrong on the radio, announcing his landing on the moon—"One small step for man, one giant leap for mankind." I remember thinking that would make a good opening line for a speech.

And here is John's cousin, who to this day still lives with his parents, moving into our dining room, now converted into a spare bedroom, where he stays for three, or maybe even six, months. And in the next one I am writing a term paper in the car on the way to the hospital to deliver my son. Here is the pair of tiny moccasins John brings back for our son from a debate trip to New Mexico. And here is Jed crawling across the carpet toward his toys. And in this one John and I are arguing, so loud we don't hear Jed fall into the bathtub we'd left filling with water even though we'd moved our hostilities into the living room. We hear him when he stands up and screams, thanks to the fact that he's still wearing his sneakers.

There I am in a sexy outfit, waiting in the hallway to surprise John coming back from a meeting. In the next one I hide my birth control pills in the nightstand near my side of the bed. When John finds them he calls me a liar and slut.

Here is Jed with me at rehearsals for my senior year dance concert.

Here we are the year before we separate, moving into another, larger apartment on the sixth floor of the same Nostrand Avenue building where we lived the four years of our marriage. I change my major from biology to modern dance and then to politics. I have an affair, which John discovers by reading my letters.

In this last scene, my mother faints in our living room. A month later she is dead.

For the art class I take to fulfill one of my last college requirements, I draw the outline of a woman's skull on a large piece of white cardboard. Into her head I paste an alphabetized set of 3 x 5 index cards and out of a collage of newspaper fashion two breasts. The rest of her doesn't exist.

I bury my mother. John misses her funeral. He has an important meeting, a debate tournament. Of course. I understand. The Society.

I throw dirt on her coffin and leave.

With the money my mother bequests I open a bank account and use the funds to rent an apartment of my own a few weeks before John agrees to move out.

Except I forget: no one ever leaves The Society. The only way out is to be expelled.

A few years after we separated John had our marriage annulled by the Catholic Church. Through some arcane canonical loophole he managed a papal order voiding a marriage that had lasted four years and created a child. He wanted to marry again and since divorce isn't acceptable to the Church you could say that his Catholic conscience required a papal dispensation. Other reasons unfolded in time.

The annulment, the custody trial, Jed's moving back years later to his father's house, those were all the parts of the puzzle of my life I tried to fit together. But the one part missing, the part I couldn't, no, wouldn't see, was the part I had played, and continued to play, by keeping the whole tale spinning my heart like a top. Finally, thinking with Hannah brought that part into focus and changed how I judged my life's events.

Thinking is like diving for pearls, bringing to the surface jewels of memory so the heart can go visiting again. And though pain isn't undone by understanding, lingering in loss no longer hampers the heart's journey toward peace.

"Basically I am happy, simply about the confirmation; the fact that I was right never to forget," Hannah wrote to a friend after visiting Heidegger for the first time in years. She wasn't oblivious to his chicanery; but nor was she forgetful or ungrateful for the force he'd been in her life. And neither am I oblivious nor forgetful or ungrateful for the force John was in mine.

When we separated, John told me I'd come back. I didn't. Instead, I went in search of another Heidegger.

{ 9 }

Who Forgives the Forgiver? My Heideggers II

Without being forgiven, released from the consequences of what we have done, our capacity to act would...be confined to one single deed from which we could never recover; we would remain the victims of its consequences forever...

Hannah Arendt, *The Human Condition*

WHEN I MET HIM THAT NIGHT IN 1971 HE WAS SITTING AT A WOBBLY WOODEN TABLE IN A CORNER OF SOME FRIENDS'

WASHINGTON PLACE APARTMENT IN GREENWICH VILLAGE. Talking, slurping soup in between sentences, he appeared not to register the fact I'd entered the room.

"This is Kathy," my friend Dina says. "Mike," he replies, and returns to some point he'd been making about passion in Peckinpah's *oeuvre*, glancing up at me long enough to tell me later, in bed, how he'd thought I was beautiful, like a frail bird, a fragile creature, too easily crushed. I'm not sure I wanted to be thought beautiful in this way. But the way he said it made it seem like what I should desire. Years later, when I read in Arendt's letters how strangeness and tenderness intertwined early in her life, this memory returns, drawing me back into its orbit and beckoning me to give an account of myself in this part of the story.

I sit down next to Mike at the table and try not to stare. He has penetrating hazel eyes and curly black hair and a smile that, when it finally appears, belies all the hurt he feels and will later cause. As he speaks he breaks off crusts of bread, piling the soft centers into a nervous mound. Over the years I get into the habit of eating the discarded crumbs.

Words fly out of his mouth like nails from an electric gun hammering ideas into conversation. It doesn't bother me. I am used to speech being a tool for mortal combat. But what's odd is how, every so often, he stops, transfixed in thought, and rubs a finger across the hollow of his cheek, as if that gesture is the only thing preventing him from disappearing into some other reality.

Why don't I run at the sight of him? I know why: He loves philosophy and politics, poetry and literature and these have become the four corners of the foundation of my new life as an intellectual. I can hardly believe how lucky I am to have met a man as fascinated with the life of the mind as he seems to be. And although I can already tell he is battling some demons, he seems willing and determined to best them; his strangeness awakens my tenderness.

The night we first met we become so immersed in conversation that we walk all the way from the West Village in Manhattan across the Brooklyn Bridge to the apartment I sublet for the summer in Brooklyn Heights. It was a tiny studio, just big enough for Jed and me. That particular night, Jed is visiting his father.

In the long hours it takes to meander to Brooklyn we cover major topics in modern philosophy along with several chapters from the novels of our respective failed marriages.

Mike's story is decidedly more dramatic than mine: his wife attempted suicide. If this should have been a clue, I miss it, mesmerized as I am by the loving way he still talks about his ex-wife and the devotion and passion with which he describes his efforts during all the months of her hospitalization to make sure she wasn't subjected to electroshock therapy. And when he describes how the lithium they'd given her to control depression had ballooned his wife to twice her normal size and then pulls a picture out of his wallet to show me how beautiful, simply beautiful she is and always will be, and that he will never get over how, after her hospitalization ended and her health returned to more or less normal, she'd left him, after all he'd done to bring her back to this side of crazy, she'd left him, I feel a pang in my heart and realize, embarrassingly, I am jealous; I am jealous and equally determined not to let this chimera get the better of me. But when we make love that first night and Mike holds my face in his hands I can't tell whether he sees her or me.

A month later, Mike moves from the room he had rented in the Chelsea Hotel after his divorce into an apartment I find for him in an elevator building on Charlton Street around the corner from the Sixth Avenue walkup I moved into a few weeks earlier. I have already fallen into a pattern of taking care of mundane things he can't seem to manage. I don't mind, I say. It's easy for me. What I don't realize is I am playing the sympathy game.

My new apartment is a small three room flat, considered "renovated" because of its chic exposed brick wall and despite its less fashionable tub in the kitchen, an adjacent sink that doubles as a wash basin and a bathroom that is literally a water closet. I pay the previous tenant a scandalously high and illegal fee called "key money," a common practice in the 1970s Manhattan rental economy. Spending the equivalent of three months' rent to claim it makes the apartment all the more precious to me. That and its location in Manhattan. I feel very sophisticated living in the city.

In the living room I set up a day bed and give Jed the small bedroom and under its loft bed he arranges his collection of vehicles and other assorted toys while I set up the easel and paints my father gave him for Christmas. Within a few weeks we make our first trip to St. Vincent's hospital to stitch up Jed's chin when he slips from the bed's ladder chasing our cat.

That fall Mike and I spend nearly every evening with Fred and Bonnie, the friends who now introduced us and who have moved from Washington Place to a larger apartment in the building next to mine on Sixth Avenue. They have renovated the apartment themselves, exposing the brick walls, refinishing the wood floors, and removing the tub from the kitchen to a bathroom created by dividing one of the long, narrow bedrooms in half. Because there are only a few shelves and no real closets, Bonnie hangs their winter clothes from a metal bar suspended in the front hallway and when I enter the apartment the first time and every time after I have to push aside several down parkas and longer wool coats to get past the front door. Along the wall on the left I notice several paintings, including a lithograph of Marilyn Monroe that looks vaguely familiar.

"Those belong to Stella," Freddie says, matter-of-factly. From his seat in the living room he can see me staring at the art. Freddie's sandy kinky hair and strong chin and especially his swagger as he leans his chair back almost to the point of tipping over remind me of James Caan.

"That's a Warhol. Andy gave it to Stella but we're keeping it here because she hasn't got any more room in her studio."

Stella is Freddie's mother, an artist who lives at the Chelsea Hotel. Everyone, including Freddie, calls her Stella. Jed learns to call her Stella, too, after the summer we vacation with Bonnie and Freddie on Martha's Vineyard when Jed works with her as her "little apprentice" in the garage on Bonnie's family property; he is charmed by Stella and her mysterious cast resin books, beautiful, impenetrable, sculptured pieces that, when I look at them now, seem to embody an unearthly sense of loss.

With his feet propped on the coffee table and one arm characteristically thrown behind him over the back of a wooden chair, Freddie is explaining to Mike how he and his brother Billy were fishing with their father in the Bahamas when they caught the gigantic marlin now hanging on the living room wall, the billed head of which has been cast in plaster and painted to a vague resemblance of what it must have looked like alive. Next to it are other paintings of Stella's and fishing photos Bonnie has taken and two small shelves holding the latest novels Freddie is reading, none of which are familiar to me.

Freddie is a writer. Every day he leaves their cluttered apartment around noon and walks to a little studio he rents near Union Square and above the maze of cheap department stores on Fourteenth Street tries to reinvent the short story. Bonnie works for a retail store as freelance writer and editor-in-chief of an in-house publication. She has long silken black hair she parts in the middle and wears gold wire rim glasses that seem to heighten the sophistication in her aristocratic Philadelphia mainline society cadence, whether she is talking about baiting line and trolling for billfish or the finer points of Freudian psychology, which she studies in her spare time. Right now the subject is tarragon chicken with carrots and biscuits, which Bonnie is cooking while Freddie grabs a beer and returns to the living room to continue his conversation about the pleasures of deep-sea fishing, sprinkling his comments with clever allusions to Hemingway.

"Why don't you and Kath come with us to Bimini this summer? You can rent the house next to ours by the water. We'll catch billfish and drink Paulie Girl beer. C'mon, think about it, man. You need one of these on your wall," he says, gesturing to the marlin.

"What about the kid?" says Mike, meaning Jed, who is playing with his trucks and cars in the living room corner but glances up when he hears he has become the subject of conversation. This particular night none of the single mothers in my building with whom I have created an informal child care pool has arranged a sleepover for the kids, so Jed has come to dinner with us. He's quieter than usual since he's just returned from visiting his father.

"Kath can figure that out." Freddie adds, annointing me the fixer.

"Maybe my father will take him for a week," I say. "I know Dad wants him to visit this summer."

"I want to see Grandpa. I want to see Grandpa...."

"No one asked you," Mike snaps. "And how the hell am I going to pay for this trip?" he says to Freddie.

"Get the old man to cover it," Freddie, says, laughing, meaning Mike's father. Freddie has a similar arrangement with his own father but on different terms. "Write out one of those checks."

Since Mike divorced, his parents have helped support him so he can finish his graduate degree. Freddie's father, a successful businessman, helps supplement Bonnie's income through a fund generous enough to allow Freddie not to have a regular job so he can continue writing and take fishing trips to the Bahamas every summer. And because rents in this part of the Village have not yet skyrocketed and are affordable enough if you manage to locate and hold onto a rent-controlled unit, they can live a comfortable enough yet bohemian lifestyle. How similar, yet different, Freddie's and Mike's ties are to their businessmen fathers. Over the years the differences will separate them and, combined with conflicted relationships to their own mothers, will shape how they each parent.

I go back into the kitchen to help Bonnie with dinner and Jed follows me.

"I'm hungry, Mommy."

"We can feed him first," Bonnie says in the instinctually caring way I come to recognize as her signal grace. We sit down at the table with Jed while he eats and when he's finished we take plates and a big pot of chicken stew into the living room, where Freddie and Mike are now revisiting poetry classes they took with John Crowe Ransom at Kenyon College in the first years they met. Over dinner, the conversation careens from symbolist poetry to modern philosophy until, somewhere in the middle of a discussion of Husserl, Jed falls asleep on the couch and I move him into the quiet of Bonnie and Freddie's bedroom.

After arguing for several hours about Hemingway and the future of the short story, about Sigmund Freud and Herbert Marcuse and Norman O. Brown, some of whom I have not yet read, we get hungry again and go for a walk down St. Marks Place toward Ratner's delicatessen on Second Avenue in the east village, where we eat potato latkes and kasha varnishkas and watch the transvestites coming in for coffee. Jed sleeps through everything including the walk.

When the night ends I bundle Jed up and go home to my apartment where I put him back to bed and try to sleep myself the several hours remaining before dawn. I get up early the next morning and take Jed with me on the subway to Brooklyn, where I teach a course on modern political theory at Brooklyn College and Jed attends the newly refurbished child care center that an organization of parents, of which I am now a co-director, helped create.

This, with few variations, becomes the routine of our lives. At the time, none of it seemed strange to me. I wanted to belong to this group of intellectuals who seem to know everything about modern literature and the vagaries of psychoanalysis and who gobble up every one of Paulene Kael's film essays in *The New Yorker*—

"You're kidding, you haven't read that? (seen that? been there?)." I want so desperately to belong that I lied.

I lied about movies I hated or didn't understand. I wouldn't admit to not having read Thomas Mann's *Magic Mountain*. I pretended to enjoy Freddie making someone into a character in his next story and as if it didn't really matter that Mike yelled at me to shut up when he's talking. I even used the excuse everyone else did for Mike's irascible rudeness: it was because of his flawed but remarkable "genius."

"He's like all incredibly bright people," Bonnie says one night. "He's moody. You just have to ignore it." (I had not yet learned that joining a group means taking responsibility for things done in its name.) Since I am not moody I wonder what this might mean about my own intellect. And when they all talk about Dr. Max, the shrink the three of them visit, I feel especially out of it, as if I must not have plumbed deeper than an inch into understanding my own *id*. Because I do not see a psychoanalyst at least once a week I presume there must be something very limited about my awareness of the hold my unconscious has on me. My need to belong begins to overwhelm me.

At first, I act as if I am not humiliated by bracketing my ego to make more room for Mike's. Later, I play up this humiliation for sympathy. Even though Bonnie has a high opinion of Mike I can count on her to come to my rescue if Mike steps over the line. She raises her hand and points a finger at him and says quietly, "Look, if you don't stop acting that way, I'm going to kick you out." Mike laughs. Yet the funny thing is, he listens. "O.K. Bonnie," he says, "O.K." And shuts up.

But the worst lie I tell is the one I tell myself by pretending not to think I should leave as soon as it seems Mike prefers when Jed isn't around. Because I don't know how else to explain why he becomes so impatient with the ordinary behavior of an active two-and a half-year old boy. All I know is Mike is uncomfortable with parenthood and it must be his lack of experience. But, of course, at twenty-two, my experience has been limited too.

Maybe that's why it seems innocent enough when Mike says we need time to ground our relationship, even if it means taking a night off from Jed. I arrange for graduate school friends of mine to baby-sit so Mike and I can have some time alone, convincing myself that all we need is a stronger foundation to become a real family. But other things seem to bother Mike too.

"Why do you have to hold his hand," he says one day as we're walking down the New York streets. "Can't he walk by himself?" And after Jed comes back from a visit with his father, talking about his Daddy, Mike says "Can't he call you Kathy? We should be

Mike and Kathy, not Mike and Mommy. And he should call his father John; how else will he ever see me as an equal?"

All this sounds bizarre yet behind it I sense a distorted yet well-intentioned effort to parent. But what I won't understand until years later is how Mike sees himself in my child. He sees himself, not my child, and he is afraid of what he sees and trying to ignore it. It's as if my expressed love for my son has brought to the surface memories of Mike's childhood disappointments, of his mother's less solicitous mothering, resurrecting primordial fears of abandonment.

And a thought tries to surface. I push it away. It terrifies me even now to remember. Could it be Mike really wants Jed to go away? How can I fix this? Because, I think if I don't fix it I'll lose everything.

Thinking back to those years I recall Hannah describing Isak Dinesen's efforts to live her life like a story "by creating a fiction and then trying to live up to it." Had I been tempted by the same kind of fantasy? Was I trying to make some story come true? But what story had I been enthralled to? I become determined to puzzle it out.

One fall night I wake up, doubled-over in pain. I can't call Mike because he doesn't have a phone. So I call Fred and in a few minutes he's knocking on my door.

"I think we'd better get you to a hospital" he says when he sees me holding my stomach.

"What about Jed?"

"Don't worry. Bonnie and I will take care of him."

I take a cab to St. Vincent's for the second time in three months. In the emergency room, three doctors examine me but cannot make up their minds about what's causing my torment. They decide on exploratory surgery.

"Please sign this consent form."

"I thought I had appendicitis."

"Probably, but in case we don't find that, we want to look further. Sign here."

After the surgery removing my appendix—and, thankfully, nothing more—I call Jed to tell him I have to stay in the hospital for a while.

"I'm mad at you Mommy."

"I'm sorry, Jed. I'll be alright in a few days."

"I'm still mad. Don't do that again."

The oddest thing is, for the week I am in the hospital, Mike becomes the perfect parent, unusually affectionate and patient, as if the fact of my surgery awakened his capacity for love, as if my absence made him feel more needed by Jed and being needed made him begin to see Jed instead of seeing himself as a child. When my scars heal, things return to what passes for normal.

One day I notice a study program in England announced at my graduate school and when I approach the department chair about taking my last courses as independent studies, he agrees. I imagine Mike and I will set up house far away from everything familiar and that the displacement will allow us to start over. I imagine I will finish my studies there; so will he. And once we are settled into a routine—I'll need only a month to arrange everything—I imagine Jed will join us and in this different place, everything will change. I imagine these things so easily I don't think anything odd about what I am proposing or how quickly John agrees to the plans.

"Take your time, don't worry," he says. "Jed can stay with my aunt and uncle on Long Island; he'll be surrounded by cousins. Go ahead, go."

I pack Jed's clothes and some of his toys in two boxes and ship them to London, along with my books and clothes and some of Mike's things. I leave New York two weeks before Mike and stay with a friend who lives near Clapham Common until I find a place to rent twelve miles from Cambridge.

When Mike arrives we take the train from London to St. Neots and are met at the station by a very aristocratic British couple who drive us three miles to Croxton, where we turn off the main road and into a circular drive that leads to The Downs, a pretentious name for a mansion into which ten New York apartments could fit. And I imagine friends visiting, each staying in a wing of the house, while along the slick wooden floors lining the halls Jed will slide his trucks and his cars and everything will be normal, or as normal as it can be, again.

But that year nothing happens like I imagine. When the time comes for my friends to bring Jed to Europe, they can't make the trip. And although I offer to come back and get Jed myself, John demurs. "He's better off staying with my aunt in the country. Finish your studies; Jed will be fine."

What I did then surprises me, even now, many decades after the fact. If I heard any threat in John's words, I ignored it. I heard what I wanted to hear. I heard someone say take it. And it wasn't just anyone; it was John, that inimitable coach, who'd told me before to take what I needed and was telling me again not to worry; I could do it, I could succeed.

I took time. Seven months without Jed. You could say I shouldn't have, that leaving my little son behind in New York wasn't a very motherly thing to do. I could say you're being judgmental or sexist. But I'd only be hiding the fact that I have thought the same thing. It wasn't a very motherly thing to do. I did it anyway. And were the clock rolled back, I can't say for certain I wouldn't do it again.

Mine was the generation of 70s feminists who tried to combine mothering with professional or work lives, begging the question of what would have to change to make such a balancing act possible or even desirable. We had different answers to that question, political programs for the future, but those did little to ameliorate what Susan Sontag once called the "immediate plight of women."

When Jed was born in 1969, I felt both totally unprepared and unequivocally eager to be a mother. As an only child reared by a mostly single "working mom," herself an only child, I'd never plumbed the mysteries of childcare; never had responsibilities for siblings. Although, like Hannah, I'd gained two stepsisters (through my father's second marriage; Arendt's mother had remarried), my sisters and I never shared a household except for a weekend here and there.

For the first six months after Jed was born I took a leave from college and became a fulltime mother and homemaker. In our Brooklyn apartment building populated with assorted lower middle class families, mostly white, husbands worked, wives scoured and cleaned, cuddled and clothed children. And shopped. Pushing caravans of baby filled strollers, the brigade of Moms ambled up and down a long avenue, stopping at the A&P, congregating in the small concrete patches of playgrounds to share stories of Johnny's first words, or Janie's first steps, or to trade news about discounts on baby clothes, or the wisdom of using the recently introduced novelty of Pampers instead of a diaper service.

I was an oddball mother. With my books and papers in a backpack, and friends from college visiting me with news of the latest demonstrations and modern dance concerts, I didn't fit.

"Why do you want to bother with all that college stuff? Who'll take care of Jed if you go back to school? It isn't right." This was pressure from the band of mothers conspiring to keep one of the pack from bolting.

But I was an oddball student too. Most of my friends weren't serious about relationships. They were serious about art or politics. I was the only one among them who had to balance care of an infant with dance rehearsals that ended at midnight, or political meetings overlapping the dinner hour.

In those days, there was no university childcare. And I was still married to John, who then lacked the inclination to help at home. So, I hired an infant care specialist to stay with Jed while I went to class and stayed up late at night writing manifestoes about the importance of cultural revolution.

I crammed the remaining year of college courses into a single semester, completed my senior choreography project and honors thesis in political science, while taking Jed with me to political meetings and rehearsals—I had decided to continue in dance but major in political science—and graduated in August 1970. That was the year of Kent State and Jackson State, of secret bombing campaigns in Cambodia. And it was the year my mother died. It was also the year I associate with beginning to realize, to paraphrase Hannah, how belonging to a group—"women," "mothers"—had become my own problem, and my own problem was political.

These were among the constellation of forces that crystallized into the context of my decision to stay in Europe for a while longer without Jed. The decision was mine; influenced by Mike, but the responsibility still mine.

Fall 1972 Mike and I spend in England. I am twenty-three. Weekdays I study in the Cambridge library, writing papers on civil disobedience and the rule of law. Evenings, Mike joins me in town for tea and scones at a quaint little shop now displaced by a Starbucks. A little later we make our way to an Indian restaurant we like on the bus line that takes us home a couple of hours later to our empty mansion where we play scrabble in the library or on the small black and white television in the sitting room watch the BBC news reporting on Nixon's Vietnam strategy. For the most part, we seem to be happy.

We make friends with the neighbors—two Aussies from Sydney, Bruce, an artist, and his wife, Libby, and their kids, Samantha and Simon. Bruce hates Americans, he tells us later over a couple of home-brewed beers. He hates Americans for the same reason he hates his own country: Vietnam. He has assumed, from the size of the place we'd rented, we must be the usual ignorant, arrogant and rich American snobs. But Libby tells him we aren't either rich or snobs. She had already ventured across the narrow road that divides our side of Croxton from theirs with a basket of fresh eggs and verified we are approachable. As for our intelligence, she points out to Bruce we are lefties who negotiated with the ruling class owners to rent the house for the same price as our apartment in New York. (Which is true; the owners decide we are the responsible sort; they care less about money than having the house looked after well).

Bruce has converted the tiny shed next to their house into an artist's studio and spends his days etching scenes of Croxton and the surrounding Cambridgeshire countryside and his evenings playing with his children and brewing ginger beer. Libby takes care of the children, which, since they are not yet in school, is a full-time job. She cooks and cans and sews their clothes and tends to the "chooks" along with managing a vegetable and flower garden. Their life is nothing like ours. I know I can't live their kind of life but I am jealous of its harmony. I begin to link together scenes from their life into a complicated fiction I must imagine mine can become.

At least once a week we have dinner with Bruce and Libby enjoying long laughter-filled evenings in conversations about art and politics. Even though the topics are like those we discuss in New York, something is different. These are friends who meet Mike and me as a couple. And they have kids.

Mike opens up and relaxes in ways I haven't seen before. In between moments of darkness that come over him unexpectedly, he becomes happier, even playful. One night, he tells me how much he misses Jed and wants to become a better parent.

So this must be the story I was trying to live: *and they all lived happily every after.* Hearing Mike want the same thing helped convince me I can make it come true.

Every week I send a small package to Jed filled with gifts from places we've visited—the London Tower, the British Museum, Big Ben. And friends in New York send weekly letters I'd written before leaving and asked them to mail to Jed in case the ones I send from Europe get lost.

I call Jed twice a month and he sounds happy and tells me all about his own vegetable garden and the games he's learned from his cousins and how he wants to get a new bike, a red one, when he gets home. John's aunt writes letters to me saying everything is fine and includes a photograph of Jed in bright green corduroy overalls and a white tee shirt and I smile when I see his blond hair.

"His hair was getting too long, so we decided to cut it," her letter continues. "We had this photograph taken before we took him to the barber." On the back of the photograph she has taped another, smaller envelope and inside it I am unsettled by the sight of several locks of Jed's hair. Years later, I find this photograph in a box of Jed's things along with some of my letters and put these in an album to save for when he leaves for college, thinking that's the next time we will be separated again.

Some weekends my friend Eric rides up from London and stays in one of The Downs' nine grand bedrooms with en suite bath, surprising the cleaning lady with his naked bag piping around the halls in the east wing. On Sundays, before leaving for London, Eric entertains the neighbors' kids, marching and playing on the great lawns and gardens of the property.

One Sunday evening, just before the fog rolls in, Mr. Harper, the gardener, has pruned the late blooming roses and left a red bunch in a vase in the small conservatory I use for my study. From the window I watch Eric prancing around the lush gardens with two small children trailing behind him and for a moment I think I see Jed in line with them until the rising mist conspires with the mournful bagpipes to push the image away.

It is damp and the winter comes colder and wetter than any we've experienced in New York. Mike's asthma worsens and we take two emergency trips to the hospital in one week. When he doesn't improve after two more trips, we leave England and The Downs and drive across France for a month, making our way to warmer Spain, settling in Almunecar, then a small fishing village on the Costa del Sol.

For two months every morning at dawn I watch men repair nets on the sandy Mediterranean beach below our deck before setting sail into the sea, dotting the horizon with their tiny wooden boats that remind me of the toy craft my father built for Jed and sailed with him on Silver Lake in Staten Island the summer before. That boat and a dozen other treasures I have packed in a box and stored in the trunk of the car, since Jed isn't coming.

By late morning the stalls in the market where I shop fill with the day's catch, mackerel and silvery anchovies, which women in black dresses scoop into newspaper cones. Along with a big bag of oranges I carry them home for our lunch and in a tiny kitchen fry fish and onions and prepare a fruit salad that Mike and I eat at a table angled toward the window in such a way that it feels like we are floating at sea.

And for those months, and many years after, that's how I felt. Adrift, at an angle, without anchor or map, compass or course.

In the face of our future's uncertainty, I must have been grabbing for something—the seduction of that "happily ever after." Why? Perhaps to avoid having to think for myself, or learn to identify what really mattered, without relying on ideology or dogma, whether about love or politics. Perhaps even to sidestep taking responsibility for acts "about which I know that I could as well have left...undone."[156]

The tricks of memory are the same as the tricks of a well-crafted story: they can convince you what happened could not have happened otherwise. But I am writing in defense of contingency.

Mike and I befriended a Spanish family who lived in a three-room whitewashed house near the edge of the town. The parents and their little raven-haired boy share one bedroom while the grandparents occupy the other. And in between these two tiny rooms they welcome us into their red-tiled dining room every Sunday for family gatherings filled with paella and beer, which we consume around two small round tables covered with muslin cloth draped over our legs so as to heighten the warmth emanating from a tiny coal stove set at our feet. In our broken Spanish, we share stories and talk about their visiting America one day. They invite us to family events and Mike takes photographs he plans to use to create an illustrated book of stories about our travels to share with Jed when we go back to the states.

One evening I bring the box of Jed's things into the house and tell the little boy, whose name I've long forgotten, to pick what he wants. His eyes light up at the Evil Knieval action figure with windup motorcycle, one of Jed's favorites.

"*Tu quiere?*"

"*Si,*" he nods. "*Por favor.*"

Even now, whenever Jed retells this story, I first recoil at the memory.

"She gave away my Evil Knieval," he says. "My favorite toy and she gave it away." He pretends it's a joke; he's laughing. But behind the laughter I sometimes have heard a little boy's fear.

I realize why I remember this story—because only recollection and what Hannah once called "reconciliation with things as they really are" can release us from reliving a single scene in our life forever and ever. Or, as she once wrote, "If I refuse to remember, I am actually ready to do anything—just as my courage would be absolutely reckless if pain...were an experience immediately forgotten."[157]

By April, Mike and I return to London. Shortly after we arrive, a friend telephones from the states with a message about something John needs me to sign. Her voice surprises me, as much because it is she, an old high school friend, who delivers the message as about what it contains.

"Church annulment? How is that possible? We have a child."

"I guess there's some special dispensation," she replies.

Weeks later I receive a letter from Jed's aunt. "I thought you were studying in Europe. I didn't know you were cavorting around with your paramour. How could you leave this dear sweet boy?" Her bluntness jolts me.

"Something's wrong," I tell Mike. "I have to go back to New York. Right away."

We leave for the states two days later.

I borrow a car and drive out to Long Island. No one knows I'm coming and when I get there no one is home. Am I too late? Has John already come to take Jed away?

Then another car turns into the gravel driveway and around to the back of the house where I have parked. I see Jed jump out of the car, laughing and when I call his name, he looks up and then, beaming with joy, runs toward me.

But what happens next I will never forget. With uncanny volition he stops mid-run with a suddenness that slams my heart like a fist. Shoulders pulled back, left hand on his hip, he utters three words of a question that rivals the one asked by the Sphinx.

"Who are you?"

I say nothing. I can't open my mouth. He stands still a few seconds longer until the world shifts again.

"You're Mommy. Mommy," he says, re-anointing me, and leaps into my open arms, laughing.

For a month we hole up in Brooklyn before I tell John our new address. It was a mean thing to do. But I needed some iota of control. Mike and I have rented an apartment near Grand Army Plaza across from the Brooklyn Museum and I enroll Jed in kindergarten at an experimental school a few blocks away. Three days a week I teach political theory at Brooklyn College and write my dissertation while Mike works at home on his psychology masters' degree. With our two bedrooms and two baths, our pet Guinea Pigs and our Volvo, we create a desirable profile. Almost normal.

I don't remember who started the chain of infidelities. Mike says I began it with the French mathematician who lived in the penthouse apartment in our building. I remind him about Irene in New York, my ex-friend, preceding the Frenchman by months. What these particular transgressions mean neither of us tries very hard to figure out. And if it should have been a sign we were ill-suited, we don't take it to heart, having gotten comfortable using each other so some unexamined dreams we each wish for might come true, while still operating under the illusion each of us is merely helping the other. If we abandoned this illusion, we would have to find a more wide-awake way to love.

A wide-awake way to love. Had Hannah discovered that many years after her love affair with Heidegger ended? Although barely able to accept her own stature as an accomplished intellectual, Heidegger had been using Hannah and her various literary connections to bring his works into English translation. Hannah agreed to help him while still acknowledging, though not to Heidegger directly, what a sly fox she thought Heidegger was.

Others have taken Hannah's willingness to do favors for Heidegger as an indication of how much Hannah remained under his spell. But could she have had other reasons for supporting him besides the obvious fact she thought his theories important?

I think Hannah chose to remember the Heidegger with all his foibles and ploys, including his insistent need for adulation and even his misguided Romantic notions about Germany's future under Hitler, and decided to accept this mischievous Heidegger into her life, along with the other Heidegger who had once made thinking come alive in that Marburg seminar room. Why?

It provided another kind of *cura posterior*, a way to reconcile herself to her own role in this dangerous yet ultimately self-enlightening episode in her life story. Even if this episode didn't cast her in a flattering light, it wasn't a chapter she wanted to disavow or even to hate. And that was how I began to feel about my own Heideggers.

The summer we returned from Europe Mike collected enough symptoms and the occasional real disease to keep us all on our toes. He and Fred compare palpitations and assorted odd lumps and glandular protrusions and sooner or later one of them concludes death is imminent. Many times we laugh at the litany of illnesses Mike "acquires" in a single year, each one more implausible than the last. Mike even makes himself the butt of a joke. But sometimes he gets lost in an obscure malady the details of which he's located in the copy of the *Merck Manual* he keeps by the bedside. I hide it, hoping the absence of the fetish will preclude magical thinking.

The season's heat matches in intensity the darkness of Mike's moods. Almost nightly, he searches an encyclopedia of symptoms and by morning, the disease is his. It could be any man's. *Crisis Masculinus*, early onset, advanced to stage four; poor prognosis. Then, when the weight of it becomes too heavy, he tumbles it into the middle of our lives. I take it. In fact, I almost welcomed the burden. But that makes me no saint.

Mike gets angry with Jed; he complains about money, about John. "Why does he get all the glory of fatherhood and none of the routine?" Not that there is nothing to complain about; John isn't blameless.

And then, sometime early in September, something snaps. Every squeak of a toy or sneeze from Jed's bedroom sets Mike on edge.

"Can't you keep him quiet; I'm trying to study."

"He's as quiet as a six-year old can be."

"Dammit, I'm leaving."

But Mike only gets as far as the door when he sees photographs of the three of us standing in his parents' backyard in Baltimore, Jed grinning and gripping Mike's waist, or laughing at Fred's birthday party on Martha's Vineyard or catching fish in Bimini and he stops in his tracks. I have put them there for effect. Melodramatic reminders of happily ever after.

Tears. Hugs. And we're all eating dinner together and laughing at the latest antics of *Monty Python's Flying Circus.*

In such moments I feel how much we really have been trying to make this family work and I glimpse the Mike I first fell in love with, the one with the winning smile and fantastic, if bizarre, sense of humor. This is the Mike who experiences the sheer pleasure of getting lost in a good story, who has a passion for thinking and the poetry of Rilke and who introduced me to the philosophy of Maurice Merleau-Ponty, forever changing the way I looked at Cezanne's shimmering paintings. This Mike has a joy for fishing and camping and bluegrass music and shares his excitement with my son and promises he will love us forever. But, yes, he is also the Mike whose too finely tuned sense of life's fragility can overwhelm him, disturbing our delicate family balance. I aim for the center.

And so it continues, this roller coaster in search of arrival, until 1975, when our family drama goes to court.

I used to think John sued me for custody of Jed because I took him to court for more child support and won. Just another round of debate. Then I thought maybe John wanted to expel me and have the court declare me unfit so I could finally be exiled from The Society forever. I am no longer certain

The judge decides I'm no Mother of the Year and writes that in his opinion. But he also says the fact that

I live with Mike without being married to him doesn't warrant taking Jed away.

We move that same year from New York to Kentucky where Mike studies for another degree, this time social work. Since we are in the South now, as my lawyer observes in his characteristic drawl, if there is another lawsuit "y'all most certainly will lose." And so here, in Louisville, Kentucky, on a date I can never remember, we pay five dollars each to two county clerks to be witnesses while a justice of the peace performs the marriage ceremony. I remember we argued on the way to the wedding.

Two years later, we move again, further south, to Wilmington, North Carolina. I have gotten a faculty position there. At first, the situation is rocky. Without a job, Mike becomes bitter.

That August, Jed returns from visiting his father, bubbling with excitement about all they've done.

"Well why don't you just go live with him then if he's so great."

"Mike, stop it," I say, and gesture for Jed to go to his room.

"And why are you always defending him?"

"Because he's the child Mike, even though you act like one."

It's difficult for children to go between their parents after a divorce. But no one ever talks about how these comings and goings wound the adults too. And if the adults in question haven't learned how to negotiate loss and separation very well, the situation can become catastrophic. Everyone feels betrayed and blames everyone else for the betrayal.

I want to fix even this.

Within a month of our moving to Wilmington, Mike finally gets a job in a mental health clinic in Jacksonville, fifty miles to the northeast, and his spirits lift. But because he has emergency duties and must live within a ten-mile radius of the clinic we move to Jacksonville and I travel 100 miles a day to teach my classes in Wilmington. Except for the boredom of the drive, I don't mind.

We rent a house in a neighborhood filled with young families and Jed starts at a new school, which he loves. He plays baseball that spring and we look like every other family cheering at the games. Mike gives Jed his old stamp collection and they frequent local stamp shows together. Jed gets hooked on collecting and decides to add law enforcement patches to his accumulating hobbies. I buy him a zip code book and he dedicates himself to writing letters to urban police departments around the country. It makes him feel important to receive letters on official police stationary in packages filled with several law enforcement insignias and one day when he proudly displays the results of his labor the thought occurs to me that he has found a way to counter-balance any vulnerability he feels in the face of Mike's unpredictable moods by surrounding himself with these symbols of power. Years later, when he moves back to New York, I pack this collection, along with the rest of his things, and they get lost somewhere in the vast warehouse of tokens from those years.

That spring when I fly to New York to defend my dissertation I am pregnant. In December, our son, Ari, is born and his arrival feels like we are beginning again. Jed takes to his new role as big brother, discovering new ways to be gentle and caring, thrilled at the bond he has with his brother. Mike seems astonished out of melancholia for a while.

In May 1978, we buy a two-story house next to the one we've been renting and in our front yard I plant a tiny dogwood tree. One evening Mike and I go walking in the neighborhood.

"You know the Chinese say if you live long enough to have a child, write a book and plant a tree, then your life is complete. You've done all three this year," Mike tells me.

I turn to him, smiling. Except he's not smiling back.

"I'm going to apply to go back to graduate school. I can't stand doing this job forever."

"But we just got settled. Why change things again?"

"Nothing's settled for me."

One afternoon I come home from teaching and find Mike sitting in a living room chair, staring at nothing, stroking his face with his finger.

"Mike, what's the matter?"

"Those dots dancing in front of my eyes. It's an aneurysm. I know it. I'm dying; something's attacking my brain."

All fall we traverse the state in search of the right medical experts. Every one of them repeats the same story: there is nothing physically wrong. Neurophysiologically speaking, his brain is intact. The more often the doctors assure him his ganglia aren't corroding, the more evidence Mike finds of a growing conspiracy. Why can't anyone admit what we all know—his life is slipping away.

"Mike, we've seen every major neurologist in the state. Isn't it time to accept the fact that nothing's wrong?"

"And you're the ringleader."

It was a Thursday when the chair of the department interrupted my teaching. "There's an emergency at home; call this number."

Dr. Ruell, the psychiatrist on call at the clinic where Mike works, answers the phone. "I need you to get here as soon as you can; I've made a deal with Mike. You'll take him to see one more doctor in Wilmington, and if the diagnosis is the same, he promises to take the medication I've prescribed and stay home until he feels better."

So I drive fifty miles to Mike's office in Jacksonville and then fifty more back to Wilmington with him. The doctor's report is as expected: no signs of any medical irregularity. Mike's problems are "in his head."

During the drive back to Jacksonville Mike is silent until we reach the outskirts of town. Then he begins to mumble. He is sick of everyone lying. But what sickens him most is the thought that after he's dead the world will go on.

"The only thing that would make it bearable, Kath, is to know you'd jump in the grave after me."

"Do you hear what you're saying? You're crazy. "

"Why, why won't you do that?"

"You can't mean it. Think of the children."

"I am. I don't want them to be with anyone else. I don't want you to remarry."

"Mike, stop it. You're fine. You just need medication. I'm taking you to Dr. Ruell right away."

"I'm dying."

"O.K. O.K. But not right this minute."

"Why don't you understand? Just say you'll go with me."

"I'll go with you to Dr. Ruell," I say. If I can get to her office, everything will be fine.

"Don't commit me. Promise you won't commit me."

What can ever make the certainty of one's death a bearable fact? Since we all are bound for that inevitable destination, it's a question each of us must face, though I suppose it's possible to ignore it. But the certainty of his own death and the certainty the world would persist after it were two facts Mike found unbearable in those years. And I knew no way then to bring him to the brink of some different precipice, to the edge of a remembered cliff where we once sat looking out at the sea at sunset, envisioning the sheer wonder of being alive, feeling being alive was both "transcendent and yet, at the same time...encompassing life and the world."

Death shows us we are nothing only if we cannot understand ourselves to be parts of this larger world. But, as Hannah once wrote,

> *by showing man his nothingness...death also points out both his source [natality, the beginning] and a possible escape from nothingness—from death. The escape is the concept of immutable being that death itself becomes. Life...borders upon eternity at the beginning as well as at the end...There is no longer any meaning to 'coming from nothing' and 'racing toward nothing.' Death itself has lost its meaning.* [158]

I didn't know how to articulate such thoughts then. And even if I had, it might not have mattered. It turns out "happily ever after" only happens when you stop living life like a story and decide to take up life as a project with no end.

Somehow Mike and I and the kids slouched along until February when letters of admission to doctoral programs started arriving and the cloud of doom under which he'd felt he was living lifted a little. He'd been accepted into a program in California and that seemed a good enough place for a new start.

It worked for a while.

Two years later, we divorced. And Jed's anger burst at the seams.

One particularly bad night Jed and I are fighting, I can't recall about what, and he calls me a bitch. I look at my son, a young man tormented by emotions he doesn't yet understand or know how to control, and I suddenly feel helpless and very much alone. I pick up the phone and call his father.

At first Jed refuses to talk. But then he agrees. After Jed calms down, his father and I continue the conversation.

"I hesitate to say this, and we won't bring it up with Jed if you don't want to; but maybe we should consider Jed's coming to live with me. We can ask him what he wants to do, let him choose." John seems sincere.

"Yes, maybe we should talk about it." I don't believe what I hear myself saying.

Years before I had a dream Jed had fallen into the sea off the back of a boat. As I reached for his hand, my arm detached from my body and when I tried to move closer to reach for him again, someone held me back. Now the dream comes back, its images reversed, and it is I who am floating, alone and out of my depths.

That summer, I attend a seminar in Massachusetts on Nietzsche and Foucault. As usual, Jed goes to New York to visit his father. Ari and I travel to Amherst and rent a small off-campus apartment in a building abutting the cemetery where Emily Dickinson is buried. At the end of the summer John and I plan to meet in New York to discuss Jed's decision. My tattered heart, heading for latitudes unknown.

One night, Jed calls me.

"Hi, Mom, what are you doing?"

"Nothing much, just reading. How about you?"

"Went to a movie with Uncle Paul. And we're ordering in Chinese."

"That's good. Where's your father?"

"He's at work, he's got some big report to finish before the end of the week and then we go to the beach house."

"Oh, yeah...did you get time to talk to each other?"

"Yeah, he told me about your being here the other day. That's weird."

"What's so weird about it; we had things to discuss."

"I don't know. It's just weird."

Seeing John and I being civil to one another wasn't a familiar sight.

"Well, John's been helpful lately. With finances and everything. It's not so unusual for us to talk about this and that."

"Yeah, 'this and that'...meaning me."

"Of course, you. We're concerned about you and school."

A few months earlier Jed had mouthed off to a teacher. She had summoned me to her office to discuss his behavior. Nothing extreme, but I was worried it might be the start of something more serious.

"Gotta go now, Mom. Uncle Paul's back with the food."

"O.K. I'll see you next week."

On the Friday before the appointed meeting Ari and I share a ride to New York with three graduate students who had advertised space available in their station wagon. Ari falls asleep in the car and I wake him when we arrive at my stepsister's house on Staten Island. The plan is Ari will stay with his cousins the next day while I meet with Jed and John.

I remember John picking me up that morning at my sister's house. I remember getting into the car and sitting in the back seat. I remember a glance from father to son, a sign to begin the conversation. And I remember being utterly unprepared for what happened next.

"Mom, I've decided to stay in New York and live with my father."

"Really?"

"Yes, I want to have a chance to live in New York."

"O.K."

"I mean, I'm not choosing between the two of you; it's not about living with my father and not living with you. It's about living in one place or another."

"I see."

But, really, I don't see anything at all.

Cultures key transitions to rites of passage, ritualized markings whose rhythms mitigate the pain of separation and loss. Children go off to college or marry or take up a job and start out on their own and though one feels pain at their leaving, it's an expected cutting of the cord. But when Jed leaves my home to live with his father at the end of his fifteenth summer, no ritual marks the event, except my packing his bags. Into boxes of folded sweaters and shirts, between baseball cards and collections of stamps, I slip notes and letters to him as if these talismans will preclude my expulsion.

Because that's how it feels: as if I'm finally being expelled. I am no longer a part of The Society. And as long as I held onto feeling negated, I was defeated. No, as long as I held onto it, I defeated myself.

Many years later I attend a reunion in New York with thirty-five former debaters and John. The debaters, now fifty- and sixty-something women, are all highly successful lawyers and doctors and accomplished businesswomen, more than you would have expected could come out of one tiny Catholic high school in Brooklyn. I hadn't planned to attend. There would be, I thought, too many painful memories.

"You have to go," Amy, says when I hesitate. "It will be good for you. Maybe it will give you a chance to let go."

I listen to one testimonial after another about how debate motivated everyone to excel and, at first, I want to run from the room screaming. Don't you get it? Don't you remember? This man who played Henry Higgins to our Eliza Doolittles admits he needed us to make him feel whole.

But I don't run. I stand to the side and use every bit of my energy to squeeze my anger down to chewable size. And I swallow. Because I've been angry too long. Because I can no longer pretend to be innocent. Because the truth is I loved him; I loved every one of my Heideggers, finally wide-awake and all on my own.

"We can no more master the past than we can undo it. But we can reconcile ourselves to it. The form for this is the lament, which arises out of all recollection."[159]

In 1950, after nearly twenty years of silence, Arendt renewed her contact with Heidegger. Though others saw, and still see, their reconciliation as a sliding backwards, a nostalgic attempt to redeem some romanticized past, I think the contact helped Hannah reclaim all the parts of her self, including ones she might have preferred to deny.

"Without being forgiven, released from the consequences of what we have done, our capacity to act would...be confined to one single deed from which we could never recover; we would remain the victims of its consequences forever..." By forgiving Heidegger his appalling mistakes, Hannah released them both from the shadows of an ignominious past and created the chance to accept responsibility for that past and learn to live with it.

So one thing I've learned from Hannah is this: forgiveness springs from facing the fact that sometimes we desire revenge against those who have or might hurt us. And this desire emerges from the heart's misbegotten project to try to stop its own pain. But the irony is pain only stops when the heart learns how to leap out of line while staying in place.

Forgiveness frees us from vengeance. And it frees both the one who forgives and the one who is forgiven by releasing them both from the consequences of some act, allowing it to come to an end. "What was done is forgiven for the sake of who did it."

Enmity has withered and in a space in my heart I discovered an opening, fruitfully empty. Having once fallen into that ignominious hole where all Heideggers must hide, I recognize my affinity with them. They beckon me to remember. To remember and to forgive.

Except one Heidegger remains to be forgiven. Please release her, release us all, from what she has done.

{10}

The Genealogy of Tribes

The directly personal relationship...exists of course foremost in real love, and it also exists in a certain sense in friendship. There a person is addressed directly, independent of his relation to the world.

Hannah Arendt, "*What Remains? Language Remains*"

WE CANNOT CHOOSE THE FAMILY INTO WHICH WE ARE BORN. And sometimes love seems so inchoate and mysterious and unworldly as to erase all logic or reason except of the lovers' own devising. Yet out of love springs forgiveness and this makes love politically relevant because it allows us to choose to reconcile with the past and act again in the future.

But what about friendship?

In the landscape of friendship, Hannah Arendt's capacity stands luminous and large. From the time she was a young woman, she surrounded herself with a circle of friends with whom she exchanged gossip, ideas about politics and philosophy, opinions on culture and the state of the world, and, occasionally, romantic partners. Perhaps the model of Berlin salon society, about which she published an important essay very early in her career, shaped her desire to create and sustain an intellectual community to nourish her. Yet Hannah's friendship circles—what later would become known as "The Tribe"—differed from those nineteenth century European salons in one important respect: hers were not comprised of "types," or representatives of different social groups, but of companions with whom she shared an equal devotion to conversation and heated debate (and a love of champagne), and to whom she gave intense loyalty, expecting it in return.

In the tiny set of rooms on Morningside Drive she shared with her husband and mother, and, later, the larger Riverside Drive apartment that hosted many a New Year's Eve party some of the most illustrious political and literary minds of the twentieth century would meet—among them Hermann Broch, Paul Tillich, Salo and Jeanette Baron, Helen and Kurt Wolff, Hans Morgenthau, Alfred Kazin, Mary McCarthy, Lotte Kohler, Elisabeth Hardwick, Randall Jarrell, Robert Lowell, J. Glenn Grey, Dwight Macdonald, W.H. Auden, Lionel and Diane Trilling. Many were, like Hannah, émigrés from Nazi-occupied Europe. Others, like Jarrell, Kazin, McCarthy, and Trilling, were American poets, writers, artists and critics whose work shaped the cultural milieu of mid-twentieth century America: the New York Intellectuals, as they came to be known. All were drawn to, and sometimes repelled by, the argumentative, opinionated, yet unceasingly electrifying German Jewish woman who held court in a shabbily furnished apartment on the upper west side of Manhattan.

In her later years, inquiring students and younger faculty from various universities might also be invited if Hannah judged their questions or projects worthy of serious conversation. "I have scheduled myself to give a department seminar on your political thought. This is one detail of a larger project I am beginning which, I hope, will result in a book on you," a young professor of political science at John Jay College in New York wrote to her in February 1975. "I am early along in this project but...would still like to meet and talk with you about a few of my early reflections on your thought." Hannah replied with an invitation to arrange a meeting, and included her home telephone number for him to call.[160]

With its high ceilings, large rooms, and grand windows, Apartment 12A at 370 Riverside Drive reminded its visitors of those pre-war buildings in Berlin. From Hannah's desk, one could look over Riverside Park and the Hudson River to the edge of New Jersey.

Entering the apartment through a foyer, you were immediately confronted by an imposing portrait of a young Franz Kafka attached to a hall closet door. Hannah had helped get Kafka's work published in English when she worked as an editor at Schocken Books and admired him as a writer she thought greater even than Thomas Mann. On another wall were arrayed some paintings of minor artists collected by Hannah's husband, Heinrich Blücher, co-host of the Tribe's gatherings.

The furnishings failed to disclose their owner was a woman who lectured on aesthetics and judgment in politics. But then, as she more than once told her students at the New School,

> *We don't deal with philosophic theories which then can or can't be applied to practical matters, but with the experience of philosophizing and the experience of the political man: or with the experience of thinking or the experience of acting.*[161]

In the living room, where Hannah received visitors with her characteristic combination of archness and wit, womanly guile and cultivated erudition, stood a high-backed sofa covered in a dismal green vinyl, worn and patched, but serviceable. Scattered across from the sofa was an assortment of armchairs and in front of it, a coffee table, on which she would serve glasses of champagne from her well-stocked supplies to closer friends on social occasions. The dining room, whose main table was covered in books, papers, and journals, served primarily as a library. Helen Wolff described it as "a cheerful apartment but by no means furnished with aesthetics in mind. [It was] a philosopher's home."[162]

This was Hannah's home against the world, providing, in the language she used in a 1974 speech given at Columbia University, a "place of one's own shielded against the claims of the public."

The shabby functionality of the apartment's decor may have been as much the result of Heinrich's strong opposition to anything that reeked of the *bourgeois* as it was the consequence of the long years Hannah and her husband scraped by with minimal income. Her close friend, Lotte Kohler, remembered Hannah talking with her in the 1960s about owning "Wisteria", a small rented cottage in the country near Palenville, where Hannah and some of her closest friends spent summer weeks from the 1940s until about 1969. Calculating how much it would cost to buy and maintain, Hannah decided she couldn't generate the necessary income, nor the time and effort to realize the project. By 1972, after Heinrich had died, when she came into some money from the settlement of her reparations claims against the German government, the idea of owning a place of her own seems to have faded.

Hannah loved being in the contentious center of things, whether quoting Goethe and Hölderlin in the original German, lecturing Saul Bellow on the literature of Faulkner, listening to Randall Jarrell reading the poetry of Wordsworth, Eliot, or Whitman to her, being celebrated in a poem written by Robert Lowell or W.H. Auden in her honor, or debating current events or philosophy with Mary McCarthy, J. Glenn Gray or Dwight Macdonald. Helen Wolff described her as "very striking...and noticeable immediately even to those who met her for the first time, was a very powerful *Ausstrahlung* [charisma]."

In *New York Jew*, his memoir of literary New York in the 1940s-1960s, Alfred Kazin attempted to explain Hannah's allure:

> *The excitement of being with Hannah was mysterious, for it reached to foundations of thought that she accepted with a kind of awe.*

> *'I have never, since a child,' she once said to me, 'doubted that God exists.'*[163]

With her, Kazin recalled in an interview more than a decade later,

> *everything...was temperament...What people responded to...was always the temperamental thing, which was very vivid...She couldn't accept criticism...But she made a very deep impression...It was this temperamental thing, which was astonishingly passionate...She was very much a woman in every deep sense of the word...There's no question that a lot of the men, poets and others who hanged around, were very much affected by her.*[164]

As a woman? he was asked. "Oh, yes, definitely."

Unsurprisingly, this erotic magnetism disturbed some of the women in the circle, including Ann Birstein (Alfred Kazin's third wife) and Diane Trilling, whose presence may have been more a function of Hannah's attachment to their husbands than to themselves. At least that was the impression Hannah gave them, either by ignoring them, or dismissing them with some curt remark.

Such conflicting images as these no longer surprised me; by now I was used to the multiple and contradictory images of Hannah expressed by people who claimed to know her.

Heinrich Blücher, Hannah's husband and salon society partner, was an autodidact who spoke in a loud, heavily accented voice, when he spoke at all. Conversation between them might set dialogue in motion until one or another of the few assembled friends, acting first as an audience, would decide to join in.

It is clear there are different attitudes toward death expressed in Plato's Apology *compared with the* Phaido. *The question is, which one is more authentically Socratic?*

As to the history of modern philosophy, it could be described thus: Two Titans—Kant and Nietzsche—stormed and demolished the heavens of the intellectual-mythical era of humanity. Then the Giants—Marx and Kierkegaard—rushed in to frolic in the ruins.

There has been a decisive break with tradition, Heinrich.

It's about time The New Leader *came to its senses and condemned [Eugene] McCarthy and the whole administration.*

How can you not understand 'the boys' are attacking that Mary's novel, The Group, because it's a best seller? They're simply jealous.

Vietnam? I agree with Lippmann and Morgenthau: this is a civil war. What troubles me more is the lying the U.S. has begun to practice.[165]

Randall Jarrell used the Blüchers as models for characters in his novel, *Pictures from an Institution*, representing their marriage as a "Dual Monarchy," the power constantly shifting between them, but always on equal terms.

In later years, Mary McCarthy recalled, Heinrich became more withdrawn.

> *I loved Heinrich...He was very explosive, very peppery. He was very reclusive, too...People would come [to the apartment] and never know that Heinrich was there. He had his own sort of separate suite of rooms...a bedroom, study, and bath...He didn't like social gatherings...And Heinrich would be there and sometimes he would listen and if the conversation sounded interesting, he would come out and take part. Sometimes he would sit there quite silently and someone would say something that he didn't like...and there was a noise like a machine gun going off. That was Heinrich.*[166]

Heinrich's reclusiveness was partly due to his deteriorating hearing. But Hannah's growing reputation and public notoriety were no doubt contributing factors. And no matter how well suited, they were temperamentally different. Hannah enjoyed large gatherings while Heinrich preferred the company of a few close friends. Still, the annual New Year's Eve party at the Blüchers' residence was a New York event whose guest list of 30 might mushroom into 80 people before the evening's end.

It became obvious to me how important an anchor friendship was in Hannah's life. Friends substituted for siblings she otherwise lacked in her youth. Even after her father's death and her mother's second marriage brought two stepsisters into her life, Hannah remained closer to friends than to family. And, despite her peripatetic existence, the remarkable thing was she managed to stay connected with some throughout the whole course of her life.

Yet over time her circle changed. After she escaped from Europe to America and her reputation as a writer circulated among a network of intellectuals and literary figures, Arendt developed new friendships. And when her controversial position on the Eichmann trial created ideological friction, friends she'd had from earlier days, like Gershom Sholem and Kurt Blumenfeld, and even some newer ones, such as Norman Podhoretz, dropped away. Following Heinrich's death in 1970, she reconnected with a few old friends from whom she'd distanced herself and began to throw large, catered dinner parties.

As important as these shifting circles were in Hannah's intellectual life, very little about them fed her emotionally. At least not in ways she readily disclosed.

There were, in fact, two types of friendship in Hannah's life—those most like her characterization of friendship in her portrait of Lessing in *Men in Dark Times,* which she called "friendship among citizens," and those she called "intimate."

> *We are wont to see friendship solely as a phenomenon of intimacy in which the friends open their hearts to each other unmolested by the world and its demands. Rousseau, not Lessing, is the best advocate of this view...Thus it is hard for us to understand the political relevance of friendship...But for the Greeks the essence of friendship consisted in discourse...The converse (in contrast to the intimate talk in which individuals speak about themselves), permeated though it may be by pleasure in the friend's presence, is concerned with the common world.*[167]

Sometimes, but only rarely, the two types were interwoven in the same friend.

"The Tribe" formed the circle of friends concerned with that common world, and much less with the intimate topics of face-to-face encounters. A very private person, Hannah shared more personal details of her life only with Heinrich and a few close friends, mostly women, in whom she confided, more frequently in correspondence than in person. But even to those closest to her Hannah offered only certain parts of herself, parceling out bits, holding back others, so that no one, perhaps not even Heinrich, held all the pieces of the Hannah puzzle at the same time. Her intention wasn't to deceive, but to protect her precious privacy.

Mary McCarthy once told a revealing story about Hannah's almost fanatical need to protect personal details of her life from public scrutiny. Having invited Hannah to lecture at their college, the organizers wanted to give a reception in her honor and asked someone if they knew what Hannah liked to drink. She liked Campari and soda, the acquaintance told them. And they promptly bought a large bottle of the *apéritif.* "Certainly not," Hannah replied when they offered her the drink at the party. "I'll have a bourbon." [168]

Old friendships, Francine Prose wrote, are like some Proustian key to the past, answering the question, "Who were we when we were friends and what has become of us?"[169]

Among her women friends, the unlikely friendship of Arendt and Mary McCarthy has been much documented and discussed, even more now since Margarethe von Trotta's film, *Hannah Arendt*, gave it its first celluloid representation. What sort of friendship was it?

Hannah Arendt met Mary McCarthy for the first time in 1944, while Hannah was working at Schocken Books. In those days, McCarthy was a striking beauty.

"If you were to make a movie of Mary McCarthy's life," someone once observed, "Grace Kelly could have played the part."[170] McCarthy's *New Yorker* short stories and her first novel, *The Company She Keeps*, were already winning her the reputation of rising literary star. With her wider connections to New York's literary scene, both of her own making and those she gained through her marriage to the critic Edmund Wilson, I imagine knowing McCarthy enhanced Hannah's network of influence. Besides her sheer beauty, that must have been part of Hannah's initial attraction to her. Equally important was McCarthy's very American angle of vision on a world of letters Hannah was about to enter. Years later, McCarthy even acted as a kind of editor for Hannah, offering suggestions, not always taken, for ways to improve Hannah's English for an American audience.

For her part, Hannah's European erudition and her mind's vitality impressed the ambitious, patrician McCarthy. Here, clearly, McCarthy must have thought, was an intellect matched with a personality worth getting to know. And wanting to spend time with someone she deemed worthy of her attention was a McCarthy character trait honed since her years at Vassar, where her own iconoclastic struggle for acceptance within Vassar's highly stratified world had been one way she tried to establish a suitable distance between her ambitions and her difficult orphaned childhood.

Frani Blough Muser, one of McCarthy's closest Vassar friends, recalled Mary "hoping to have a salon. Interesting people and all that. She'd imagined herself as a figure from literary history...So she put herself in a salon, like Madame de Staël."[171] Hannah Arendt proved a perfect avenue to that kind of rarefied society.

Yet, the connection between the women was a decidedly two-way street, bringing Hannah to the attention of more of the New York intellectuals. And, when occasions required, it gave both women another woman to share gossip about the jealousy of the *Partisan Review* "boys" toward women's success, and the envy some *PR* wives exuded about the attention these two commandeered from "the boys."

But McCarthy also had a reputation for being an acerbic wit, possessing a sharp, satiric tongue and little restraint in its exercise. Some months after their first acquaintance, the relationship between the two women hit a major roadblock at a gathering at the home of Phillip Rahv, editor of the recently resurrected *Partisan Review*, and a former lover of McCarthy's. As McCarthy told the story years later, she'd made a comment about Hitler's declining popularity in France, which she thought amusing. "So I said...'You know, I feel sorry for Hitler, because he'll never achieve this dream of his of being loved by all these people that he's conquered.' " Hannah was none too pleased.

> *There was a terrible sort of explosive sound, which was Hannah Arendt going off like a machine gun. She turned to Philip and...said, 'Rahv! Must I come to America to hear this kind of talk in the house of you, a Jew.' She didn't speak to me for two years.*[172]

Despite this rocky start, the improbable friendship between Hannah and Mary McCarthy found a way to begin again and lasted nearly three decades, nourished by both the intellectual and emotional sustenance each offered the other.

Becoming each other's fans sheltered them from various storms of attack they sustained from different quarters. McCarthy's 1949 novella, *The Oasis*, a thinly veiled satire of the self-aggrandizing projects and limited moral imaginations of leftist intellectuals of the type at the center of *Partisan Review*, had been published to the outrage of several in New York literary circles, who recognized themselves in several of her characters, among them Philip Rahv, who later tried to sue to stop the book's being brought out in a larger imprint by Random House.

"I just read *The Oasis*," Hannah wrote to McCarthy in 1949, "and must tell you that it was pure delight. You have written a veritable little masterpiece."[173]

Hannah's supportive note gave McCarthy some measure of relief from the widening criticism her book was receiving. Later, when Hannah experienced an even greater tempest following the publication of *Eichmann in Jerusalem*, McCarthy returned the favor with a vigorous defense of her friend's work.

> *What can be done about the* Eichmann *business, which is assuming the proportion of a pogrom. Whether you answer or not (and I still feel it would be best if you answered somewhere, even if not in* PR*), I am going to write something to the boys for publication.*[174]

"The boys" was the well-chosen put-down the two women used, representing awareness that their acceptance into this elite inner circle of intellectual men was tinged with more than a modicum of hostility. If "the boys" were intent on treating McCarthy—and, to a lesser extent, Hannah—as an interloper in the house of literature and criticism, each woman activated whatever connections she had at her disposal in defense of her friend. For her part, McCarthy published a scathing reply in *Partisan Review* to Lionel Abel's polemic against Hannah and *Eichmann in Jerusalem*, which had appeared earlier in the same magazine.

Yet, their intellectual support of each other didn't rule out giving criticism or providing alternative insight. "I've read your book [*The Origins of Totalitarianism*], absorbed, for the past two weeks, in the bathtub, riding in a car, waiting in line in the grocery store. It seems to me a truly extraordinary piece of work," McCarthy exclaimed in a letter to Hannah. And then added an objection: she thought Hannah's explanation of totalitarianism gave too little weight to the role of the "fortuitous" in its development. After finishing McCarthy's *The Group*, Hannah wrote to her:

> *I liked* The Group *very very much, it is quite different from your other books...You have won a perspective, or perhaps rather: you have arrived at a point so far removed from your former life that everything now can fall into place. You yourself are no longer directly involved. And this quality makes the book more of a novel than any of your other books.*[175]

Unafraid to judge, both women practiced a form of truth telling that, in its more strident tones, bordered on arrogance, the kind of arrogance neither begrudged the other.

Perhaps it was mutual admiration for this burnished, self-confident truth telling that cemented the friendship between Hannah and McCarthy. Certainly the affection each displayed for the other was genuine and deep, even if the attraction between them was difficult for many in their circle to comprehend without trying to explain it away as a kind of intellectually advanced *folie à deux*. "How you came to view the friendship," Frances Kiernan wrote, "would always depend in large part on how you felt about McCarthy and on how willing you were to subscribe to her belief that Arendt was both truly good and truly brilliant."[176] And, no doubt, on how you felt about Hannah.

But, I wondered, how many outside such an intense and devoted friendship as theirs—especially those lacking anything comparable in their own lives—can understand what really happens between such friends? Reflecting on my own friendships brought me closer to understanding what makes the truly passionate ones last is the same thing threatening to unravel them—a delicate, yet highly combustible mixture of self-disclosure, shared viewpoints, and fantasy.

Littered throughout the correspondence between these two women are recommendations for books to read and write, places to visit, and ways to think about current issues. Yet the undertone of their dialogue expresses a growing intimacy and fervor, whether engaging topics worldly or personal.

After a 1968 letter from Paris catching Hannah up on the latest news among their friendship circle, as well as events in her own personal life, McCarthy wrote "I must stop. I miss you very much. More than ever recently." And Hannah replied: "Each time I receive a letter from you I realize how much I miss you. Times are lousy and we should be closer to each other. I guess I have been depressed all winter." Not only the "daily news" which was "like being hit over the head" but Heinrich's continuing health scares troubled Hannah all the time.[177]

The most private self-revelations, though, came from McCarthy. Hannah disapproved of her being too open, McCarthy told an interviewer in 1988. "She thought that was all very American and that one should hide things. Actually I don't think she hid much herself, but that was her principle."[178] McCarthy held back very little. Flagrantly effusive in public and private about all her excesses, she frequently used her letters to Hannah to unload the emotional consequences of her many romantic liaisons and marriages, or to seek advice, sometimes even engaging Hannah in her intrigues.

Sometime in the fall of 1956, McCarthy started an affair with an Englishman named John Davenport. She was supposed to meet Hannah in Amsterdam in October, but wrote to tell her plans had changed; she was staying in London with her lover. Then she enclosed several postcards written to her husband at the time, Bowden Broadwater, to create the illusion that she and

Hannah were traveling together and asked Hannah to mail then to Bowden. Hannah complied.

The affair with Davenport continued into the following spring until McCarthy learned from another friend of Davenport's about the darker, more treacherous sides of her lover's personality—Davenport was a pathological liar and drunk who fabricated his own ancestry to gain entry to British society. This sad story became the narrative thread of a long letter to Hannah. "The truth is," McCarthy wrote,

> *I still care about him, just as much as ever, though perhaps this feeling would not last if I saw him in actuality...Oh, Hannah, isn't it awful? I still would do anything for him...but what can I do?*[179]

Two weeks later came Hannah's reply:

> *[H]e did not want to be saved by you either. And this is the reason why I think you were right not to see him...[Y]ou had to be frightened away; and he must have known that it would take rather drastic measures to achieve this. Certainly, there is a great deal of cruelty in all this; but then you can't expect someone who loves you to treat you less cruelly than he would treat himself. The equality of love is always pretty awful. Compassion (not pity) can be a great thing, but love knows nothing of it.*[180]

One of Hannah's other close friends, Lotte Kohler, claimed Hannah couldn't understand McCarthy's promiscuity. There's no question, as McCarthy herself knew, that she and Hannah didn't see eye to eye about McCarthy's trumpeting of women's sexual experiences, as she did rather audaciously in her fiction. But if Hannah couldn't understand it, she didn't condemn it, any more than she did other friends' extramarital affairs. Instead, she suggested McCarthy simply couldn't have it both ways—if she wanted to lead a promiscuous life, she ought to accept the choices she'd made and take responsibility for them. Self-pity wasn't a trait Hannah tolerated.

In 1960, trying to obtain a divorce from Broadwater in order to marry her next, and last, husband, Jim West, McCarthy once again turned to Hannah, complaining about Broadwater's lingering resistance and asking Hannah to intercede on her behalf. Again, Hannah complied, agreeing to help in her own way. But not without chastising McCarthy for her impatience:

> *You say you cannot trust him. Perhaps you are right, perhaps you are wrong, I have no idea. But it strikes me that you can forget so easily that you trusted him enough to be married to him for fifteen years...You write that it is just 'too ridiculous' for the two of you (Jim West and you) to be the 'passive*

> *fools of other people' If you want to look at the matter in these terms at all, then it seems to me rather obvious that you both are the victims of your own, self-chosen past. This may be inconvenient but it is not ridiculous, unless you wish to say that your whole past was not only a mistake, but a ridiculous one.*[181]

And then, after lecturing her, Hannah closed her letter with this: "Mary, my Dear, I miss you! Much love and the best of luck. Yours, H."

In a recent post on "Page Turner," *The New Yorker's* online book blog, Michelle Dean complained the image of Arendt's friendship with McCarthy in von Trotta's film was a "flat portraiture," arguing it represented the conversations between these two "ferocious minds" as if they had been dominated by exchanges "about men and love." In reality, Dean contended, their friendship formed a "close intellectual bond," serving as a "bulwark against their naysayers."

All this is true; but to me it underplays the complexity and intimacy of Hannah's relationship to Mary McCarthy. In an age when, as Dean notes, "women hunger for models of intellectual self-confidence" the pair's friendship is certainly a source of inspiration, an exemplar of women "talking about ideas among themselves." But this model also risks a portraiture that is flat, dispassionate and disembodied so it's important to pay attention to the complex role of the erotic in this and Hannah's other female friendship. Even in her letters to McCarthy "about men and love," Hannah's conceptualization of judgment and responsibility—her "ideas"—shine forth. And this complexity of thought is no less evident in the relatively unexplored significance of less known, though not lesser, female friends who came into Arendt's life, and sometimes left prematurely.

I confess to having been as much beguiled by the centrality of Hannah's friendship with McCarthy as anyone. No doubt the extensive correspondence between them, along with their celebrity, contributed to my enthrallment, over-shadowing the significance any other friendships may have played in Hannah's life. Still, as open and loving as Arendt was with McCarthy, I couldn't help thinking the intimacy between them was bounded by a margin of revelation which Arendt would not cross. Arendt's brutally honest mentoring of McCarthy in matters of the heart seemed to be a barrier behind which she kept her most self-revelatory feelings and fears to herself. Even though she talked with McCarthy about her concerns for Blücher's health and her feelings about her former lover, the notorious Martin Heidegger, Arendt didn't speak in the voice or with the vulnerability any woman, no matter how intellectual, might use to express her most intimate fears or joys with her "closest woman friend."

Then, while researching Elżbieta Ettinger's archives, another woman, an early acquaintance from Hannah's days in Germany came into sharper focus: Hilda Fränkel. And so did more angles of Hannah.

Hannah had met Fränkel in Frankfurt around 1930 through the theologian Paul Tillich. Fränkel may already have been Tillich's lover before both of them left Germany in 1933, he for America with his family and she for Argentina with hers. But by the time Hannah reconnected with the pair they were both living in New York and, despite Tillich being married, the affair between them was in full swing. Although they were worlds apart in background and education—Fränkel worked as Tillich's secretary at Union Theological Seminary but otherwise kept her distance from the intellectual world in which Hannah mostly circulated—they were drawn to each other.

For Hannah, friendship thrived on equality, but only in the sense of a shared commitment to independent thinking and a willingness to take risks. Hilda Fränkel possessed these characteristics to an extraordinary degree. Her perceptive intelligence and willingness to talk frankly, yet privately, about even her sexual life and erotic encounters endeared her to Hannah.

Hannah's own marriage was more remarkably stable than others in her New York circle. Despite Blücher's affairs, some of which she knew of and tolerated, their marriage was relatively conventional. Yet, she refrained from judging the extra-marital dalliances, especially in the case of those she liked. She might criticize her friends' choice of partners, but not the fact of their having more than one at a time.

In fact, Lotte Kohler recalled, Hannah loved hearing stories about love affairs, fiction filled with adventure and romance. Hilda Fränkel was very open about such things. Gifted with what Hannah called an "erotic genius," there was a matter-of-factness about Fränkel's narration of her amorous liaisons, which Hannah received with amusement and more than a little admiration for the sexual freedom the stories expressed and the ease with which they were told. Once, she told Hannah, Fränkel had no money to pay the electric bill. So she invited the bill collector to her home and went to bed with him to discharge the debt.[182]

For several years, Hannah had been deepening her friendship with Fränkel. Then, illness interrupted their lives. When Hannah left for an extended trip in late fall 1949—her first journey to post-war Europe and the occasion for her initial reunion with Heidegger—Fränkel was already in the final throes of a losing battle with cancer. Wracked with pain and heavily dependent on morphine to dull it, yet dreading the thought of never seeing her dear friend again, Fränkel was determined to hold on until Hannah came back to New York. They wrote each other frequently, sharing news of their respective "journeys," and complaining about their "men."

In Hannah's absence, Heinrich took over the role of watchful guardian of Hilde, bearing gifts Hannah sent her from abroad. But he couldn't match the comfort Hannah could provide when Fränkel grew impatient with Tillich. "Yes, men are rather heavy baggage," Hannah wrote. "Nevertheless, one cannot get along without them. That's true."

For her part, Hilde goaded Heinrich any time Hannah worried about his tardy correspondence. And she supported Hannah's reconciliation with Heidegger. Writing to Hilde about her first meeting with Heidegger, Hannah recounted the episode as one of tragicomic proportion, Heidegger appearing "like a dog with his tail between his legs." But then she observed, "Basically I am happy, simply about the confirmation; the fact that I was right never to forget."[183] And Hilde replied, "I'm so proud of you about H[eidegger], as you are proud of me."[184]

As death drew nearer, both women began to reflect on the particular meaning this friendship had in their lives: "Darling," Hannah wrote to Fränkel

> *I can hardly tell you how much I owe you, not only for the loosening up which comes from intimacy with a woman like I have never known before, but for the happiness of closeness, a happiness never to be lost, and all the greater since you aren't an 'intellectual' (what a hateful word), and therefore are a confirmation of myself and my true belief. I so long to talk with you and cannot imagine how I should live without you, incredibly impoverished, as if suddenly condemned to silence about the most important things when I have just learned to speak.*[185]

While in Europe, Hannah had also reconnected with another old friend Ann (Annchen) Mendelsohn Weil. Hilde was gladdened by that news, hoping this old friendship might fill the gap left by her own death.

> *Hannah I am so glad that you saw Annchen and that you could help her...Don't tell her about me, just be good to her...Shouldn't you bring Annchen [back to America] with you? It would be a rescue for her and for you a close person. Couldn't she replace me in your life?*[186]

Hannah demurred:

> *Annchen...no, Hilde, what you are to me she could never be because you and I are close on a level which she doesn't even know...The happiness that I've found with you grew even more intense because you are leaving and because pain too became part of it.*[187]

Hilda Fränkel's death, in 1950, came only a short while after Hannah returned from Europe. The loss was surely horrific for her.

Two years later, on another European trip, Hannah wrote to Heinrich about a new depth she had reached in her friendship with Annchen, despite a falling out they'd had about Hannah's portrayal of Jews in her writing. "Spending time with Annchen was simply marvelous. We reached an intimacy in which we were fully attuned to each other; it lay like a warm wrap around our shoulders."[188] Recognizing the importance of this friendship to his wife, Heinrich responded. "I am happy that in spite of everything Annchen and you are so close again, and that in a true friendship everything is reconcilable."[189]

Still, I couldn't help thinking Hannah never again had the same kind of intimate woman friend she'd found in Hilde Fränkel. Perhaps because the two women had connected first and foremost emotionally rather than intellectually and at a time when Hannah was not yet well known, Hannah had been able to be vulnerable with Fränkel as with no one else. Though she may have exchanged confidences in conversations with other women—notably, Lotte Kohler, to whom she entrusted her personal correspondence with Heidegger—I doubt Hannah found a match for her connection with Hilde Fränkel.

What it must have been like for Hannah to lose such a close friend with so much of her life still ahead of her. Thinking about my own friendship history, I imagined the pain of such a separation must have been difficult to bear.

Her friendship with Mary McCarthy persisted until Hannah's death. Other women also managed to get close to Hannah, at least up to a point. And that was no simple thing to achieve, since Hannah's standards for companionship, and her notorious impatience with women she considered to be mere appendages of men in her circle, were extremely high and not infrequently off-putting.

In 1961, a 37-year old scholar of Renaissance history and literature named Rosalie Colie was teaching at Wesleyan University when Hannah Arendt became a visiting fellow at its Center for Advanced Studies. It was only a few months after Arendt had covered the Eichmann trial in Jerusalem, and her report on it was yet unwritten. Still, her reputation already well established, Arendt cut an imposing figure among the scholars on Wesleyan's campus, where she gave a seminar on Machiavelli and revised her manuscript of *On Revolution* for publication.

Colie attended Hannah's public talks and wrote her an adulatory note in January 1962, including a poem by Yeats she thought related to *The Human Condition.* Although the note began with the formal salutation "Dear Miss Arendt" its conclusion indicated the seeds of a friendship had been planted that term: "It surely was fine to have had the luck to hear you and see you this term. I look forward to next year, and before then, to dinner in NY, which I shall make good on."[190]

For her part, Hannah was impressed with Colie, whom she later described in a 1967 letter of recommendation to Oxford, where Colie was to be appointed as a Talbot Research Fellow in a program specifically designed for women, as "one of the most erudite women I have ever known." Two years later in a letter attached to Colie's appointment at Brown University she added to this assessment that besides Colie's "profound erudition," she was an excellent teacher

> *rather strict in her demands and still very much beloved by her students...She is very civilized, sophisticated, extremely well-read in all branches of literature, witty, full of spirit. I am sure you will be glad to have her as a colleague.*

When Hannah returned to Wesleyan in 1963, the friendship between them deepened and Hannah began integrating Colie more closely into her circle; Colie soon counted both Hannah and Hannah's husband, Heinrich Blücher, among her close friends. The two women began to correspond more consistently about books, interpretations of literature and history, sharing observations on politics and the general state of the world, gossip about academia, along with details of their personal lives. Unfortunately, only Colie's side of the initial exchange remains in Hannah's archives:

> *Kierkegaard is my most unfavorite author of all authors of any age...[He] strikes me as just plain sick and rather emotionally scrofulous at that...Is existentialism a real thing? I find I don't know what anyone means by existential...A severe limitation, on campus.*
>
> *With all the desperate family conclaves and babysitting, I haven't done any work, read any books or thought any thoughts.*
>
> *I went to give a bad lecture at Vassar and there discovered that you, Hannah, were the object of praise for the courage of the Eich*-mann *articles...My lecture was on the failure of revolutions in 17th century Holland...It got me started on thinking about something*

> *that 'comes next' namely 17th century republicanism and its failures...The climate here for three days has been heavenly: the willows, whether weeping or plain, are saffron yellow and lovely; the weeping willows are like fountains of gold.*

By now, Colie was signing her letters to Hannah "Much love" or "Love from Posie."

Like almost everyone in literary New York in 1963, Colie followed the publication of Hannah's controversial series about the Eichmann trial in *The New Yorker*, and with great enthusiasm:

> *Well, another week, another* Eichmann *chapter. It is still very good: the only thing of course—this didn't happen to me until this one, the third—is that it is really difficult to read about such a subject while meandering through the jewelry, etc., ads in the back of the* New Yorker.

By mid-March the *Eichmann* essays were causing quite a stir, much more than Hannah had anticipated her thesis about the 'banality of evil' would generate, though both Heinrich and some colleagues had already sent warnings of the brewing crisis to her in Europe.

Arendt left for a much-needed vacation after the intense work on the Eichmann trial and *On Revolution.* Colie intended to travel to Europe later that spring to meet her. "No sure news yet on my flight, but

I will let you know. Then we have to figure on renting a little car and tooting around in it. Can you imagine?" But those plans were interrupted by Colie's acceptance of a new job at the University of Iowa's Comparative Literature Department. As she wrote Hannah on March 19, 1963:

> *I am going to go to Iowa: it is a good job. Full professorship, in both English literature and history, which is ideal...I feel a thousand years younger all of sudden, as if the albatross had gone off my neck and I could start to be a human being again instead of such a fake...The Iowa thing may ruin our summer plans. [S]han't get paid until September and have no dough.*

After Hannah returned from Europe, Colie spent a week with her in August 1963 before moving to Iowa. "It was a wonderful week. You were as always hideous about money. I have a thing too, but you must build up my ego by letting me pay! Important morale-builder." They visited together in December. But the drive back to Iowa that winter convinced Colie she'd moved too far from the east coast. "As you said all along," she wrote to Hannah the following March, "it is too damned far away. And winter, when one is frozen in, is not a good season to come to that realization in."

Colie felt herself to be a pariah, a fact she attributed in part to "growing up in a socialist and French household in the thirties, amidst men [her father included] who had spent four of the very worst years of their lives at the front." She was also a pariah in the sense of having a vagabonding kind of academic career, unusual for the times.

But though nearly a generation separated the two women in age, it mattered little to their friendship, except perhaps in one important regard: Colie appeared to rely more on Hannah for emotional support than the other way round.

During her first fall semester in Iowa, Colie managed to get some modest work done on her manuscript on the use of paradoxes in Renaissance literature and art. By spring, she felt more overwhelmed by her schedule. And, she confessed to Hannah in mid-March, 1964, another development interrupted her concentration on work:

> *I am falling in love, as usual, most inappropriately [to a married man], though a pretty wonderful person (naturally—my rule: never fall in love with anyone you don't like). This lends piquancy to the season, but also interferes with straight thinking, hard work, and all that.*

Another letter followed in April reporting Colie was busy again "refurbishing...old stuff, but at least the thing [her poetry] is functioning again. A relief: in all senses (I think, damn it, it has to do with LOVE. This offends me somehow)." She also invited Hannah to lecture "on a subject of your choice (preferably, if it still is preferable to you, on civil rights) in the autumn."

Hannah replied: "What I really would like to know about is 'Falling in Love'. I am constantly thinking about the poet problem...let's discuss it, but in person."

The occasion came in May 1964, when they met in Chicago, where Hannah then held an appointment at the University of Chicago's Committee on Social Thought. By then, the *Eichmann* controversy had become even more heated; Hannah felt the consequences personally. With the exception of Hans Morgenthau, most of the Chicago faculty shunned her. Hannah must have welcomed Colie's visit as additional relief in an otherwise stressful setting.

In advance of their May get together, Colie sent Hannah a short letter, which, in retrospect, proved an ironic commentary on the later course of Colie's life:

> *Am working like mad...[H]ave recomposed Locke and am bursting to do the whole thing, but PARADOX must come first. Am now on the horrible paradoxes of love. Then*

> *suicide (a natural progression, I frequently think).*

Such topics must have littered their conversation. While only fragments of their letters over the next year survive, they indicate Arendt began to worry for Colie's health, and did whatever she could to help her friend find much-needed stability in her life. Still, it was enough to give me insight into the complex roles Hannah assumed in her friendships with women, roles far more emotionally resonant than other portraits of Hannah as a cool, somewhat distanced observer of human behavior had ever rendered her.

Colie came to Chicago in spring 1965 to lecture as part of her application for a position there. The experience proved disappointing; she wrote to Hannah asking for any enlightenment as to what had happened. "I find myself thinking about it and puzzling it out, and feeling cross (God knows, at myself, as much as anything else, for thinking of it so gloriously, and then for being let down). But above all, curious." Hannah answered almost immediately. Unable to get any clear information, she speculated about why Colie had been rebuffed, cautioning Colie not to let the matter overwhelm her:

> *It still seems pretty clear to me that S [probably Leo Strauss] is the culprit—which is especially nasty as he had ample to time to*

> *protest before you even knew anything about it, and throughout this time was quite enthusiastic. Probably all calculated. Such things happen everywhere as we both know. Universities are like monasteries, full of intrigues. For S, it was probably a way, his way, of getting even with me for what? I have not the faintest idea but suspect for not having read his books. But Posie, please, I understand how unpleasant the whole business was and I couldn't be sorrier, but now forget it. Don't worry the little wound until it grows into something monstrous, which it is not.*

But the "little wound" did worry Colie. Adding to this, by 1966, Colie's three years in Iowa convinced her she needed something different.

The following summer, the tragic death of a colleague's young child, combined with the deterioration of her relationship with Curt Zimansky, alluded to two years before, made her feel all the more miserable about life in Iowa. "The summer has revealed that my feelings about Curt, though very deep, were not the sort that really wanted to share life as married people must." She'd been much more deeply affected by the child's death, she confessed to Hannah, than the loss of Curt; in some ways, she admitted, she must have contributed to the love affair's demise.

> *I think I told you: there was trouble brewing anyway, because I was at work and he was not, and probably never will be. You said, don't urge him. I did, though, whenever he expressed—it was fantasy—notions of writing this or that: and he did mind, because he knows he isn't going to do it.*

The next year Colie landed a visiting position at Yale, which was "very good. Very therapeutic," she told Hannah. And the summer after that, partly through Hannah's support, she won a fellowship to Oxford, giving her a year of research support, free from teaching and, most importantly, free from the depression she experienced at the thought of having to return to the Midwest.

Just before leaving for England in 1967, Colie wrote an enthusiastic letter to Hannah, thanking her for support and providing details of her upcoming trip, along with continuing a conversation about Locke generated by an essay Colie had written and sent to Hannah. She also seemed buoyed by steps she'd taken to improve her brother's health (he was an alcoholic), "stick[ing] him into a hospital to be dried up, first of all, then to be 'treated'...for the longest possible time...three months." As for the relationship with Zimansky, although it had apparently limped along, Colie reported "Curt" to be withholding of

> *what he thinks and feels, so though he does lovely things (like fix the doorbell and so forth) from dawn to dark, he keeps that part of him away... I nag, too: and have fallen foul of the worst of my habits...which is fatal. I'll not do that when I get back from Europe! Or I'll try not to...Love to you both, as usual. And see you soon, in Europe somehow.*

But what she didn't admit to Hannah until some months into the Oxford appointment was how she'd faced a serous health challenge and spent most of the summer recuperating from an operation before leaving for England. And then, meandering across accounts of her Yale experiences, her letter landed on the following announcement: "Also fell in love: I think for real. Certainly a real person. Unexpected, genuine grown-up man, for a change; not self-doubting intellectual of the sort I meet a lot, and certainly no parasite—the opposite." Although he was still married, Colie claimed there was

> *no chaos and counterclaims from the wife...If the arrangements go through, then life will alter, and it may be absolutely heavenly. If they don't then life will still be patchy, but okay. You once said, Hannah, about another thing, that things arranged themselves. This will, I think; it seems to be doing so.*

The man in question was Willis Lamb, a theoretical physicist who had won the Nobel Prize in 1955 and was twelve years older than Colie. "When possible, may I bring him around? He will be scared, but not scared, nice, that."

After berating Colie for not being more forthcoming about her health—"Please write about your health in detail...such things are important and one should know about them"—Hannah replied: "[Y]ou always can bring around whomever you wish. As for being scared, I am scared to death of theoretical physicists." And she closed the letter with Christmas and New Year's greetings, and a poem, an old German carol, she thought appropriate:

Es ist ein Ros entsprungen,
aus einer Wurzel zart,
wie uns die Alten sungen,
von Jesse war die Art
und hat ein Blümlein bracht
mitten im kalten Winter,
wohl zu der halben Nacht.

[Lo, how a rose e'er blooming,
From tender stem hath sprung.
Of Jesse's lineage coming,
As men of old have sung;
It came, a flow'ret bright,
Amid the cold of winter,

When half spent was the night.]

As it turns out, Willis Lamb's divorce did not proceed uneventfully. Despite difficulties, Colie said she felt happy—"and I want to record that"—and hopeful that, after the next year in Toronto, she and Willis would land in a place where they'd both have academic positions. "I mind being part of a package: would rather just be me, if that's possible...I'm more rigidly feminist than I had realized."

In the end, Willis remained at Yale and Colie was hired at Brown in 1969, where she held an endowed professorship and, in January 1972, became the first woman to chair an academic department there. Yet, a mere six months later, Colie was dead, the result of what published obituaries called a "boating accident" on an offshoot of the Connecticut River near the house she shared with her husband in Old Lyme.

In fact, her death was a suicide.

Lillian Bulwa, a colleague of Colie's, wrote to Hannah in Switzerland to inform her of Colie's death, enclosing the London *Times* obituary. Yet, Hannah sensed immediately the real circumstances of Colie's death:

> *[I]t was suicide, wasn't it?...Needless to say—*
> *I am more distressed than I know how to say.*
> *I had not heard from her in years; she must*

have been many times in New York without coming to see me.

Although Hannah claimed she hadn't heard from Colie "in years," in the Library of Congress I found two letters in her papers from Colie's time at Brown, written nearly two years apart—one in October of 1969, and the other in March of 1971. They reveal Colie struggling to make sense of a world gone awry, wanting to become excited again about teaching, but concerned her students seemed withdrawn "from political action, political life and—in some quarters—even from thinking about politics." And, she admitted, she worried she, too, was somehow avoiding "thinking about what is happening." Although Colie referred to public events, the passages could easily be read as a gloss on Colie's private life.

Had Hannah worried for her friend's stability or tried to reach her in any way? Having only recently experienced a major loss in her own life—Heinrich died in October 1970—it might have been more difficult for Hannah to perceive another's pain. And yet, when she heard about Colie's death, it was suicide that came immediately to mind.

"Yes, it was suicide," Bulwa wrote back to Hannah, "but, it seems to many of her friends, avoidable." Perhaps avoidable. But, for Hannah, not having been able to help her friend prevent such an end would now become one more fact to which she would have to reconcile.

These stories revealed a side of Hannah not usually captured in more traditional portraits. Yes, she was intimidating, judgmental, arrogant, and not easily moved from an opinion once formed. But she was also a woman of deep feeling, with an appreciation for the vagaries of the human heart. Those she allowed to come closest saw and came to depend upon that. Perhaps a little too much.

Considering my own closest friendships I began to comprehend the cost.

{ 11 }

Who Were We? What Has Become of Us?

Something is happening or has happened to our friendship, and I cannot think...I am being over-sensitive or imagining things.

Mary McCarthy to Hannah Arendt, September 9, 1974

For heaven's sake, Mary, stop it, please. *I say that of course for my own sake and because I love you, but I think I also may say it for your sake.*

Hannah Arendt to Mary McCarthy, September 12, 1974

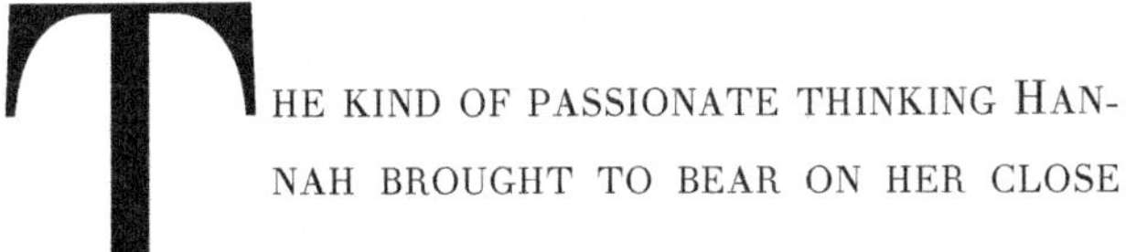

THE KIND OF PASSIONATE THINKING HANNAH BROUGHT TO BEAR ON HER CLOSE

Kathleen B. Jones

FRIENDSHIPS WITH WOMEN MADE PASSIONATE THINKING LOOK LIKE A WHOLE-BODIED, WHOLE-MINDED AND, YES, INEVITABLY DISAPPOINTING ENTERPRISE. Not for the less nimbly minded or the weak hearted.

Who were we when we were friends...

I could mark the changes in my own life by the comings and goings of best friends, the women with whom I have gotten as close as you can get without falling in love. Though, truth be told, sometimes I have fallen. When I felt my world splitting, these women helped bind it; I thought we'd always be friends. But I've traveled far from who I was then and that journey's cost me most of those friends in the process.

...and what has become of us?

My first best friend was Moira. She lived in a rambling green-shingled Victorian house next door to my grandparents' second-story apartment on Lenox Road in Brooklyn. In between us stood the vacant lot where Moira and I once built a makeshift fort out of bits of discarded lumber, metal and cloth. One day my grandfather nailed a wide piece of plywood for a platform in between the limbs of a tree and attached a ladder of wooden planks to the trunk and we climbed up to our very own world, carving our initials into the tree's branches, sharing secrets, pretending not to be lonely. I was eight when I met Moira. And when I saw her again, five summers ago in Florida, forty years after we'd lost touch, I was eight again and almost as giddy.

I'd just ended a twenty-year friendship. Surfing the Internet one night for old friends and acquaintances, I sent an email and found Moira. At the time, she was unemployed and living in Tampa. "Puts a roof over my head until I find another job," she'd said when I'd asked how she decided on Florida.

"I'll come see you in June," I told her.

In late June, I met Moira for dinner at a seafood restaurant near the harbor. Except for being inches shorter and a little heavier than I remembered, she looked almost the same as those Brooklyn days when we used to roll down the grassy hills outside Kings County Hospital, rolling and rolling, until we were too dizzy to stand.

"I was sitting on my grandparents' porch, putting on my new skates. You rolled by on yours. 'Hey, girlie,' you said, 'wanna play'? And that was it; after that we were best friends, Kathy and Moira." I slide into the semicircular booth, where the hostess has directed us.

"I said that? I said 'Hey Girlie'?" Moira laughs, slipping in next to me, her voice gravely from a pack-a-day habit she began not long after those rolling down the hill days. "I guess I was a smartass even then."

"You were pretty bold. Good thing, too, because if you hadn't been I might still be sitting on that porch."

"Hey, do you remember the haunted house on New York Avenue, the one near the library?" she asks, pulling a Marlboro out of her pack. "O.K. if I smoke?"

I nod and keep on talking. "You told me a witch lived in that house near the library and watched us behind her curtained window. And if we stopped too long in front of it, she'd grab us."

"You believed me?" Moira blows smoke over her shoulder and it curls toward the bay window. Small blue boats bob in the water. The sun ripples gold across the incoming tide and I follow its beacon back to that June Moira and I were fourteen, strolling the boardwalk in Atlantic City eating cinnamon doughnuts we'd bought hot off the bakery conveyor belt, that summer she dared me to walk sugar-lipped up to some boys she said were cute enough to ask them to join us on a ride called the Caterpillar, knowing how much I wanted to bounce into their arms, into romance, into some fairy tale of an escape out of Brooklyn.

"I believed everything, including your story about meeting Ringo and Paul while you were waiting in line to get into the Beatles concert at Shea Stadium."

"God, I was awful," she says, shaking her head. I notice her auburn hair would mostly fade to grey, like mine, if she didn't color it. "I never even went to that concert."

"Hey, do you remember the monkey bars in the Winthrop Street playground? I couldn't understand how you were able to balance running around on the top."

"I used to run around the top of the monkey bars?" Moira laughs, raising her cigarette to her lips, while her other hand shades her eyes. A sliver of sun slides across her freckled face. There are tears in her eyes. How habitual we once were to each other.

"Don't you remember?" I lean back in the booth and smile and look at the boats and the dock and think another year will go by and then another and each one will be added to the forty already separating us from the memory of how completely we knew each other once, at a certain age, in a certain time, and won't ever be able to again.

Who were we when we were friends and what has become of us?

In my first year in college I met tall Sharon with the ash blond hair falling around her face like the branches of a willow. Sharon, who spoke with surprising rapidity for a girl who grew up in Buffalo, lived a crazy life at Bensalem, an experimental, communal college into which she transferred our second year, and whose anarchist principles introduced me to the counterculture, the anti-war movement and casual sex with her brother.

Some years later, in graduate school, I befriended Regina. We had political science and a lot more in common. We were both parents of small, very active boys; we'd both studied modern dance with Paul Sanasardo; and we were both attached to men who were psychologists in need of treatment themselves.

The year Regina got cancer I was in a downward spiral. While she battled doctors in New York who wanted her to take the easy way out—just cut off the breast and be done with it—in California I was trying to decide whether to stay married to Mike. Sometimes it isn't watching someone close to you die but watching her succeed at staying alive that gives you the courage to change.

In my Kentucky period, my best friend was Susan. Diplomatic and caring, she saw me through the drama of Mike's affair, helped move Mike out of and back into our apartment and sent us all off with a bang to North Carolina. The relationship she forged with my son, Jed, was her greatest gift; a gift of the reciprocating kind, allowing her to discover wells of motherly feeling she never knew she had.

I still have a letter Susan wrote weeks after Ari was born. "Dear Jed," it reads, "I know you're excited about your new baby brother. You are going to be such a great big brother to him! It's a little scary, isn't it, being the big brother? You get sort of afraid that your

Mommy will be so busy with the baby she'll forget about you. That's how I felt when my little sister was born. But don't worry. Your Mommy loves you. She always will. She'll still take you to concerts and games. She just needs you to help her now. You'll do that, won't you? I know you will. Love, Susan."

The North Carolina years were a dry spell in terms of best friends and the time in my life when I needed them most, which perhaps explains their absence.

Then we moved to California and I met Liz.

For twenty years Liz and I were best friends and as long as it lasted I thought our friendship was based in openness and honesty and measured its power by the fact that whenever she and I were together we made ourselves and everyone else laugh. And we were together often.

The ability to be with friends who mattered to her whether or not Heinrich came along was something I'd so admired about Hannah and had long struggled to find for myself. Even though we were married and our friendship sometimes included our respective husbands it was easy for Liz and me, easier than I'd known possible, to find time for "us" alone.

But what made it seem so real also made it seem permanent and its ending even more awful to bear. Because, when it ended, it felt as if it took friendship itself in its wake.

Liz and I shared an office for several weeks before we even set eyes on each other. It was spring and we both had been recently hired to teach introductory courses in the same department at the university where I'd spend the next two and a half decades explaining the concept of gender. Based on a cursory glance at the objects prominently featured among the contents from her purse strewn on her desk—a brush with long blond hairs clumped in its bristles, a Clinique compact, a small mirror and a magenta-colored lip-liner pencil that looked as if it had been chewed not sharpened—I concluded I wouldn't like her.

One afternoon I let my class out early after a quiz and headed to the office to grade papers. I was surprised to see someone sitting at the desk near the window. The cascading wavy golden hair and lipsticked smile me told me it was Liz.

She was talking on the phone and scribbling notes in a large blue folio I recognized as *The New Yorker* diary. Holding up a finger to signal the conversation would end in a minute she gestured me in. I walked over to my corner of the room and deposited my books on a shelf. Arranging the papers I'd brought from class into a neat pile I selected one and pretended not to eavesdrop. Later I would learn how important a tool overhearing conversations could be, an indispensable device in the business of covering each other's ass.

"I thought I'd never get that one off the phone," she said, walking toward me with an outstretched hand. "You must be Kathleen; I'm Liz. Should we go for a coffee? I've got a few minutes before class and need some kind of pick-me-up after the day I've had."

"What part of New York are you from?"

"Grew up in Queens in a kind of UN international community," she laughed. "I thought I'd covered the accent."

"It's the way you said coffee. I'm from Brooklyn. And call me Kathy, please; my father's the only one so far who's ever gotten away with calling me Kathleen."

We became inseparable; so much so that if mutual friends or acquaintances happened to spot me at a party or a meeting without her the first question I'd be asked was "Where's Liz?" Neither of us did anything to dispel the notion that we were our sister's keeper. In time, taking care of each other turned out to be our Achilles heel.

In the early days of our friendship Liz lived in Del Mar with her husband in a condo they'd scraped enough money together to buy just when the market had started to climb. Years later they sold that condo at a good profit and moved into a large California ranch house with three bedrooms and four baths and a stone fireplace with a double hearth in a more pretentious, upscale community, the same house that fifteen years later Liz would be forced to sell to avoid foreclosure.

It was Liz who explained the facts of life to Jed one day after school when I was stuck at a meeting. She was driving him home in "Mickey Mouse," her black *Karmann Ghia*, and had left her overstuffed purse open near his seat on the floor.

"What's this?" Jed asked, pulling out a tampon from the overflowing bag.

"That's what women stick in their who-ha," Liz responded, as calmly as if she were explaining how to tie shoelaces, and continued to drive.

"What for?"

"Because of their periods. Women bleed once a month and use those things to stop the blood from leaking all over."

"Why do women bleed?"

"It's part of the process of making babies."

"Oh."

It occurs to me now, recounting this story, the child in the car couldn't have been Jed. He already was old enough to know about sex. It must have been Ari. And this memory slip reflects my relationship with Liz as much as the story itself. She was so completely a part of my life it seemed she had always been there. Had been; always would be.

In those days she was ready to handle any emergency and never considered any panic attack too small to be serious. The day Mike finally moved out I called Liz and she came over, reminding me, while pulling chairs into places vacated by the removal of half of the furniture, that all I was missing was some silly glass table she'd never liked anyway and we'd find just the right thing to replace it.

I could count on Liz to attend my children's school events if I was ever out of town at a conference. Not only would she appear in designer-perfect attire and greet all the teachers by name, introducing herself as my sons' godmother, she'd take photographs and send them along to me with a letter describing event highlights. And though she wasn't the first person to whom I confessed my love for Amy, I didn't have to; she already knew, accepting it without the need to ask me, like other friends have and still do, "How did that happen? What made you fall in love with a woman?"

We had a way of caring about each other that seemed entirely non-judgmental and free of the competition that sometimes beset women's relationships. I thought about Hannah's friendship with Mary McCarthy, the way one came to the aid of the other even if it meant participating in some charade, like when Hannah sent those postcards to Bowden Broadwater on Mary's behalf. But though she participated in the duplicity, Hannah still lectured Mary, chiding her to face the pattern of her life.

It was like that for a long time between Liz and me. But later, some dimension of that kind of judgment—not being judgmental, but being able to offer guidance when it's needed, hoping your friend will take it to heart or offer a good enough reason not to—became overshadowed by some tragically flawed affinity that contributed to its ultimate failure.

What bound us so terribly tightly was a shared history of crazy mothers. In Liz's case, hers walked out when Liz was in her early teens. She'd turn up now and then, on the telephone or in a letter, and then disappear again as quickly and completely as if she'd never come back.

When it became apparent her mother was nowhere to be found, Liz promptly lied about her age—she was sixteen at the time—to secure a job in a furniture store in Manhattan to help pay the rent on an apartment she shared with her boyfriend. "How old am I today?" she would ask me every year on her birthday. "I lied about my age for so long I can't remember."

Lying, it turns out, was her strong suit and in the beginning watching her manipulate situations only made her more beguiling because magnanimity was at the core of her deception. She didn't try to get away with something only for herself; the wider purpose of her mendacity was the greater good.

Liz had an eye for how to work a room and never came away empty-handed. With an uncanny ability to remember everyone's name the first time she met them, when she met them again she'd smile, shake hands and, with a light touch on the shoulder and a seductive wink—"So nice to see you again"—Liz would charm the person into thinking the only reason Liz had come to the party, the meeting, or whatever gathering she was attending, had been because she just knew that person would be there. She was especially effective with people who had a lot of money.

One year, decades before such strategies became all the rage at universities, Liz concocted a bold plan for raising money to endow a scholarship fund for women's studies students and called all the bigwig feminists she could think of to come to our university, give a lecture to an auditorium sized crowd for a small fee or none at all and, oh, by the way, Ms. Steinem wouldn't mind attending an invitation-only cocktail party for heavy hitter donors, would she? No Ms. Steinem wouldn't. Gloria Steinem, Bella Abzug, Shirley Chisholm, Angela Davis, one after the other they came, swelling the university coffers along with Liz's pride.

Hannah's description in Rahel Varnhagen of the pathway to parvenu-hood Rahel took resonated the more I thought about Liz:

> *Those who are resolutely determined to rise, to 'arrive,' must early accustom themselves to anticipating the stage they hope to attain by simulating voluntary appreciation; must early set their sights higher than blind obedience...must act as if they were performing freely, and as their own masters...By this fraud the pariah prepares society to accept his career as a parvenu.*[191]

In retrospect, this seemed to describe Liz's strategy perfectly.

The thing is, Liz told stories so well—"it's because of that one year I studied acting," she'd explain—that everyone believed her. I know I did; I wanted her to succeed. And I also wanted to be there to enjoy the fruits of her labors when she did. So I cheered her on. I did more than that; I helped cover her tracks.

At first the lies were small ones, the dog-ate-my-homework kind you might tell when you're buying time for something you've promised to do but either forgot or failed to complete because you'd been inadvertently distracted. "Yes, I mailed that check last week; I'm surprised you never got it. I can put another one in the mail now, if you'd like, but when you get the first one, would you mind returning it? I need to keep all my records straight." Or the sort that get you something for nothing. "I don't believe you can't find the reservation we made last week for dinner. And it's my friend's birthday! I'm sure you don't want me to disappoint her." Then we branched out.

In those days after my second divorce, I was struggling financially to support myself and two children on a lecturer's salary supplemented by meager child support and had to rent out the spare room in my house to a boarder to help cover expenses. Even with the extra income, near the end of the month I was often strapped for cash. Liz would come to the rescue. Whether or not she had anything left in her account, she'd write me a check. Depositing it would buy me a few days before my own account was fully depleted. By the time her check had bounced twice, I would have been paid and been able to cover the fees and pay her back. Of course, when she got into an equivalent jam, I was expected to bail her out, which I did.

Once a particular creditor had been harassing her for months and she'd held him off as long as she could with the usual stalls. When she couldn't buy any more time, she concocted a better scheme, one entailing fabrication of a medical doctor complete with appropriate license number and business stationary, whose correspondence documenting her debilitating illness would postpone the penultimate stage of collection before default. She placed the order, posing as the doctor's administrator, and we drove to the Jiffy Print a few days later to collect the box of linen water-marked paper with matching cream-colored envelopes. Liz composed an appropriately curt note, which she typed and I signed, and then mailed it to the creditor. The harassment stopped long enough for her to raise the necessary funds, buying things on another credit card, returning them for cash.

I suppose what allowed me to justify such questionable charades was my sense of the moral rectitude about helping the proverbial needy friend. And the fact that said friend always seemed to offer the same kind of boundless, unmitigated support to me.

One afternoon a few months after Mike and I separated I was in my university office when the phone rang. It was Mike and he was in a particularly belligerent mood. I hung up on him and the phone rang again. I said I had to go to class and hung up again. On and on it went like this—me unable not to answer the phone, him unable not to call—until the moment arrived for my class to begin.

I remember hearing the phone ringing down the hall as I entered a room filled with eager undergraduates prepared to grapple with Marx's theory of surplus value. But when I opened my mouth, nothing came out.

With the last ounce of self-control I could muster, I walked out of the classroom, went back to my office and called Liz.

"Get out of that office and away from that damn phone and come over here right away," she said. "When I see you, I'll know what to do."

I don't remember how I found my way across the campus to the seminar room where Liz told me she'd be waiting with another colleague but the minute she saw me standing at the door, she grabbed her bag, quietly left the room, having already made sure my classes were covered for the rest of the week, scooped me into her car and drove me to the therapist with whom she'd arranged an emergency appointment. And she did this in one seamless move.

It began to seem our friendship functioned best when one of us was in crisis until crisis became all there was. There is a steep price to being take care of and it's felt most acutely when being taken care of is taken away.

Sometimes I trace the beginning of her decline to the year Liz and Louis's marriage came apart. It was a shock, even to Liz. They were supposed to have moved back to New York together. Louis had landed an exciting new job and Liz already had several leads for a new career for herself. A few months before she was to head east with Louis the department gave a grand going away party for her and another colleague, who was taking a position at a small liberal arts college in the Midwest.

In pictures taken that day she's wearing a bright red vest and at the buttoned up neck of her crisply ironed white shirt I can see the delicately carved broach I knew she coveted and had purchased for her as a *bon voyage* present from the department. Head slightly cocked at an angle, her face beams with what looks like joy. But when I cover that smile with a small slip of paper I can see behind it; there is sadness pooling in her eyes. Had she had another of her famous premonitions? Did she know even then Louis would leave her?

Whether the decline began then, or a few years later, after Liz reinvented herself as the high-powered CEO of a local woman's health clinic, putting herself on the firing line in the national abortion debate to the point of keeping a bullet-proof vest in the trunk of her car, or, later still, after her daughter had been born and the man she was living with, the child's father, got fired on a sexual harassment charge, or whether it was shortly after Liz herself lost the last executive position she ever held and, when the settlement money ran out, stopped paying her bills and began to drink more and pop even more pills—whenever it began it should have been apparent where it would take us.

She'd disappeared on me once before. It was right after Louis left her and she hadn't yet figured out what to do next. My turn to come to her rescue. I drove up to her place on weekends, sometimes stopping at her favorite restaurant to get take-out lasagna and a bottle of good red wine. We'd hang out and gossip. If she was feeling "too fragile" to stay in the house we'd meet for a movie, the more escapist the better; one that offered several days respite from depression that year was *Black Widow*, whose tag line—"She mates and she kills"—had an appropriately sinister, retributive appeal.

Then one day she stopped answering the phone. I left one message, then another, then a dozen more until I gave up.

For months her silence continued until a mutual friend told me Liz had turned to her for help.

Years later, I deciphered the pattern—Liz had at least two friends on whom she could rely for almost anything. If she didn't call one of us, she'd contact the other. But just in case, waiting in the wings were a few more acquaintances, knowing little of her history. I'm convinced that, at first, she did this to protect those of us closest to her from exhaustion. It can't always have been so the right hand wouldn't know what the left hand was doing.

But in the end, Liz expanded her tribe to include circles of people who didn't even know other circles existed, making it less likely any one would counsel against another's coming to her aid. She was so successful at manufacturing saviors that on the day the chorus of us assembled in the admitting room of the rehab unit where she'd been taken we numbered so many the coordinator had to move us to a larger room, where we spent the ten minutes before Liz was brought in for the intervention overcoming our shock by introducing ourselves to one another.

We were supposed to go around the room, each one telling Liz how much she was loved and wanted her back and would help her if and only if she acknowledged she needed help. Her father said he would go first and the minute he opened his mouth Liz started to cry. She seemed genuinely upset.

I felt ashamed for having doubted her even for a second. Reprimanding myself, I held tight to what she said next—"Thank you all for your love. I feel loved and I want to get better"—clutching it like some security blanket of truth. We fell into each other's arms and she smiled and whispered she was sorry and I meant it when I said, "You know I would do anything for you. Anything." We laughed when she asked if that included getting her some perfume.

"You know what I like."

"Of course," I said, "I'll get you some Coco."

Oh, but how wide is the latitude of compassion, how long the longitude of denial? Not wide enough and too long. In the space of a deserted heart, such lines never meet.

By the time I visited her again she was complaining. She didn't belong here, she said; the place was filled with drunks and junkies. She had no patience for such stupidity. She wanted to leave.

"And Kath, what were you thinking when you bought me this shirt. It's not my color or style. It makes me look terribly fat and like some old maid," she said and held up a striped cotton sweatshirt I'd bought her as if it were some filthy rag I'd found in the garbage. "Return it. Get me something nicer."

> *There is nothing so reassuring as a person's listening to reason...For what blasts human relationships is never alienness or baseness or vanity but only the ignoring of this appeal...If the appeal fails, if the other refuses to listen to reason, there remains nothing human, only...eternal differentness and incomprehensible otherness...*[192]

Listening to Liz rationalize the disaster she'd made of her life, I wondered if she'd forgotten I knew who she was or that we'd played this game many times before. It dawned on me that Liz thought what had happened to her was the world's mistake and she was determined to prove the world wrong, not by taking up her life, but by inventing another.

> *'Real' meant to her the world of those who were socially acknowledged, the parvenus as well as the people of rank and name who represented something lasting and legitimate. This world, this society, this reality, had rejected her.*[193]

I took the shirt, shoved it into the shopping bag, walked out of the room, got into my car, drove home, and, except in dreams, didn't see her again for years.

The other night, I dreamt Liz and I were traveling together again to some unidentifiable land. It would be a long journey so we packed several large suitcases, filling them not only with our clothes, but also with other mementoes. There were baby's shoes, children's paintings, a lover's old shirt, family photos, unpaid bills and letters and documents, a few toys, a jumble of cloth and paper and plastic, an entire life's transcript, if you knew how to read it. For a while, we drove in a car and then parked on the side of the road and started to walk. At first we were alone and then hundreds joined us. Liz said she was tired so I agreed to carry the bags.

Before us loomed an enormous station, a transportation center from which thousands were departing.

But the closer we got the farther behind Liz fell until someone ran up to me to say Liz couldn't continue.

"She has to get back to the car; she forgot her medication. If she doesn't take it you know what will happen. Leave your bags here and take these to her," she said and handed me four empty shopping bags.

I turned toward the road and saw Liz in the distance ahead moving toward the car, but as I started walking the road turned into a staircase just like the one in that famous Escher painting and I couldn't tell if I was going up or down. Then I remembered the suitcases I'd left behind and asked a passing porter what would happen to my things. "They'll send them on without you and you'll have a few days to claim them; after that, they'll give them away."

Every now and then an old friend appeared on the stairs and I'd ask for help. "Can you take these to her?" But each one refused. I ran faster now, down a long corridor that led outside to a ramp and at the top of it I came to a dead end and through the thick glass wall blocking my path, I could see Liz, leaning against the car, calmly waiting, arranging her hair, as if nothing unusual had happened. I called to her, but she couldn't hear me

It's never easy to let go of someone you love, even if you know they're behaving erratically. It's especially hard if the person you love has been the child of an elusive mother, and it feels nearly impossible if you've had that same experience yourself. Because then, when you reach for that person, extend a caring hand and pull them out of the pit again, you are, at one and the same time, the hand extended and the one holding on for dear life. And somehow you know you're acting out some kind of repetition compulsion but you think, if I do this one more time, just this one more time, it will be the last. But of course it can't be the last time because the only way to mitigate fear of abandonment is to continue the cycle or overcome the fear.

A thick wall of glass, seeing but neither hearing nor being heard, not because I am indifferent—I can see her and that causes pain—but because I no longer can stand my appeals being ignored. And I wonder if that was how Hannah felt about Rosalie Colie.

I used to think death was the ultimate separation; that ghosts were spectral traces of the deceased. But the living can haunt us too.

Sometimes when I drive north on Interstate 5 in California I catch a glimpse of a golden Mercedes sedan ahead of me and as it exits near the Del Mar fairgrounds I imagine it's Liz and begin to follow her to her house for another evening of Chinese food and movies and gossip. We pass near the super market and she calls me on the mobile phone to remind me not to forget the cream for morning coffee and while I'm there why don't I get a bottle of her favorite Chardonnay, she's almost out. I can't see her car on the winding road ahead but I continue the few miles to the entrance of her subdivision and as soon as I turn the corner thin strands of smoke curling out of the chimney tell me she's already started a fire in the hearth to take the chill off the November night.

We finish the spare ribs off first and move onto the Singapore fried noodles and I ask her to save some for tomorrow because I like to eat them for breakfast. I'll spend the night; it's too late to drive home and, anyway, no one's home tonight. We stay awake late laughing at Letterman and then Liz pushes the automatic timer on the TV and falls asleep.

Then I remember she's gone. And so is the woman I was when I loved her.

The centrality of friendship as a theme in *Men in Dark Times* came through so strongly Mary McCarthy told Hannah she thought the book to be

> *very maternal...*mutterlich, *if that is a word. You've made me think a lot about the Germans and how you/they are different from us. It's the only work of yours I would call 'German,' and this may have something to do with the role friendship plays in it, workmanly friendship, of apprentices starting out*

> *with their bundle on a pole and doing a piece of the road together.*[194]

Hannah replied, saying she wasn't sure why McCarthy thought the book was 'German.' But she heartily embraced the idea of friendship that McCarthy had characterized: "And of course friendship in the sense of 'doing a piece of the road together'—as distinguished from intimacy. Thanks!"[195]

Doing a piece of the road together. Though coming from different backgrounds, this pair of friends engaged in shared dialogue about a common world for many years. Through face-to-face conversations and letters, their communication wandered across the terrain of politics, connecting them even when they were apart through commentaries about world events and local gossip, about wars and politics and love and family life. They crafted a friendship bond as powerful as any intimacy that might have happened between them had they been lovers.

There still is one close old friendship like this in my life.

> *My dearest friend: sometimes do you not wonder what happened to our young selves? Our dreams of social justice? The difficulty now to speak of this, social justice, our trip to Salvador: does it not look far, far away, as if it happened years and years ago?*

In a box of memorabilia stored in the attic are two plastic placemats, one green and one black. Atop each sprout monuments and buildings, the signature shapes of two famous skylines—New York (black) and Paris (green). A designer's tiny trademark is stamped in the corner. "*Taïr Mercier, Paris*" it reads. And the date: 1986, the year Françoise, who gave them to me, emigrated to the United States, the year before we met.

"Why this need to figure out a new founding of our friendship," she wrote to me after a time when I had caused her pain.

> *I was using these terms as well last summer. But then, I have been thinking: there cannot be any new founding: it has already had a foundation. Spring, 1987...the encounter. Foundations grew [out] of the thousands [of] hours we shared together, on the phone, at the movies, on the dance floor, traveling in other countries, cooking together, getting drunk together, hurting each other, finding solace in each other, taking some distance, meeting again... We do not change deeply... We lie less to ourselves...How to say the beauty of an encounter, its incredible richness, the luxury it represents in this world. We can cherish it as a souvenir or continue to enjoy it.*

Kathleen B. Jones

Politics brought us together, the politics of gender, and complicated our friendship right from the start. But politics and love for the world keeps it going.

It began in a classroom at a University we each had reached through individual, labyrinthine journeys. Along a trajectory shaped by the anti-Vietnam War and Women's Liberation movements of the 60s and 70s, mine led out of New York, through Kentucky and North Carolina and finally reached California; hers followed lines whose colonial origins she traced from French Indo-China to *Île de la Reunion* and then detoured through Algeria and into the French Women's Liberation Movement of early 70s Paris, until she arrived on that same Californian shore.

How bizarre our paths ever crossed.

What could ever constitute anything like a common world between a woman who grew up in Brooklyn, New York, in a working-class family, and a woman who grew up in Réunion Island, in a family of Communist activists, witnessing repression at an early age, leaving her island for Algeria and later, for France? The answer now strikes me as perfectly simple: the awareness that we share a common world comes from doing a piece of road together.

I decorated the wall of my old study with posters, including one announcing a conference on colonialism and gender; my name and hers are on the list of presenters. Strange to think now how those intertwined forces of colonialism and gender conditioned our meeting at all and yet not at all strange because our ongoing dialogue about those topics has sustained our friendship for nearly thirty years. In conference halls and classrooms, in restaurants and government buildings, and in different private and public landscapes around the world, passionate conversation has shaped this friendship, one "that makes political demands and preserves reference to the world."[196]

It strikes me how this description of friendship is too abstract. Because real passion grounds this kind of friendship, too. And there also was, there is, love and desire, a love for each other continuing to be in the world at all and a desire for that world to become better, the kind of love and desire driving us into numerous research projects about women's movements, past and present, and even taking us to dangerous places, both in the world outside and in the world between us.

Yes, we ate and drank together, cooked and danced together; we wrote and published essays and visited archives to document women's revolutionary struggles. And then, in summer 1991, we decided to travel to El Salvador to interview women working for women's rights. From there we intended to journey to Panama to interview others who had experienced American intervention first hand. We eventually got to Panama and completed those interviews, but in a decidedly different state of mind than we'd anticipated. Because, in Salvador, we'd been arrested and imprisoned for more than 36 hours, having naively—or could it have been unconsciously intentional?—taken the wrong road together at the wrong time.

This is not the time to tell the prison story or to narrate the complicated years of friendship that led up to it, but a time to report the friendship continuing after.

Who were we when we were friends and what has become of us?

In a picture of us taken the day after our release we are sitting together on a stone bench in San Salvador, a few miles away from the prison, wearing brightly colored skirts, mine a silk one Françoise made for me the summer before. Her arms encircle my waist. I have my right hand on top of her left, and her right hand rests atop them both. We are smiling. We are still alive.

I do not know then how far she will go to rescue me, until rescue me she does, away from my last Heidegger, and so far away from the woman I had been it soon begins to seem possible to her we will become more than the closest of friends, possible that the intimacy we once shared will become permanent, as much as anything in the peripatetic life she lives can be.

I do not think I felt the same way, though I must have let her think so.

I do not know then how much I will hurt her.

By the next summer, a year later, I am living with Amy and another year goes by before Françoise and I even touch on the subject of what has happened, and not happened, between us; about why I am with Amy and not with her. She is angry. And pained.

Do we need to find another foundation for our friendship?

She had first thought so; I had agreed.

We'd been corresponding all year about her research. Long, detailed letters about her new work on the politics of psychiatry and colonialism, about the unacknowledged consequences of the history of slavery in the history of France and the *Outre-mer*, France's far flung colonies.

> *After the first finds in the Archives about the 1848 period, I felt quite excited. The trials also appeared to be good material...But I have had difficulty with the part on political discourse...I get depressed when I see the effects of these years of Cold War rhetoric on people: a disgust for politics; a fear of being separated from France; and anti-Communism of the worst kind; totalitarian*

politics...And I will not even start with the machismo that reigns here.

And about my own research and the book on authority I had just published.

About your book: perhaps your feeling is close to [another writer's]: It is yours as long as you write it, less when it is thrown into the world...I am very glad it is out and very proud of you.

This kind of conversation is the sort we always have had, still have. But beneath the lines of her letters I read an almost inarticulate undertone of sadness and sense her displacement.

I have a strange feeling here," she writes about being back in her native island. It is one "of extreme familiarity and of not being at home. There are moments when I feel very comfortable, surrounded by familiar things. And then, at other times, I feel extremely alien. I do not feel at home."

She returns to the U.S. to finish writing. A year passes and a different kind of letter arrives.

Why this need to figure out a new founding of our friendship... it has already had a foundation...As Rilke wrote: 'We must accept our existence as much as we can; everything, even what is extraordinary must be possible. It is after all the only courage we are asked to assume: to be courageous when confronted

> *with what is most strange, incredible, inexplicable.' Why renounce the incredible chance of our encounter...its incredible richness, the luxury it represents in this world. We can...continue to enjoy it.*

And continue we have.

> *I am faxing to ask you something specific. You have to feel absolutely free to refuse to do it...A month ago, the newspaper* Temoinages *asked people to write letters of support [for my brother]. I was wondering...if you could write a letter of support...*

I wrote the letter. She reports on its impact:

> *Yesterday, Réunion called me. Very moved by your message...Yesterday...[my brother] on TV interview...thanked people who had shown solidarity, you among them....So,* voila, *wanted to let you know what has happened... (You were the only one in the US to respond....) Thank you again.*

Years pass. We see each other less frequently. But the connection sustains.

> *Hi My Dearest—Well, life shifts and one door closes and another opens...We are moving to Bristol, UK!! I thought you'd be excited about this news! I can hardly believe it, after 32 years of living here in CA, moving on!!! Easier to visit France from England,*

> n'est-ce pas*?? Are you still living in the same place in Paris? And what about François [her lover]? Meanwhile, the Republicans can't lie enough, pretending to feel the pain of ordinary people, while raking in billions for themselves. Whatever happened to the idea of real republicanism? It's a lost art. All my love, K.*

She writes back:

> *Apartment still there and François as well, but the girl is a nomad...something happened in my former life I suppose. Well, a little less than before and I even said no to a job at Brussels at European Parliament partly because I was tired of commuting and sleeping in foreign spaces...You know I turned 60 last January 23rd? Did not quite register...Went to Yunnan for Xmas: very interesting, very cold, very tiring, not a vacation more 'study'. Looking at next superpower: well nothing new, very poor and very rich people. Cannot wait to see you! Love, F.*

Volo ut sis. I want you to be. That phrase of Augustine's Hannah liked to quote best captures the heart of the closest friendships.

The trouble is we change, and only those friendships able to change along with us can last. I am lucky this one has survived.

No, not lucky. Grateful.

A year after Heinrich's death, Hannah traveled with McCarthy and her husband, Jim West, to Greece, including to many of the places Hannah had been with Heinrich on an earlier trip. "I know it was painful for you to revisit so many of the places you had been with Heinrich," McCarthy wrote to Hannah after returning to New York. "That has never happened to me, to repeat an experience, with different people, that I'd shared with someone now lost...I can only hope the good outweighed the disagreeable or discordant." And then, in an affectionate offering to her friend, McCarthy recounted a dream she'd had the night before:

> *I had a vivid dream about Heinrich. He had risen from the grave, literally a resurrection. He came out of his grave very merrily, dressed in outdoor clothes and wearing a little checked cap. It turned out that, though he'd been buried, he'd been alive all the time, just playing possum, it was a little joke he'd played on us. I was very much surprised and noticed that you weren't and said to myself, 'Hannah has known all along.'*[197]

Hannah replied indirectly to McCarthy's worries:

> *During the last months I have often thought of myself—free like a leaf in the wind...And all the time I also thought: Don't do anything*

*against this, that is the way it is, let no 'autocratic will' interfere...Let me come back once more to the 'leaf in the wind.' It is of course only half true. For there is, on the other hand, the whole weight of the past (*gravitas*). And what Hölderlin once said in a beautiful line:* 'Und vieles/Wie auf den Schultern eine/Last von Scheitern ist/Zu behalten—*And much/ as on your shoulders/ a burden of logs/ is to bear and keep.'—In short: remembrance.*

Much, much love. Yours, Hannah.[198]

{ 12 }

Love of the World

If we want to be at home on this earth, even at the price of being at home in this century, we must try to take part in the interminable dialogue with the essence of totalitarianism.

Hannah Arendt, *"Understanding and Politics"*

FOR A LONG TIME NOW, I'VE HAD HANNAH'S VOICE IN MY HEAD. A friend recently asked why I found her so compelling.

Because of her hesitations, her inconsistencies and reversals, I said. Earlier in my life, I wanted everything to fit. Now, I crave ambiguity. Give me the rough edges, the bags under the eyes and the wrinkles of truth.

Kathleen B. Jones

Because Hannah's writing makes me think. Not only what appears on the page, but also how it got there.

Because she wrote during and about life in dark times and still managed to fall in love with the world, in love with its durability, its persistence beyond any one individual's life.

Because her work unsettles just about every hallowed way to understand modern history and politics.

All these reasons are behind my motivation to direct a seminar for schoolteachers on the political theory of Hannah Arendt, as I have done every summer for the last six years.

We gather together on the campus of Bard College, where Hannah and her husband, Heinrich, are buried. The teachers come from all parts of the country and different backgrounds to spend five weeks of their summer vacation immersed in Hannah's essays and books.

Our discussions frequently become heated. Used to thinking of history in terms of causes and effects, the historians who join the seminar contest Hannah's theory of history as a process of "crystallization." Finding no ordinary linear narrative in her explanation of what or why Nazism happened in the middle of Europe in the 1940s, they are left with Hannah's unsettling assertion that the past did not have to turn out as it did.

Where is the comfort in that? And while the literary scholars appreciate her story-telling approach, they still puzzle over is usefulness as a window on the past.

Yet, regardless of discipline, as the "Antisemitism" section of *Origins* unfolds, I can feel the seminar scholars becoming increasingly agitated at Hannah's apparent refusal to read anyone's history as a genealogy of eternal victimhood, including the history of the Jewish people with whom she insistently belonged. One summer in particular, the agitation reached the boiling point.

We had begun, as usual, with Hannah's report on the Eichmann trial. As expected, her indictment of the leadership of the Jewish councils for cooperating with the Nazis by providing lists of names of those to deport struck a raw nerve among many. One participant, Ariel, had reacted angrily to that material. By the time she finished the first chapters of *Origins* her reaction had gone from hostility to rage.

"This is unbelievable; even in this book she's blaming Jews for doing what they had to do to survive. As a Jew, I am offended by her idea that Jews were in any way responsible for the creation of conditions that led to the *Shoah*."

"Do you think that's what she is saying?" I ask.

"Well, she's blaming the court Jews of the 17th and 18th centuries for supporting the monarchies that helped create nation-states and then later, in the 19th century, she attacks those Jews who sought to assimilate, blaming them for trying to survive in an unwelcoming environment. It sounds like she's holding them responsible for what happened later. What choice did they have? Given the social conditions she describes, how could she have expected Jews to behave differently? They did what they had to do to survive."

"Does that mean these Jews were not responsible for their actions?"

"For what they did then, sure they were responsible. But not for what happened later. The Nazis did that all by themselves. I mean, they convinced people there was a Jewish world conspiracy."

"But why was that idea so convincing?"

"Because Jews have been the brunt of hatred for millennia. We studied the history of anti-Semitism in Hebrew school."

"We studied a lot of things in Hebrew school," Bettina, another participant interjected. "Including how the Holocaust justified the establishment of the state of Israel as a Jewish state. But when I lived in Israel for several years I heard other sides of the story. So I guess Arendt's point about responsibility has made me question how this history has been and is being taught. What's been left out of the story?"

"The Holocaust was an attack on Jews. Isn't that enough to give Jews the right to a state? We have the right to protect ourselves from another extermination campaign," Ariel retorted.

"I don't disagree," Bettina explained. "But what kind of state? And at what price? We took land from other people, denied them rights to establish our own state."

"Before Jews settled the area, the desert was barren. We made the land productive."

"I heard that story in Hebrew school, too. Jews made the desert bloom. But what about the way of life of those who were already there?"

"Look, why are Jews always being held up to standards higher than the rest of the world. How about the United States? Didn't Americans do the same thing? Americans took the land from the Indians. So please explain why it's O.K. for Americans and not for the Jews. America is for the Americans and Israel is for the Jews. What's the difference?"

"Maybe there isn't much of a difference. I think that's what Arendt is saying. That the problem is the nation-state and how it uses different, I don't know, different categories like race or ethnicity or some other marker to keep some people out, to make them stateless. Look, remember how in *Eichmann* Arendt wrote that the real crime the Israeli court was confronted with was the extermination of the Jewish people and that was a crime against humanity perpetrated upon the body of the Jewish people?"

"Yes, I certainly do. And I got really mad at what she said next. That 'only the choice of victims, not the nature of the crime, could be derived from the long history of Jew-hatred and anti-Semitism.' Like attacking Jews, trying to wipe us all off the face of the earth, isn't enough of a crime."

"No," Bettina continued. "She's saying it's so serious a crime that everyone, not only Jews, but all of humanity should condemn it. The Jewish question isn't just a question for Jews."

"It's a question for Jews first. Because the rest of the world hasn't cared much about Jews except to use us and then try to make us disappear. That's why we have to defend ourselves. No one else will. Even Hannah Arendt said 'If you are attacked as a Jew you must defend yourself as a Jew.' That means we have to stand up for ourselves, as Jews."

"True. But we can't just be for ourselves; we also have to live among different peoples."

"Including people who want to destroy us? We have to survive first."

At this point I intervened, offering another citation from Hannah.

"Maybe there's a way to bring the two sides of this debate together. In a 1941 essay Arendt wrote, using Hillel's famous statement: 'As Jews, we want to fight for the freedom of the Jewish people, because "If I am not for me—who is for me?" As Europeans we want to fight for the freedom of Europe, because "If I am only for me—who am I?" ' "

"Well, that doesn't really solve the problem. After all, there are Jews who aren't European," responded Ariel.

"You know," another seminar commented, "what I've been wondering the whole time we've been reading Arendt, and now, even more, listening to this discussion: What is a Jew? A member of a religion or a race or...?"

"Well...that depends," Bettina responded. Ariel nodded in agreement. "Not just religion, because, I mean, I'm Jewish, but I'm not religious. But, I wouldn't agree that Jews are a race. That's what the Nazis said. The whole idea of race is a fiction."

"Race may be a fiction to you but it's a reality for me," one of the African-American seminar members pointed out. "I've been reading ahead in the section on Imperialism in this book and I'm furious. At one point I wanted to throw the book out the window. I mean, she has some nerve calling Africans 'savages.' That sounds pretty racist to me."

And so we dive back into *Origins* and the discussion opens into the wide range of thinking about race and racism that Hannah's theories always provoke.

In *The Origins of Totalitarianism*, her masterful analysis of the rise of Nazism, Hannah Arendt outlined the social and political factors she said drove "the Jewish people into the storm center of events" and made "the Jewish question and antisemitism...the catalytic agent...for the rise of the Nazi movement...for a World War of unparalleled ferocity, and finally for the emergence of the unprecedented crime of genocide in the midst of Occidental civilization."[199] That "this seemingly small and unimportant Jewish problem...had the dubious honor of setting the whole infernal machine in motion" was, in her words, an "outrage [to] our common sense."[200]

Despite the outrage, Hannah took seriously the fact that antisemitism formed the core of Nazi ideology and explained how its widespread acceptance set the stage for the Final Solution—the extermination of the Jew—to become the official purpose of Nazi policy. But she not only refused to accept the idea that the choice of victims was accidental, she also resisted explanations absolving the Jewish people of any responsibility for the development of those disastrous circumstances in which they found themselves in the middle of Europe in the 1930s.

To Hannah, the idea of "eternal antisemitism" as the unbroken continuity of the persecution of Jews beginning at the end of the Roman Empire and continuing into the twentieth century was a dangerous fallacy. "Comprehension," she wrote, "does not mean...deducing the unprecedented from precedents."[201] She thought interpreting the virulent political form of antisemitism at the core of Nazi ideology as if it were only a more modern variant of "eternal antisemitism" inherently negated "the significance of human behavior" and bore "a terrible resemblance to those modern practices and forms of government which, by means of arbitrary terror, liquidate the very possibility of human activity."[202] Instead, she argued, we must bear consciously the burden that the horrific events of the twentieth century placed on us and examine the behavior of both the perpetrators and their chosen victims in historical perspective.[203]

It's not so difficult to understand that perpetrators of murderous crimes had the choice to behave differently and should be held responsible for their actions. In fact, we are so used to accepting the reasoning that if someone's actions cause another harm the one doing the harming is fully responsible for the damage done we become reluctant to excuse the perpetrator simply because her life's circumstances gave her few options, and especially not just because everyone around her was behaving equally badly. What's harder to swallow is the idea that any actions or attitudes of the chosen victim might have contributed in some way to their initial selection for attack. So when anyone contests the victim's absolute innocence we are likely to recoil in horror and accuse the person of blaming the victim.

But when Hannah turned to Jewish history she found there "certain aspects of Jewish history and specifically Jewish functions during the last centuries" that, for her, contained "elementary clues to the growing hostility between certain groups of society and the Jews,"[204] clues she thought Jews had ignored or misread to their increasing peril.

> *What actually happened was that great parts of the Jewish people were at the same time threatened with physical extinction from without and dissolution from within. In this situation, Jews concerned with the survival of their people would, in a curious desperate misinterpretation, hit on the consoling idea that antisemitism, after all, might be an excellent means for keeping the people together, so that the assumption of eternal antisemitism would even imply an eternal guarantee of Jewish existence.*[205]

Not stopping at this biting observation, Hannah carried her indictment of the concept of "eternal antisemitism" further by holding Jews as least partly responsible for their own predicament:

> *The more surprising aspect of this explanation...is that is has been adopted by a great many unbiased historians and by an even greater number of Jews. It is this odd coincidence which makes the theory so very dangerous and confusing. Its escapist bias is in both instances the same: just as antisemites understandably desire to escape responsibility for their deeds, so Jews, attacked and on the defensive, even more understandably do not wish under any circumstances to discuss their share of responsibility.*[206]

To the question of why the Jews of all people were the target of such genocidal enmity the idea of eternal antisemitism offered the "question begging reply: Eternal hostility." Hannah would have none of it. "Modern anti-Semitism," she wrote, "must be seen in the more general framework of the development of the nation-state, and at the same time its source must be found in certain aspects of Jewish history and specifically Jewish functions during the last centuries."[207]

To put it bluntly, Hannah criticized the actions and inactions of specific groups of Jews in the centuries preceding the twentieth for contributing to the development of the constellation of events that crystallized in the rise of Nazism and the extermination of six million Jews. Was her theory, then, nothing more than a textbook case of blaming the victim?

Hannah's iconoclastic perspective on Jewish history not only put her at odds with almost every other study of Holocaust history, both in her time and ours, but also transformed her into *persona non grata* within the Jewish community itself. Small wonder, then, that she outraged people all over again when she reiterated her ideas about Jewish responsibility in *Eichmann in Jerusalem*, her report on the trial.

Why was it so important for her to judge the behavior of those who had been targeted as enemies of the Nazi state? Why couldn't she be satisfied with condemning the perpetrators of genocidal crimes? Didn't her after the fact moralizing reveal a fundamental insensitivity to Jewish suffering?

In *Eichmann* she criticized Jewish leaders for their role in providing the Nazis with lists of the names of Jews to be sent for deportation. And she did so in especially caustic prose.

> *[I]f the Jewish people had really been disorganized and leaderless, there would have been chaos and misery but the total number of victims would hardly have been between four and a half and six million... To a Jew, this role of the Jewish leaders in the destruction*

> *of their own people is undoubtedly the darkest chapter in the whole dark story.*[208]

Among other things, her opponents accused her of being wickedly arrogant and callously indifferent to the plight of the victims, whose hour to tell their stories to the world had finally come with the Jerusalem trial. Notable among them was her close personal friend, Gershom Sholem.

"In the Jewish tradition," Sholem wrote in a series of letters he exchanged with Hannah in 1963,

> *there is a concept, hard to define and yet concrete enough, which we know as* Ahabath Israel*: 'Love of the Jewish people'. In you, dear Hannah, as in so many intellectuals who came from the German left, I find little trace of this.*

In a word, he said, Hannah was "heartless."

"You are quite right," Hannah responded.

> *I am not moved by any 'love' of this sort, and for two reasons: I have never in my life 'loved' any people or collective—neither the German people, nor the French, nor the American, nor the working class or anything of that sort. I indeed love 'only' my friends and the only kind of love I know of and believe in is the love of persons. Secondly, this 'love of the Jews' would appear to me, since I am myself Jewish, as something rather suspect...I do not*

'love' the Jewish people, nor do I 'believe' in them; I merely belong to them as a matter of course, beyond dispute or argument.[209]

Many wondered how she, a Jew and escapee from a detention camp for Jews in Gurs, France, could be so hostile to her own people. She must be one of those self-hating Jews! Such inferences amounted to an attack on her person, Hannah herself once wryly observed in an interview following the *Eichmann* controversy. And to such an attack, she would offer no defense.

You do not love the Jewish people; you do not even believe in them. What kind of a Jew are you?

Hannah Arendt had been haunted by these questions long before *Eichmann in Jerusalem* brought them into the open. And because the answers she formulated to "the Jewish question" were often paradoxical her location in the pantheon of Jewish intellectuals has been considered by many to be tenuous at best. Gershom Sholem severed his friendship with Arendt over the *Eichmann* controversy. And, despite the fact that she personally escorted youth to Palestine in 1936, she is nowhere to be found among the righteous among nations honored at *Yad Vashem*, the Israeli memorial to the Holocaust.

"I merely belong to the Jewish people as a matter of course, beyond dispute or argument." But, of course, the dispute and the argument have persisted.

Exactly what does belonging to any people entail? The strange thing is, this is the same question Hannah Arendt formulated for herself, first, in her biography of Rahel Varnhagen, and continued to explore in a series of essays on Jewish history written in exile from Germany, which became the basis for her study of antisemitism in *The Origins of Totalitarianism.* And she carried that question into essays about Zionism and the establishment of the state of Israel in the 1940s, allowing it to resonate in the articles written for *The New Yorker,* which ultimately became the basis for *Eichmann in Jerusalem,* and even in essays and correspondence written in the later 1960s and early 1970s. In fact, it's no exaggeration to say that the Jewish question, the question that Hannah said the 1933 burning of the Reichstag transformed into a political question for her, remained the most enduring provocation in her life. The perplexing fact is how it also remained a question to which she gave no unequivocal and certainly no metaphysical answer.

Or is it so perplexing after all? It seems to me her refusal to settle the matter once and for all of what being or becoming a Jew meant was the only acceptable position she could take, given her background and life experiences.

Hannah Arendt was a secular Jew whose experience of being a Jew was conditioned by both her German and Prussian heritage. Many commentators, Ettinger among them, have made much of the tension they claimed Hannah experienced as a German Jew.

Having been exiled as a Jew from Germany, and surviving for many years as a stateless person, first in France and later in America before becoming a U.S. citizen in 1951, certainly shaped her identity. She once said she had learned from her mother to respond to being attacked as a Jew by defending herself as a Jew and she did this on every occasion she was vilified, whether by non-Jews or by her own people, by insisting on her Jewish identity. But she also called on others to do the same thing.

Her years as a stateless person forever shaped her understanding of nationalism. To Hannah, the rise of the modern nation-state, with its increasingly exclusionary idea of citizenship, defined as an attribute belonging to a "people" identified ethno-biologically, created the conditions displacing millions of people from one country after another and, without any reliable authority to guarantee their protection, deprived these now stateless persons of the most basic rights. The nation had conquered the state, Hannah wrote, transforming "the state from an instrument of law into an instrument of the nation" and giving "national interest...priority over law long before Hitler could pronounce 'right is what is good for the German people.'"[210] What factors had led to these conditions?

Hannah wrote that World War I and its aftermath "touched off a chain reaction in which we have been caught ever since and which nobody seems able to stop..."

> *Inflation destroyed the whole class of small property owners beyond hope for recovery...Unemployment...reached fabulous proportions...Civil wars...were...bloodier and more cruel than all their predecessors...[and] were followed by migrations of groups who...were welcomed nowhere and could be assimilated nowhere. Once they left their homelands they remained homeless, once they left their state they became stateless; once they were deprived of their human rights they were rightless, the scum of the earth.*[211]

After the war ended, "every political event added a new category to those who lived outside the pale of the law."[212]

Never in the majority in their resident countries, and with significant international ties, Hannah thought Jews were especially vulnerable to denationalization.

But she didn't consider the disaster of statelessness to be an exclusively Jewish problem, seeing it instead as a crisis likely to spread, engulfing ever increasing numbers of people now regarded as disposable.

She defined the problem of statelessness, emerging most extensively and catastrophically in Europe around the Jewish question, as a crisis confronting humanity as a whole. That events of the twentieth century had driven so many millions into a "barbed-wire labyrinth" demonstrated to Hannah that neither history nor nature could ever guarantee human rights to any person or group.

> *Humanity has in effect assumed the role formerly ascribed to nature or history...[and] in this context...the right to have rights, or the right of every individual to belong to humanity, should be guaranteed by humanity itself. It is by no means certain whether this is possible.*[213]

Recognizing "the right to have rights" must be undertaken as an uncertain project by humanity as a whole led Hannah to refuse to define her identity as exclusively Jewish. She was, she always insisted, a Jew and also a German, characteristics neither of which she considered to have been obliterated when she also become a "naturalized" American citizen. Yet, as much as she continued to identify with German culture and the

German language she didn't withhold criticism of Germany's own darkest chapters.

In 1959, on the occasion of her acceptance of the Lessing Prize, Arendt took the opportunity to remind her mostly German audience in the starkest of terms of who she was—a Jew expelled from Germany in a time out of joint—and what it meant to embrace that identity.

> *[F]or many years I considered the only adequate reply to the question, Who are you? to be: a Jew. That answer alone took into account the reality of persecution... When I use the word 'Jew' I do not mean to suggest any special kind of human being, as though the Jewish fate were either representative or a model for the fate of mankind...In saying, 'a Jew,' I did not even refer to a reality burdened or marked out for distinction by history. Rather, I was only acknowledging a political fact through which my being a member of this group outweighed all other questions of personal identity.*[214]

Asserting that she was a Jew was Hannah's political response to the situation at hand and reflected her principle: "in times of defamation and persecution...one can resist only in terms of the identity that is under attack."[215] So I read her insistence on her identity as a German, even after the war, as an equally political response, a specific resistance to any theory attempting to explain away the world's past by seeing Nazism as nothing more than the most recent and predictable evolution of German culture.

Still, Hannah's efforts to embrace all the facets of her background as a German and a Jew, and as a German Jew who had become an American, continue to befuddle and even anger many studying her life and her work.

Elżbieta Ettinger, for instance, never seemed to grasp fully the meaning of Arendt's complex identity. In the many interviews Ettinger conducted she struggled to come to terms with Arendt's "loyalty" to what Ettinger frequently and derogatorily defined as the "German *Geist.*" Becoming convinced that Hannah's being German fatefully compromised her Jewishness, time and again she pushed her Jewish interviewees toward a similar interpretation. Some, of course, insisted on an alternative interpretation.

Alfred Kazin told Ettinger he saw Hannah Arendt as "different from all the other German Jews I've known and I've known a great many." He thought Hannah wanted to bring Jewish life back on different more literary and spiritual principles. But, he added, she was understandably a little weary of Jewish history. "I think she was weary of being Jewish," Ettinger retorted.[216]

To Ettinger, and to many others today, what had happened in Germany came as no surprise. It was merely the natural evolution of German history, making the Nazi extermination project the logical and predictable result of a specifically German form of anti-Semitism, "built up through the centuries by scholars from Luther to Fichte, Herder, Kant, Hegel, Wagner. The Nazis entire vocabulary...was created by these philosophers—Hitler added only technology."[217]

"You know what I don't understand is why [Hannah Arendt] or anyone else would be so surprised by what the Nazis did," Ettinger told Holocaust historian Saul Friedlander. "Don't you think the Germans are capable of doing just about anything?"

"I'm sure that the Nazi regime reached the point which astounded everybody and that's what is the amazement that comes through...in the *Origins of Totalitarianism*," Friedlander replied.

Ettinger didn't agree; Nazism, she insisted, was distinctly German. And she regarded Hannah's insistent "Germanness" as much more than a simple factor shaping her Jewish identity. It represented a fundamental betrayal.

More recently, Deborah Lipstadt interpreted the significance of Hannah's background as a German Jew similarly. Acknowledging that "[*Eichmann in Jerusalem*] and the controversy it aroused put [the Eichmann] trial on the intellectual map," Lipstadt nonetheless attacked Hannah's interpretation of the Holocaust as a crime against humanity perpetrated on the body of the Jewish people and rejected this point of view. Instead, highlighting Hannah's "personal [German Jewish] disdain for Israel that bordered on anti-Semitism and racism,"[218] along with caricatures of Middle Eastern Jews found in Hannah's correspondence during the trial, Lipstadt considered Hannah's viewpoint that the Holocaust was an "unprecedented" event to be the misguided result of upper class German Jewish upbringing, which included a limited and distorted perspective on Jewish history.

> *Hannah Arendt...seemed unable to acknowledge that the Final Solution...was not a great rupture in all that had come before, but was the outcome of the anti-Semitism that was scripted culturally and theologically into the bedrock of European culture...[S]he was torn between her Jewish roots and the universalism of the intellectual world to which she was wedded.*[219]

In the end, Lipstadt concluded, Hannah constructed "a version of the Holocaust in which anti-Semitism played a decidedly minor role,"[220] an odd conclusion to reach, I thought, about someone who had spent most of her life tracking anti-Semitism's history in Europe, including the very specific role it played in the Final Solution.

Yet I have come to think Hannah's insistence on belonging to the Jewish people while refusing to be a "Jew in general" marks her distinctively political approach to the question of what identity means in general. If, to Hannah, being "Jewish" is neither simply a matter of birth, nor of religion, then it becomes a fact of political life, only one among many other possible ways to define the plurality of the human condition.

Being an exiled German Jew in the twentieth century gave Hannah a particular perspective: In an increasingly globalized world we have all become refugees, wandering far from some imagined promised land of our ancestors, searching for a new way to be at home in a world where we might connect with and live with others with whom we have no evident or common ties binding us together as a people, except the shared fact of having been born.

What we share is the capacity to act as if we belong together in the same world, approaching each other in the context of "prevailing world conditions at a given time." This means, as Hannah described in her Lessing speech,

> *in the case of a friendship between a German and a Jew under the conditions of the Third Reich it would scarcely have been a sign of*

> *humanness for the friends to have said: Are we not both human? It would have been mere evasion of reality and of the world common to both at that time...In keeping with a humanness that had not lost the solid ground of reality, a humanness in the midst of the reality of persecution, they would have had to say to each other: A German and a Jew, and friends.*[221]

To me, this passage is a gloss both on the types of friendship Hannah cherished and the kind of "friendship" she negotiated among her many complicated parts. "The promise of reconciliation," writes Daniel Maier-Katkin, "which is neither forgetfulness nor an averted glance, but a full-bodied recognition of the human condition, is that it preserves the possibility of love...and friendship, as Hannah understood, is the foundation of all humanity."[222]

Our shared human condition is one of plurality: we are each the same, that is human, in such a way that no one is the same as anyone who has ever lived, lives now, or will ever live. We are each the same in a unique way. And each of us is born, Hannah once wrote, for no particular reason or purpose, for no specific task except to interrupt life's ending by beginning something new.

Birth gives everyone the chance to take up life, to go somewhere new, to find a road not yet taken, leaving behind marks of who she has been. And with these marks of remembrance a life story can be told, making anyone's life matter through its telling. But because what a life's story means depends on others' responding to it, story-telling needs a public world, a world filled with others who make my own story matter maybe even more than it matters to me.

Without all those others, any life story would remain meaningless. It turns out we really do need others to see what we see, hear what we hear, touch what we touch, comprehending the truth with their own senses and in their own hearts. Without others' recognition, our lives don't make much sense.

Sometimes the fact that the world can exist without us, both before we are born and after we die, overwhelms. But being born into a world that already exists creates possibility. Because when something new comes into it every one already here gets the chance to live with the novel and the strange, to dwell, as a poet once said, in possibility. The trouble is that's never so easy to do. In fact, it can be pretty frightening. Too often, we corral the familiar, try to avoid the unanticipated, resist the unprecedented and out of the ordinary.

Two women helped me. One directed me to a room where I could undress, while the second waited outside. Now wrapped in a towel, I stood before a deep pool.

Was the water cold? But I thought better than to ask. Instead I began reciting the Hebrew prayers memorized during my months of study with the rabbi: *Barukh ata Adonai Eloheinu melekh haolam, asher kid'shanu b'mitzvotav v'tzivanu al hat'vila.* (Blessed are You, Lord, our God, King of the universe, who has sanctified us with His commandments and commanded us concerning immersion) And then I stepped into the pool and sunk deeper, slowly covering my naked self in the waters.

I felt myself sinking, becoming a child again. But what was strange was how, at the same time, I remained aware of my adult self watching that child. Helpless, witless, and utterly without knowledge, she was being held in the arms of her godmother before the baptismal font of her youth, but that long forgotten embrace was rocking the child to the rhythm of even more ancient sounds: the Hebrew blessing, *Shehecheyanu.* I held my breath, diving deeper still. *Baruch atah Adonai eloheinu melech ha'olam shecheyanu v'kiy'manu v'higyanu lazman hazeh.* (Blessed are You, our God, Creator of time and space, who has supported us, protected us, and brought us to this moment).

That day, following my immersion in the *mikvah*, I took the Hebrew name, *Yaffa.* And that same day, my older son bathed himself in the ritual bath and became *Jedidayah.* Together we joined the tribe of Israel. And my younger son, born a year after my conversion, became a member of that tribe through me.

I felt humbled becoming a Jew. And yet, like so many other Jews I know and have known, I consider myself a non-believer, though my hesitation, or more precisely, general resistance to religion makes me no less Jewish or spiritual. Being a Jew is something I have chosen to be.

But is it really so simple as that?

You do not love the Jewish people; you do not even believe in them. Then what kind of a Jew are you?

What kind of a Jew am I? I am *Yaffa*, daughter of lapsed Catholics, Geraldine and Edward, mother of Ari, Jew by birth and Jed, Jew by conversion, spouse of Amy, who affiliates with no religion, step-sister to Susan and June, who have taken their own spiritual paths, grandmother to Julia, soon to be Bat Mitzvah, along with her twin sisters, Natalie and Ava, (none of whom would be in this world without the technology of artificial insemination) and grandmother to Kellan and Tanner, sons of Ari and Meghan, who were married by a rabbi in a wine vineyard in Southern California and have baptized their children, awaiting further notice about their sons' own predilections. All of which is to say I am a not so unusual secular member of a wandering tribe of story-tellers whose polity, though grounded in remembrance, does not wish to be bound by blood or land and has not yet been founded.

A few years ago in London, I went to a National Theatre production of David Mamet's searing play, *Edmond.* As I waited for the theatre to open, I wandered around an exhibition of photographs of different European scenes called "Then (thirty years ago) and Now." Two sets of photographs captured my attention.

The first set depicted the Costa del Sol. Then, only a few scattered hotels interrupted the curve of sandy beach unfolding as wide and white as the eye could see. Then, it was the landscape one noticed. Now, littered with hotels and restaurants, the landscape looked cluttered. The built environment had eclipsed everything; only a lone tree common to both images remained of once naturally lush surroundings.

The second set was taken on a street corner in an older section of Stockholm. Between then and now, little in the physical landscape had changed, but in the photograph taken thirty years after the first, the graceful red brick building still standing on the same corner had become a mosque. Now, in the surrounding streets, walked women in headscarves and veils and bearded men returning from prayer.

Images of centers shifting and being shifted and of anxieties provoked by these changes occupied me as I found my seat in the darkening theatre.

Thirty years ago, I remembered standing on that same Spanish hillside. Twenty years ago I had walked those Stockholm streets. How disconcerting the unfamiliar can be. And then, onstage, the play began to enact the most extreme response possible to the kinds of changes those photographs invoked.

Edmond is the story of a successful white businessman bored with his life. He has learned from a fortuneteller that he is in the wrong place. So he leaves his wife and his home and sets out on a quest to discover where he belongs in the world. Soon after, he is attacked on the street and descends into a howling labyrinth of sexual and racial violence and retribution, an unbridled, stream-of-consciousness misanthropic rage at everyone and everything. As if he could reduce the world to himself, his behavior defies all logic, however perverse.

Edmond is homeless; he is lost. Only at the end of the play, in prison, does he begin to wonder if "every fear hides a wish." He has been afraid of everyone and wanted to destroy everything he'd come to fear. Behind this fear, he says, is his wish: not to be alone in the world. And now his wish has come true: Edmond is imprisoned for life in a cell with a black man.

"Do you think there is a Hell?" Edmond asks at the end of the play.

"I don't know," the Prisoner says.

"Do you think that we are there?" Edmond persists.

"I don't know, man."

And is there a place we go when we die, Edmond wonders.

"I don't know," the Prisoner says. "I would like to think so."

"I would too," says Edmond, and then kisses The Prisoner good night.

Overwhelmed by the play's violence it took a long while for that kiss to sink in. Then I began to think of it as a peculiar kind of political sign; I began to see the kiss as a provocative, revolutionary act.

Even in the prison we make of our lives it remains possible to start something new.

Do you really think that's possible?

Do you really imagine it's not?

I don't know; I would like to think so.

I would too.

No force of history or law of nature automatically prevents the worst or the best we can do from happening. The terrifying fact of being human is simply this: we are free to be and do whatever we can imagine. And that is both the curse and the blessing of our human condition.

It has taken me a long time to accept this. I spent most of my professional life explaining away the inhumanity of some—mostly men toward women—and the compliance of others, including myself, by pointing either to historical conditions, ignorance, or fate. But lately it's become harder for me to ignore what Hannah once said: no awful thing happens inevitably or because of the will of the gods but results from a failure to think.

Writing under the horizon of what she called the "society of the dying," the system of concentration camps where some people transformed others into "ghastly marionettes with human faces" reliably marching toward death, Hannah appalled her readers by saying that even under fascism freedom was possible. For the most part, she wrote, it was ordinary people who had done evil things to each other; when they were ordered to hurt others, they complied. They had become joiners, unable to think for themselves.

To her critics, Hannah sounded as if she expected the impossible to happen in a world that events beyond anyone's control had created. But she thought no automatically generated combination of conditions had inexorably led the majority of Germans and millions of others to comply with the terms of the Final Solution. In fact, the more horrible thought Hannah kept thinking was that the death camps were something that "should never have been allowed to happen."[223]

What made this thought more horrible was it meant that whatever debauchery the camps embodied, however dehumanizing they had been, what caused the depravity was neither the chance confluence of circumstances nor the predictable end of history's lock stepping march. Such awful events happened because some people acted horribly and the majority did nothing to stop them.

Hannah thought Nazism had shown the world something extraordinary—that we humans were capable of anything imaginable, which meant we really were free to be and to do whatever we wished.[224] If, in the shadow of the camps, the idea of freedom had become a merely abstract concept, to Hannah that signaled how successfully the camps changed what we like to call "human nature." Their murderous success included the horrifying effectiveness of a humanly designed system to exterminate all trace of human spontaneity from the earth.

I think Hannah would say the specter of extermination still haunts us. If, when someone administers control without thinking, whether against a whole people or only one person, we say "nothing can be done to stop it," then we act as if there is little to defeat our own march toward death. Not necessarily a physical death. But the death of thinking is a death nonetheless. Because if nothing stands in the way of life's movement from a beginning to some predictable end, then freedom is nothing more than a dream. And without the ability to feel "the shock of experience"[225] domination can become complete.

Hannah said that doing something or setting something in motion, beginning again, makes freedom identical with being born. Each of us "is a new beginning, begins...the world anew."[226] Being human means being able to create something new out of what already has happened. And she called this capacity for new beginnings politics.

To her, politics was hope's activation in an otherwise desperate present. It was hope brought to life because action signaled that what had already happened didn't have to continue to happen, and wouldn't unless we did nothing about it. And that was why, she said, spontaneity or the political birth of the possible has always been what dictators and ideologues try hardest to kill by ordering birth and controlling death and destroying the memory that anything unpredictable ever happened in between.

The trouble is, as Hannah well knew, this same irreversible and unpredictable character of action can also generate despair. Because what has already happened will continue to happen if we do nothing about it. And we would turn away from life in despair and hold freedom contemptible, she said, if it weren't for the fact that this isn't the end of the story.

We have come out of dark times. And even if now we have entered dark times again, whether in our private or public lives, we still have the capacity to tell stories. And if some suppress these stories, or try hard to make them disappear into "holes of oblivion" by erasing every record of "all deeds, good and evil...all traces" of what ordinary people have done, even under extraordinary circumstances, the consoling fact is that nothing human is ever that perfect.

> *There are simply too many people in the world to make oblivion possible. One...will always be left alive to tell the story...[and] the lesson of such stories is simple and within everyone's grasp. Politically speaking, it is that under conditions of terror most people will comply but some people will not...it did not happen everywhere. Humanly speaking, no more is required...for this planet to remain a place fit for human habitation.*[227]

One left alive to tell the story. Between reckless optimism and feckless despair, story-telling illuminates moments of release created by forgiving those who have harmed us and casts into relief the islands of security we generate by making and keeping promises. Stories help us remember to forgive, releasing each other from one deed's confinement; they also slow us down and remind us to promise to stop moving fast forward long enough to be at home in the world for a while.

That's why I want to remember that kiss.

In a dream I am attending a conference. The meetings are being held in a large hall. I walk down a long corridor to find the room where I am scheduled to read my paper. But at the end of the corridor I come upon two rooms each with a posted sign. One says "Creative Performance" and the other "Academic Presentation." To which do I go? Where do I belong? I move back and forth from one room to the other, unable to settle.

I have this dream when I begin writing this book. A year later, I leave the university.

In another dream I am visiting an old farm, my great-grandfather's farm in Connecticut. It is early morning. The earth is muddy from the waters of a river overflowing its banks, spilling down the slope toward the house. A barn with an attached corral stands in the near distance. I walk toward it. An old cow is asleep in its dung. I kick it and the animal turns into a lizard-like creature, an alligator, and slithers down a ramp into the deep, deep mud. An old man emerges from the barn. I notice another younger man lurking nearby. The property is littered with debris—old tires, broken furniture, bits of clothing, and dangling wires. The old man asks if I want to help clean up. I say yes. He begins to arrange the discarded things into a heap. I wander nearer the bottom of the slope, closer to the house, where the younger fellow has gone, and try to occupy him in helpful chores. He's edgy, angry, resistant. The old man calls to me. He's arranging old rusted toys—trucks, fire engines, and other miniature vehicles—in a red wagon. Do I want to keep these, he asks. Yes, of course, I say. He clears the area, making it orderly and clean. I can see a place to plant things, I say. We can grow food. The old man tells me he was homeless. Not exactly homeless, he corrects himself, but without purpose. He wants to help me plant, make things grow. And we set about preparing the cleared space together.

At first I think the dream is about my two ex-husbands. Only much later do I realize I am the two men in the dream, the older one who wants to accommodate the past and find a place in the present to grow, and the younger one who is intent on remaining angry and resistant to change.

I have this dream a few days before my fifty-fifth birthday, a week after my retirement from the university.

In a third dream, a year to the day before I completed this manuscript, I am standing with my first husband in a deep ravine. Above us, on either side, are the buildings and lights of a city. The place reminds me of underneath the boardwalk in Coney Island, except it's deeper, more angular, like the southern California aqueduct. Concrete walls rise to the city above.

I am on a long trip. We have arranged to meet. As we talk old feelings return, memories of love. He hugs me, tells me he loves me. I am traveling, I say; I have to go. He knows that, he says; he doesn't want me to stay.

Ahead of me lies a narrow tunnel. To get where I am going I know I must walk through it. At first, I hesitate. Then a voice says, It's O.K.; no one is in there to hurt you. But it's dark; there are no lights and I am afraid. Suddenly a woman with a young child comes up to the entrance. She is carrying a suitcase and a tall walking stick. I've decided to go through the tunnel and am relieved we'll be traveling together. I help her into the cramped space and take the walking stick.

Ahead are several pathways, but I seem to know which one to take. I walk faster. Go ahead, says the woman with the child, we'll catch up with you. Soon I come upon an underground city filled with people and many shops and houses. I don't stop.

After several more turns in the road, I see a bright light and can hear the ocean. I am near the end. I leave the stick by the tunnel's opening and walk into my home. And there I find Amy waiting.

Kathleen B. Jones

In the end, all I remember is love.
Sustained and sustaining.
Enduring.
Love.

Notes

[1] *Between Past and Future (BPF)*, (New York: Viking Press, 1969), 3.

[2] *Rahel Varnhagen: The Life of a Jewess (RV)*, First Complete Edition, ed. Liliane Weissberg, (Baltimore and Chicago: Johns Hopkins University Press, 1987), 83.

[3] Hannah Arendt, *The Human Condition (HC)*, (Chicago: The University of Chicago Press), 192.

[4] *HC*, 8.

[5] Hannah Arendt, *Men in Dark Times (MDT)*, (New York: Harcourt Brace & Company, 1968), 20.

[6] *MDT*, 21.

[7] *MDT*, 22.

[8] *Hannah Arendt and Martin Heidegger: Letters, 1925-1975*, *(HA/MH)* ed. Ursula Ludz, (New York: Harcourt, 2004), 50.

[9] *The Jew as Pariah*, ed. Ron Feldman, (New York: Grove Press, 1978), 76-7.

[10] "'What Remains? The Language Remains': A Conversation with Günter Gaus," in *Hannah Arendt, Essays in Understanding, 1930-54 (EU)*, ed. Jerome Kohn, (New York: Harcourt Brace, 1994, p. 4-5.

[11] *EU*, p. 5.

[12] Sheila Isenberg, *A Hero of Our Own: The Story of Varian Fry*, (New York: Random House, 2001).

[13] "Personal Responsibility Under Dictatorship," in Hannah Arendt, *Responsibility and Judgment (RJ)*, ed. Jerome Kohn, (New York: Schocken Books, 2003), 19.

[14] *RV*, 85.

[15] *EU*, 12.

[16] *RV*, 248.

[17] *Correspondence: Hannah Arendt, Karl Jaspers, 1926-1969 (HA/KJ)*, eds. Lotte Kohler and Hans Saner, (New York: Harcourt Brace, 1992), 16.

[18] *HA/KJ*, 17-18.

[19] *HA/KJ*, 18-19.

[20] *HA/KJ*, 19.

[21] *HA/KJ*, 22.

[22] *HA/KJ*, 23-24.

[23] *HA/KJ*, 25.

[24] *HA/KJ*, 29.

[25] *HA/KJ*, 31.

[26] *HA/KJ*, 36.

[27] "The Jew as Pariah: A Hidden Tradition," in Hannah Arendt, *The Jewish Writings (JW)*, eds. Jerome Kohn and Ron Feldman, (New York: Schocken Books, 2007), 297.

[28] *Ibid.*

[29] I am indebted to Liliane Weissberg's wonderful introduction to her edition of *Rahel Varnhagen* for the inspiration behind "slipping into her skin." Weissberg, op. cit, 5. It helped clarify my own interpretation of

Arendt's story telling as a "structured montage." Ibid., 50.

[30] *I Could Tell You Stories*, (New York: W. W. Norton, 2000), 27.

[31] *RV*, 103.

[32] *Love and St. Augustine (L&StA)*, eds. Joanna Vecchiarelli Scott and Judith Chelius Stark, (Chicago: University of Chicago Press, 1996), 100, 102, 108.

[33] *All About Love: New Visions*, (New York: William Morrow, 2001), 76.

[34] *Ibid*, 136.

[35] *Elżbieta Ettinger Papers, 1922-2001 (EEP)*; Correspondence with Helen Wolff, 1991-92, MC 579, folder 26.27. Schlesinger Library, Radcliffe Institute, Harvard University, Cambridge, Mass.

[36] "Woman in Dark Times," *New York Review of Books (NYRB)*, June 24, 1982.

[37] *NYRB*, October 21, 1982.

[38] *Ibid.*

[39] *EEP*; Interview with Alfred Kazin, March 27, 1990, MC 579, folder 20.11. Schlesinger Library, Radcliffe Institute, Harvard University, Cambridge, Mass.

[40] *EEP*; Research Notebook, MC 579, folder 21.1. Schlesinger Library, Radcliffe Institute, Harvard University, Cambridge, Mass.

[41] *The Beginning of the Journey*, (New York: Harcourt Brace, 1993), 147.

[42] *EEP*; Interview with Diane Trilling, March, 1990, MC 579, folder 20.11. Schlesinger Library, Radcliffe Institute, Harvard University, Cambridge, Mass.
[43] *EEP*; Interview with Irving Howe, March 31, 1990, MC 579, folder 20.11. Schlesinger Library, Radcliffe Institute, Harvard University, Cambridge, Mass.
[44] *Ibid.*
[45] *A Lifetime Burning in Every Moment: From the Journals of Alfred Kazin*, (New York: Harper Collins, 1996), 106.
[46] *EEP*; Interview with Pearl and Daniel Bell, Jan. 2, 1990, MC 579, folder 20.11. Schlesinger Library, Radcliffe Institute, Harvard University, Cambridge, Mass. See also Kazin's journal entry, January 18, 1964.
[47] *New York Jew*, (New York: Vintage Books, 1979), 299.
[48] *EEP*; Interview with Alfred Kazin, March 27, 1990, MC 579, folder 20.11. Schlesinger Library, Radcliffe Institute, Harvard University, Cambridge, Mass.
[49] *When Men Were the Only Models We Had: My Teachers, Barzin, Fadiman, Trilling*, (Philadelphia: University of Pennsylvania Press, 2002), 7.
[50] Elisabeth Young-Bruehl, *Hannah Arendt: For Love of the World*, (New Haven: Yale University Press, 1982), 272.
[51] *EEP*; Interview with Michael Denneny, December 26, 1992, MC 579, folder 20.12. Schlesinger Library,

Radcliffe Institute, Harvard University, Cambridge, Mass.

[52] *Ibid.*

[53] *EEP*; Correspondence with Helen Wolff, 1991-92, MC 579, folder 26.27. Schlesinger Library, Radcliffe Institute, Harvard University, Cambridge, Mass.

[54] *JW*, 466.

[55] *EEP*; Interview with Melvyn A. Hill, January 1, 1993, MC 579, folder 20.13. Schlesinger Library, Radcliffe Institute, Harvard University, Cambridge, Mass.

[56] *Ibid.*

[57] *Ibid.*

[58] *EEP*; Melvyn A. Hill to Elżbieta Ettinger, April 23, 1993, MC 579, folder 17.13. Schlesinger Library, Radcliffe Institute, Harvard University, Cambridge, Mass.

[59] *EEP*; Melvyn A. Hill to Elżbieta Ettinger, April 25, 1993, MC 579, folder 17.13. Schlesinger Library, Radcliffe Institute, Harvard University, Cambridge, Mass.

[60] *HA/KJ*, 457.

[61] *EEP*; Interview with Mary McCarthy, June 25-26, 1988. MC 579, folder 17.13. Schlesinger Library, Radcliffe Institute, Harvard University, Cambridge, Mass.

[62] *Ibid.*

[63] *EEP*, Correspondence with Helen Wolff, 1991-92, MC 579, folder 26.27. Schlesinger Library, Radcliffe Institute, Harvard University, Cambridge, Mass.

[64] *Ibid.*

[65] *Ibid.*

[66] *EEP*; Interview with Lotte Kohler, June 19, 1990, MC 579, folder 20.12. Schlesinger Library, Radcliffe Institute, Harvard University, Cambridge, Mass.

[67] *Within Four Walls: The Correspondence Between Hannah Arendt and Heinrich Blücher 1936-1968 (WFW)*, ed. Lotte Kohler, (New York: Harcourt, 1996), 41.

[68] *Between Friends: The Correspondence of Hannah Arendt and Mary McCarthy, 1949-1975 (BF)*, (London: Secher & Warburg, 1975), 75.

[69] *Ibid.*, 78-9.

[70] Special Collections & Archives, Olin Library, Wesleyan University, Middletown, CT., *Elisabeth Young-Bruehl Papers*, Box 4, Interview Notes, Interview with Anne Weil, July 3 [n.d.], 2.

[71] *Ibid.*

[72] *WFW*, p. 201.

[73] *EEP*; Interview with Lotte Klenbort, May 23, 1993 MC 579, folder 20.13. Schlesinger Library, Radcliffe Institute, Harvard University, Cambridge, Mass.

[74] *EEP*; Interview notes, Interview with Lotte Kohler, March 25, April 1, 1990, MC 579, folder 20.11. Schlesinger Library, Radcliffe Institute, Harvard University, Cambridge, Mass.

[75] *EEP*; Interview with Lotte Kohler, June 19, 1990, MC 579, folder 20.12 and 20.11. Schlesinger Library,

Radcliffe Institute, Harvard University, Cambridge, Mass.

[76] *BF*, 269.

[77] *Ibid.*, 271-2.

[78] *EEP*; Interview with Michael Denneny, December 26, 1992, MC 579, folder 20.12. Schlesinger Library, Radcliffe Institute, Harvard University, Cambridge, Mass.

[79] *EEP*; Interview with Melvyn A. Hill, January 1, 1993, MC 579, folder 20.13. Schlesinger Library, Radcliffe Institute, Harvard University, Cambridge, Mass.

[80] Daniel Mendelsohn, *The Elusive Embrace*, (New York: Vintage, 1999), 65.

[81] *RV*, 141.

[82] Mendelsohn, *op. cit.*, 73-4.

[83] *RV*, 246.

[84] *Ibid.*, 245.

[85] *Ibid.*, 157.

[86] *Ibid.*, 164.

[87] *Ibid.*, 159.

[88] *Ibid.* 175.

[89] *HC*, 186, emphasis in original.

[90] *BF*, 168.

[91] Hannah Arendt, "Some Questions of Moral Philosophy," in *RJ*, 97.

[92] *Eichmann in Jerusalem (EiJ)*, (New York: Viking Penguin, 1963), 252.

[93] *Ibid.*, 276.

[94] "Some Questions of Moral Philosophy," in *RJ*, 50.

[95] *EiJ*, 125-6, emphasis added.

[96] "Some Questions of Moral Philosophy," in *RJ*, 50.

[97] *Ibid.*

[98] *Ibid.*, 56.

[99] *EiJ*, 18.

[100] Karl Plank, "Thomas Merton and Hannah Arendt: Contemplation after Eichmann," *The Merton Annual*, 1990, vol. 3: 132.

[101] *HC*, p. 246.

[102] *HC*, p. 246, 247.

[103] Hannah Arendt, *The Origins of Totalitarianism (OT)*, (New York: Schocken Books, 2004), 7.

[104] *Ibid.*, 627.

[105] *Ibid.*, 630.

[106] *Ibid.*

[107] *HC*, 9.

[108] *Ibid.*, 11.

[109] *OT*, 631.

[110] *L&StA*, 51-2.

[111] *MDT*, 97.

[112] Ludwig Bemelmans, *Madeline*, (New York: Simon and Schuster, 1939).

[113] *MDT*, 109.

[114] *HC*, 71, 72.

[115] Hannah Arendt, *On Revolution (OR)*, (New York: Viking Compass, 1965), 84.
[116] *MDT*, 109.
[117] *OT*, 456, 453, 455.
[118] *The Mother Knot*, (New York: Random House, 2004), 74.
[119] Hannah Arendt, "Introduction into Politics," in *The Promise of Politics (PP)*, ed. Jerome Kohn, (New York: Schocken Books, 2005), 129.
[120] Arendt, Hannah---Correspondence---Beerwald, Eva (stepsister)---1938, 1948-1975, *Hannah Arendt Papers*, Box 1, Manuscript Division, Library of Congress, Washington, D.C.
[121] *WFW*, 92.
[122] *Ibid.*
[123] *Ibid.*, 93.
[124] *Ibid.*
[125] *Harrison, op. cit.*, 76-7.
[126] *Ibid.*, 79, 82.
[127] *HC*, 168.
[128] *A Natural History of the Senses*, (New York: Vintage, 1991), 96.
[129] Hannah Arendt, *The Life of the Mind*, (New York: Harcourt Brace, 1978), "Thinking," 133.
[130] Abstract of Elżbieta Ettinger Biography, http://oasis.lib.harvard.edu/oasis/deliver/~sch01225. Accessed May 30, 2012.

---

[131] *EEP*; Letter of Elżbieta Ettinger to Melvyn Hill, March 3, 1993, MC 579, folder 17.13. Schlesinger Library, Radcliffe Institute, Harvard University, Cambridge, Mass.
[132] *EEP*; Fellowship Proposal to the National Endowment for the Humanities, 1993-95. MC 579, folder 20.7. Schlesinger Library, Radcliffe Institute, Harvard University, Cambridge, Mass.
[133] *Ibid.*
[134] *EEP*; Letter of Elżbieta Ettinger to Melvyn Hill, March 16, 1993, MC 579, folder 17.13. Schlesinger Library, Radcliffe Institute, Harvard University, Cambridge, Mass.
[135] *EEP*; Letter of Elżbieta Ettinger to Mary McCarthy, May 21, 1988, MC 579, folder 26.1. Schlesinger Library, Radcliffe Institute, Harvard University, Cambridge, Mass.
[136] *EEP*; Interview with Mary McCarthy, June 25-26, 1988, MC 579, folder 26.1. Schlesinger Library, Radcliffe Institute, Harvard University, Cambridge, Mass.
[137] Elżbieta Ettinger, *Hannah Arendt/Martin Heidegger*, (New Haven: Yale University Press, 1995), 22.
[138] *Ibid.*, 23-4.
[139] *Ibid.*, 15.
[140] *Ibid.*, 10.

[141] *EEP*; Interview with David Jaroff, Jan. 13, 1991, MC 579, folder 20.14. Schlesinger Library, Radcliffe Institute, Harvard University, Cambridge, Mass.

[142] *EEP*; Correspondence with Saul Bellow, March 14, 1998, MC 579, folder 17.8. Schlesinger Library, Radcliffe Institute, Harvard University, Cambridge, Mass.

[143] *HA/MH*, 3.

[144] *Ibid.*, 78.

[145] *Ibid.*, 4.

[146] *Ibid.*, 11-12.

[147] *Ibid.*, 29.

[148] *Ibid.*, 16-17.

[149] *Ibid.*, 31.

[150] *Ibid.*, 25-26.

[151] *Ibid.*, 31.

[152] *Ibid.*, 34-35.

[153] *Ibid.*, 50-51.

[154] *MDT*, 27.

[155] *Ibid.*, 29.

[156] Arendt, in *LM*, "Willing," 14.

[157] *RJ*, 94.

[158] *L&StA*, 75.

[159] *MDT*, 21.

[160] Correspondence, Universities and Colleges, 1947-1975, n.d.---City University of New York, New York, N.Y., *Hannah Arendt Papers*, Box 36, Manuscript Division, Library of Congress, Washington, D.C.

---

[161] Courses---New School for Social Research, New York, N.Y.---"Philosophy and Politics: What Is Political Philosophy?" lectures and seminar---1969 (1 of 2 folders), *Hannah Arendt Papers*, Box 58, Manuscript Division, Library of Congress, Washington, D.C.

[162] *EEP*; Correspondence with Helen Wolff, 1991-92, MC 579, folder 26.27. Schlesinger Library, Radcliffe Institute, Harvard University, Cambridge, Mass.

[163] *Op. cit.*, 305-6.

[164] *EEP*; Interview with Alfred Kazin, March 27, 1990, MC 579, folder 20.11. Schlesinger Library, Radcliffe Institute, Harvard University, Cambridge, Mass.

[165] Paraphrased from excerpts in *WFW* and *BF*.

[166] *EEP*; Interview with Mary McCarthy, June 25-26, 1988. MC 579, folder 17.13. Schlesinger Library, Radcliffe Institute, Harvard University, Cambridge, Mass.

[167] *MDT*, 24.

[168] *EEP*; Interview with Mary McCarthy, June 25-26, 1988. MC 579, folder 17.13. Schlesinger Library, Radcliffe Institute, Harvard University, Cambridge, Mass.

[169] "Introduction", *The Friend Who Got Away: Twenty Women's True-Life Tales of Friendships that Blew Up, Burned Out, or Faded Away*, eds. Jenny Offill and Elissa Schapell, (New York: Broadway Books, 2005), xviii-xix.

[170] William Abrahams quoted in Frances Kiernan, *Seeing Mary Plain: A Life of Mary McCarthy*, (New York: W.W. Norton, 2000), 270.
[171] *Ibid.*, 81.
[172] *Ibid.*, 305.
[173] *BF*, 1.
[174] *Ibid.*, 149.
[175] *Ibid.*, 145.
[176] *Seeing Mary Plain*, 353.
[177] *BF*, 211.
[178] *EEP*; Interview with Mary McCarthy, June 25-26, 1988. MC 579, folder 17.13. Schlesinger Library, Radcliffe Institute, Harvard University, Cambridge, Mass.
[179] *BF*, 46-7.
[180] *Ibid.*, 49-50.
[181] *Ibid.*, 103-4.
[182] *EEP*; Manuscript Drafts, 2000. MC 579, folder 19.2. Schlesinger Library, Radcliffe Institute, Harvard University, Cambridge, Mass.
[183] Correspondence, General, 1938-1976, n.d.---Fränkel, Hilde---1949-1950, Feb 10, 1950, *Hannah Arendt Papers*, Box 12, Manuscript Division, Library of Congress, Washington, D.C.
[184] *Ibid.*, February 14, 1950.
[185] *Ibid.* January 8, 1950.
[186] *Ibid.* December 7, 1949.
[187] *Ibid.*, March 2, 1950.

[188] *WFW*, 173.

[189] *Ibid.*, 181.

[190] This excerpt and all those that follow from the Colie/Arendt correspondence are from the following source: General, 1938-1976, n.d.---Colie, Rosalie Littell---1962-1972, *Hannah Arendt Papers*, Box 12, Manuscript Division, Library of Congress, Washington, D.C.

[191] *RV*, 199.

[192] *RV*, 153.

[193] *Ibid.*, 177.

[194] *BF*, 224.

[195] *Ibid.*, 232.

[196] *MDT*, 25.

[197] *BF*, 290.

[198] *Ibid.*, 294, 295.

[199] *OT*, 7.

[200] *Ibid.*, 11.

[201] *Ibid.*, xxvi.

[202] *Ibid.*, 18.

[203] *Ibid.*, 7.

[204] *Ibid.*, 19.

[205] *Ibid.*, 16-17.

[206] *Ibid.* 16.

[207] *Ibid.*, 17.

[208] *EiJ*, 116-117.

[209] *JW*, 466-67.

[210] *OT*, 351.

[211] *Ibid.*, 341.

[212] *Ibid.*, 353.

[213] *Ibid.*, 379.

[214] *MDT*, 17-18.

[215] *Ibid.*

[216] *EEP*; Interview with Alfred Kazin, March 27, 1990, MC 579, folder 20.11. Schlesinger Library, Radcliffe Institute, Harvard University, Cambridge, Mass.

[217] *EEP*; Correspondence with Michael Denneny, MC 579, folder 17.10. Schlesinger Library, Radcliffe Institute, Harvard University, Cambridge, Mass.

[218] *The Eichmann Trial*, (New York: Schocken Books, 2011), 149, 152.

[219] *Ibid.*, 183, 187.

[220] *Ibid.*

[221] *MDT*, 23.

[222] *Stranger from Abroad: Hannah Arendt, Martin Heidegger, Friendship and Forgiveness*, (New York: W.W. Norton, 2012), 348.

[223] *EU*, 14.

[224] *OT*, 456.

[225] *OT*, viii.

[226] *BPF*, p. 165; *OT*, 466

[227] *EiJ*, 232, 233.

CPSIA information can be obtained
at www.ICGtesting.com
Printed in the USA
BVOW03s0828300617
488223BV00001B/46/P